Monetary Policy and Taiwan's Economy

ACADEMIA STUDIES IN ASIAN ECONOMIES

Series Editor: Sheng-Cheng Hu, *Director, Institute of Economics, Academia Sinica, Taiwan*

Titles in the series include:

Economic Efficiency and Productivity Growth in the Asia-Pacific Region
Edited by Tsu-Tan Fu, Cliff J. Huang and C.A. Knox Lovell

Food Security in Asia
Economics and Policies
Edited by Wen S. Chern, Colin A. Carter and Shun-Yi Shei

The Economic Analysis of Substance Use and Abuse
The Experience of Developed Countries and Lessons for Developing
Countries
Edited by Michael Grossman and Chee-Ruey Hsieh

Productivity and Economic Performance in the Asia-Pacific Region
Edited by Tsu-Tan Fu, Cliff J. Huang and C.A. Knox Lovell

The Economics of Health Care in Asia-Pacific Countries
Edited by Teh-Wei Hu and Chee-Ruey Hsieh

Monetary Policy and Taiwan's Economy
*Edited by Gerald P. Dwyer, Jr., Jin-Lung Lin, Jia-Dong Shea
and Chung-Shu Wu*

Monetary Policy and Taiwan's Economy

Edited by

Gerald P Dwyer, Jr.

Federal Reserve Bank of Atlanta, USA

Jin-Lung Lin

Academia Sinica, Taiwan, ROC

Jia-Dong Shea

China External Trade Development Council, Taiwan, ROC

Chung-Shu Wu

Academia Sinica, Taiwan, ROC

Edward Elgar
Cheltenham, UK • Northampton, MA, USA

339,509512
I61m
1998

© Gerald P. Dwyer, Jr., Jin-Lung Lin, Jia-Dong Shea and Chung-Shu Wu 2002

Published by
Edward Elgar Publishing Limited
Glensanda House
Montpellier Parade
Cheltenham
Glos GL50 1UA
UK

Edward Elgar Publishing, Inc.
136 West Street
Suite 202
Northampton
Massachusetts 01060
USA

A catalogue record for this book is available from the British Library

Library of Congress Cataloguing in Publication Data
International Conference on the Conduct of Monetary Policy (1998: Taipei, Taiwan)
  Monetary policy and Taiwan's economy/ edited by Gerald P. Dwyer, Jr ... [et al.].
     p. cm. — (Academia studies in Asian economies)
  Includes bibliographical references and index.
  1. Monetary policy—Taiwan—Congresses. 2. Banking law—Taiwan—Congresses. 3. Taiwan—Economic Policy—Congresses. I. Dwyer, Gerald P. II. Title. III. Series.

HG1297 .I58 1998
339.5'0951249—dc21

                                                    2002021260

ISBN 1 84064 986 0

Printed and bound in Great Britain by Bookcraft, Bath

Contents

Part III Banking Regulation

Tables

Figures

Contributors

Ronald W. Anderson Professor, Department of Accounting and Finance, London School of Economics and Political Science, London, UK.

William G. Dewald The Retiring Research Director, Federal Reserve Bank of St. Louis, Sedona, AZ, USA.

Gerald P. Dwyer, Jr. Vice President, Federal Reserve Bank of Atlanta, Atlanta, GA, USA.

DeAnne Julius Former Member of the Monetary Policy Committee and currently a Non-executive Director of the Bank of England, London, UK.

Jin-Lung Lin Research Fellow, The Institute of Economics, Academia Sinica, Taipei, Taiwan, ROC.

Georg Rich Former Chief Economist of the Swiss National Bank, Zurich, Switzerland.

Jia-Dong Shea Chairman, China External Trade Development Council, Taipe, Taiwan, ROC.

Chung-Hua Shen Professor, Department of Money and Banking, National Chengchi University, Taipei, Taiwan, ROC.

Philip Turner Head of Secretariat Group, Monetary and Economic Department, Bank for International Settlements, Basel, Switzerland.

Delano Villanueva Former Advisor, IMF and Director of Research, South East Asian Central Banks (SEACEN), and currently Economic Policy Consultant, USA.

Chung-Shu Wu Research Fellow, The Institute of Economics, Academia Sinica, Taipei, Taiwan, ROC.

N A

Acknowledgments

Academia Studies in Asian Economies serves to assimilate the findings of research conducted by the faculty of the Institute of Economics, Academia Sinica and studies presented at conferences sponsored by the Institute.

The Institute of Economics is one of the 25 research units of Academia Sinica, the leading academic institution in Taiwan. Its goals are to conduct and promote academic research in economics, Its faculty conducts research in all areas of economics, with emphasis on issues related to Asian economies. To promote economic research, each year the Institute organizes a number of international conferences on Asian economies. The papers included in this volume were selected from those presented at the International Conference on the Conduct of Monetary Policy, held at the Institute in June 1998. Over one hundred and twenty conference participants from six countries contributed papers and discussed issues concerning monetary policy in US and in Asia-Pacific region.

Many individuals and institutions contributed to the success of this conference and this volume. We owe a special debt of gratitude to Governor Fai-nan Perng and the Economic Research Department of the Central Bank of China, Taiwan. Without their generous financial support, this conference would have not been possible. Our thanks also go to Dr. Sheng-Cheng Hu, former director of the Institute of Economics, for his encouragement and support during various stages in organizing this conference and editing this volume. The staff of the Institute has provided efficient logistic support and Ms. Li-Ping Wen has offered excellent assistance in preparing this volume.

PART I

Introduction

NIA

BK Title:

1. Editors' introduction

Gerald P. Dwyer, Jr., Jin-Lung Lin, Jia-Dong Shea and Chung-Shu Wu

1. INTRODUCTION

An International Conference on the Conduct of Monetary Policy was held in Taipei during the Asian financial crisis, a crisis with far-reaching effects on Asia. Banking problems were a more important factor in the crisis than problems with monetary policy, but monetary policy in response to the crisis had the potential of being an ameliorative or an aggravating factor. The importance of both was clear by the time the conference was held. What was not clear was whether the Asian crisis would spread from Korea, Indonesia and Malaysia to Taiwan, an issue of obvious importance to the Republic of China. The importance of monetary policy and banking regulation and any information that might be garnered at the conference was evident in the seriousness with which the conference was treated by officials in Taiwan.

The crisis and its ramifications were of more than intellectual interest. Parts of the conference were attended by the Minister of Finance as well as both the Governor and Deputy Governor of the Central Bank of China. Presenters included a member of the Monetary Policy Committee of the Bank of England, the Research Director of the Swiss National Bank and the Research Directors of the Federal Reserve Banks of St. Louis and Chicago in the United States. Economists employed by the Bank for International Settlements and the International Monetary Fund also presented papers.

The chapters in this volume examine both fundamental aspects of monetary policy and supporting banking regulation that can mitigate problems created by unsound monetary policy. In this introduction, the relationships between the contributious and the analytical innovations are emphasized.

3

2. MONETARY POLICY

The first three chapters examine the role of monetary aggregates in monetary policy. Perhaps ironically given at least some of the academic literature's recent denigration of the informativeness of monetary aggregates in monetary policy (e.g. Estralla and Mishkin 1997; Stock and Watson 1999), all of these chapters are by economists associated with central banks, one with the Swiss National Bank and the other two with Federal Reserve Banks in the United States. It would be extraordinarily misleading to claim that monetary aggregates play an important role in monetary policy around the world as of this writing, and the papers arguably are responses to questions raised about monetary aggregates' role in monetary policy.

Georg Rich examines the behavior of central banks targeting a monetary aggregate and what distinguishes such a central bank from one that is targeting the price level. Essentially, it has been claimed that 'Not only do most central banks explicitly ignore monetary aggregates, but even central banks that claim to target the aggregates ignore them'. The Swiss National Bank, where Rich is Research Director, is one of the central banks that uses monetary aggregates as intermediate targets. Hence, this issue is of immediate importance to him as well as to others interested in whether monetary aggregates have any role to play in monetary policy. Rich's argument is simple but powerful. Over shorter periods of time, say a year, monetary policy has a more immediate effect on monetary aggregates than the inflation rate. A central bank may deviate from the monetary targets for one of two reasons: the central bank may be attempting to stimulate the economy even though the ultimate price-level objective is being sacrificed; the central bank may be accommodating a change in the demand for money. If a central bank deviates from its monetary targets because it is deviating from a policy of long-run price stability or low inflation, this deviation will be apparent more quickly in the monetary aggregates than in inflation. By indicating a monetary target, a central bank can be forced to explain the reason for the deviation and, if the low-inflation policy has political support, forced to undo its actions. Hence, the incentive to deviate is less than it would be without an intermediate monetary target. If the central bank deviates from its monetary target because of a change in the demand for money, the monetary target forces the central bank to explain that deviation. If the monetary authority is deviating from its monetary target to generate revenue from the government or to stimulate the economy, it will have to use subterfuge to hide its intent or it will have to explicitly disavow its inflation target. As Rich indicates, this process can increase private agents' confidence in the central bank's pursuit of a low-inflation policy.

William G. Dewald uses simple predictions from the quantity theory of money as a basis for an intriguing measure of a central bank's credibility. The quantity theory suggests that money growth is related to nominal income growth and inflation but not real income growth. Using annual-average and ten-year average data for the United States for 1897 to 1996, Dewald shows that these relationships appear in the ten-year averages. He then examines the relationship between monetary policy and interest rates, illustrating the positive relationship between nominal interest rates and inflation rates over longer periods.

Dewald provides empirical content to a notion often used and seldom measured – a central bank's credibility. Given the long-run nature of the relationship between the monetary aggregates and inflation, it is most convincing to do this in terms of long-term expectations. Long-term interest rates can provide a measure of long-term expected inflation with an independent measure of the expected real interest rate. A measure of the expected real interest rate over long periods of time is difficult to come by using United States data.[1] It is well known that real interest rates are positively related to real income growth if real interest rates primarily change due to increases and decreases in total factor productivity. To take a bolder position, the growth rate of real income can be interpreted as the real yield on real assets.[2] If this is so, then the nominal long-term interest rate less the growth rate of real income provides a measure of expected inflation over the bond's term to maturity. As Dewald's prior analysis indicates, the growth rate of real income is at least largely independent of monetary policy. Hence, this measure of the expected inflation rate over ten years provides a measure of households' expectation of the consequences of monetary policy. If *credibility* is defined in terms of zero expected inflation, then the closeness of the gap between Treasury bond rates and the growth rate of real income is a measure of the central bank's credibility. Dewald provides evidence that this measure is consistent with United States experience since the 1950s.

Gerald P. Dwyer, Jr. examines whether monetary aggregates are a leading indicator of inflation, or whether monetary aggregates are uninformative about future inflation. This is a limited role for monetary aggregates in the formulation of monetary policy. Even this limited role, though, has been called into question by some championing real variables as leading indicators of inflation and by those advocating targeting inflation directly. Dwyer uses data for the United States from 1953 through 1997 to examine the link between M2 growth and inflation. He shows that there is little or no relationship between inflation and money growth over short periods of time and a closer positive relationship over longer periods of time. The lack of such a link is to be expected from earlier evidence. He shows, though, that there is a closer link between the growth of nominal income and money growth over periods as short as a year or a quarter than between inflation and money growth. Averaging nominal income growth makes little difference to the relationship while averaging inflation over periods as long as three to five years manifests a much closer relationship between inflation and money growth than do averages over shorter periods. The positive contemporaneous correlation between money growth and inflation over longer periods indicates that sustained changes in money growth are related to sustained changes in inflation, but it does not provide direct evidence that money growth helps to predict inflation. In the last section of the chapter, Dwyer shows that money growth does indeed help to predict inflation. In fact, he shows that money growth does a credible job of predicting inflation even over the early 1990s, a period seen by many as putting the nail in the coffin of money growth's usefulness as a leading indicator of inflation.

DeAnne Julius examines the role of the Bank of England's inflation forecast in the United Kingdom's pursuit of the inflation forecast determined by the government. She explains how monetary policy has operated in the United Kingdom since the inception of the Monetary Policy Committee in 1997 and how deviations of the inflation forecast from the target feed into Bank of England actions. The Bank of England's rules create a degree of transparency rare if not unknown before in monetary policy. Seldom does a central bank have a well-defined target, let alone is that target public information.[3] In addition, the Monetary Policy Committee on which Julius sits is required to publish explicit inflation forecasts every quarter, forecasts on which substantial effort by committee and staff members is expended. Julius's main point is that, contrary to what one might expect from the academic literature, a fair amount of judgment is important for determining the optimal response by the Bank of England to deviations of the forecast from the target. This argument dovetails nicely with Rich's: having a target and projected deviations from it does not immediately imply how a central bank should respond.

Philip Turner examines the role of exchange-rate policies in the Asian crisis. He presents evidence that Asian countries pursued exchange-rate policies that led to loose monetary policies in the first half of the 1990s. His evidence indicates that monetary authorities were quite willing to have low interest rates when this supported a fixed exchange rate but they were reluctant to raise rates when the pressure on the exchange rate required tighter policy. In fact, he argues that this reluctance probably exacerbated the Asian crisis. He argues that these countries are unlikely to return to as tight a targeting of the exchange rate and that monetary policies focusing on domestic factors with a role for the exchange rate are more likely to be sustainable.

Chung-Shu Wu examines a related important aspect of monetary policy in many countries, the relationship between the exchange rate, capital flows and central bank intervention. Wu uses quarterly data on the exchange rate between Taiwan and the United States from 1987 through 1997 to estimate the relationship. In a small country such as Taiwan, it is more likely that exchange-rate intervention is effective than in a country such as the United States or the United Kingdom. Wu develops a model using portfolio analysis as well as trade. He separates net capital flows into net foreign direct investment and net foreign portfolio investment to determine whether these two forms of capital flows might have a different relationship with the exchange rate. Because he includes relative price levels in the United States and Taiwan in the estimated equations, Wu's estimates can be interpreted in terms of both nominal and real exchange rates. In terms of general research results, perhaps Wu's most interesting finding is that capital inflows have a negative relationship with exchange rates for foreign direct investment but not for portfolio investment. Perhaps most interesting from the standpoint of the conference is Wu's finding that the Bank of China's intervention in the foreign exchange market does affect the value of the New Taiwan dollar. Purchases of United States dollars by the Bank of China increases the value of the Taiwan dollar relative to the United States dollar. It is improbable that this effect is due to a change in the supply of dollars of any magnitude. Hence, either the intervention changes the current or expected future supply of New Taiwan dollars or affects the exchange rate through some other channel, an issue left to future research.

Chung-Hua Shen examines whether monetary aggregates or interest rates might be useful intermediate targets in Taiwan. He does this by focusing on whether these variables are reliably related to the growth rate of real Gross Domestic Product (GDP). It might seem that it would be more consistent with other chapters in this volume and elsewhere to focus on inflation or the growth of nominal GDP. Shen shows that there is at best a loose relationship between inflation and money growth in Taiwan, possibly due to supply shocks and capital flows. He does not examine nominal GDP because he argues that the press in Taiwan associates it with discretionary policy. He finds that the growth of a monetary aggregate, M2, helps to predict real GDP over the whole period but this informativeness for prediction is far from stable. Shen suggests that this unstable relationship may be due to financial deregulation in the late 1980s and 1990s, but adding mutual fund shares to M2 makes little difference in these results. He also finds that various interest-rate measures helped to predict real GDP before the 1990s but none of these measures are informative in the 1990s. He concludes that there is little support for using an intermediate target in monetary policy in Taiwan and it may be more useful to skip directly from instruments to monetary policy goals in Taiwan's rapidly changing economy.

3. BANKING REGULATION

In the light of the Asian crisis, Delano Villanueva discusses the role that banking regulation can play in insuring that banks do not magnify shocks to other parts of the economy. Villanueva argues that a sound banking system is important for the implementation of monetary policy. He defines a sound banking system as a competitive and efficient banking and payments system. He argues that an unsound banking system complicates monetary policy by introducing noise into the transmission of monetary policy to the rest of the economy and by creating situations where the central bank operates as a lender of last resort with uncertain consequences for inflation. Unsound banks can also constrain monetary policy's ability to respond to capital flows because the desired policy may worsen the banks' situation and because it may heighten the possibility of runs on the banks. Villanueva also discusses factors that create situations of unsound banking. After noting the primacy of an unstable macroeconomic environment for creating banking system fragility, Villanueva details other empirically important sources of such fragility and how banking regulation and supervision can help to support sound banking.

It might seem at first glance that banking reforms in Eastern Europe are hardly related to the Asian crisis. However, the restructuring banking systems in Asia has important similarities to restructuring banking systems in Eastern Europe after the fall of communism. As Anderson explains, restructuring the banks in Eastern Europe was a critical part of restructuring the economies. To take the most trivial thing but one with profound implications, many firms could borrow as desired from banks without fear of consequences of failure to repay loans. As Anderson explains, setting up legal definitions of default and consequences of default are important parts of making firms accountable for their choices. Many of these same issues arise in Asian countries, including the lack of any legal counterpart to bankruptcy. Anderson's essay compares the financial reforms in the Czech Republic, Poland and Hungary and their implications for efficient operations of those economies. While it will be some time before the implications of reforms in Asia are clear, it is clear that legal provision for consequences of not honoring debt contracts and reorganization of the banking systems are important parts of any resolution of the Asian crisis. The experience in Eastern Europe holds lessons in terms of the importance of financial reform and in terms of the relative costs and benefits of alternative methods of reforming financial systems.

4. CONCLUSION

Those of us attending the conference found the papers informative about both monetary policy and banking regulation. In combination, these papers demonstrate that monetary policy and banking regulation can be improved by sound economic analysis. Given the timing of the conference, a pertinent question is: Could the Asian crisis have been avoided by application of the points made in these papers? In an abstract world, perhaps; in the world in which we live, no. The points made in these papers can contribute to better policy, even if they are more likely to effect marginal improvements than large changes.

NOTES

1. Some countries have inflation indexed bonds that can be used to construct a measure of expected inflation over long periods. The United States Treasury bonds indexed for inflation, TIPS, may provide such information in the future but in 2000, they lack liquidity and it is uncertain whether they and other federal governments will be retired until Social Security

deficits create new issues of government debt.
2. This proxy for the real interest rate also has been analysed by Friedman and Schwartz (1982, pp. 274–76, Chapter 10.)
3. There is a certain irony in this development at the Bank of England, arguably a source of much of the mystique surrounding central banks.

REFERENCES

Estrella, Arturo and Frederic S. Mishkin (1997), 'Is there a role for monetary aggregates in monetary policy?', *Journal of Monetary Economics,* **40** (October): 279–304.
Friedman, Milton and Anna J. Schwartz (1982), *Monetary Trends in the United States and the United Kingdom: Their Relation to Income, Prices, and Interest Rates, 1867–1975,* Chicago: University of Chicago Press.
Stock, James H. and Mark W. Watson (1999), 'Forecasting inflation', *Journal of Monetary Economics,* **44** (October): 293–335.

PART II

Monetary Policy

E31 £43
£51
£52

2. Inflation and money stock targets: is there really a difference?

Georg Rich

1. INTRODUCTION

Inflation targeting looms large in the current debate on monetary policy. In the early 1990s, New Zealand, Canada, the United Kingdom, Sweden and several other countries adopted a new approach to monetary policy, based on explicit inflation targets. The increasing popularity of the new approach triggered a lively discussion on the merits of inflation targeting. At first, the debate was largely confined to central banks. More recently, it has started to capture the attention of academic economists. Bernanke and Mishkin (1997), Mishkin (1999), Bernanke, Laubach, Mishkin and Posen (1999), in particular, have thoroughly examined the experience accumulated by central banks with inflation targets.

Mishkin (1999) also compares inflation targeting with alternative approaches such as setting targets for the exchange rate, for the growth in the money stock, and for nominal income growth. He concludes that inflation targeting is superior to the alternative approaches considered in his study.

In this chapter, I attempt to assess and extend Mishkin's analysis. I focus on the differences between inflation and monetary targeting. The emphasis on these two approaches is motivated by the fact that my employer, the Swiss National Bank (SNB), targeted money from 1975 to 1999. However, at the end of 1999, the SNB decided to abandon monetary targeting and to shift to a policy approach based on an inflation forecast. Therefore, Mishkin's study is of particular interest to us.

Although I confine my analysis to inflation and monetary targets, I do not wish to convey the impression that the other approaches are not worth discussing. For small and medium-sized countries, including Switzerland, exchange rate targeting is often an attractive alternative. Nevertheless, Switzerland has not followed the example of other small countries that chose to peg their exchange rate to a major currency or to a currency basket. Our preference for a floating exchange rate derives from the fact that we have greatly benefited from our efforts to pursue a largely autonomous monetary policy aimed at maintaining price stability through tight control of money growth. The principal benefit consists in a level of interest rates lower than anywhere else in Europe. Relatively low Swiss interest rates are explained to a large extent by the high credibility acquired by the SNB.[1]

Mishkin (1999) maintains that inflation targeting has several advantages over monetary targeting:

1. Monetary targeting makes sense only if a stable relationship exists between the inflation rate and the growth in the monetary aggregate targeted by the central bank. Moreover, the central bank must be able to control the target variable. In the case of inflation targeting, by contrast, the problems arising from velocity shocks are largely irrelevant.
2. Inflation targeting is easily understood by the public and therefore highly transparent. The simplicity and transparency of inflation targeting also strengthens accountability of the central bank. The public is able to monitor the activities of the central bank. It may thus compel the central bank to account for its policy actions.
3. Inflation targeting, through its effect on accountability, reduces the likelihood that the central bank will pursue time-inconsistent policies. The public debate will be focused on what the central bank is best able to do: To achieve and to maintain price stability in the long run. However, as Mishkin emphasizes, central banks with inflation targets do not disregard other policy objectives. At least some of them take great pains in trying to explain to the public to what extent they are able to pursue output, employment and other objectives without jeopardizing price stability in the long run.
4. A major drawback of monetary targeting, as was practiced by such countries as Germany and Switzerland, is that the central banks concerned frequently failed to meet their targets. This reduced the usefulness of monetary targets as a means of communicating the central bank's intentions to the public.

The last point 4 raises an intriguing question: If Germany and Switzerland had been following inadequate targeting procedures, why were they still relatively successful in keeping inflation low? After all, in both Germany and Switzerland, inflation, as measured by the CPI, averaged roughly 3 percent over the last quarter century. This figure is lower than in virtually any other country.

Mishkin (1999) answers this question by arguing that both Germany and Switzerland adopted a 'hybrid' form of targeting. They combined elements of inflation and monetary targeting, but in practice their strategies resembled inflation, rather than monetary, targeting. A similar opinion is expressed by Bernanke and Mihov:'[I]t might be argued that inflation goals, rather than money growth targets, are the driving force behind German monetary policy' (1997, p. 1026). However, this interpretation of German and Swiss monetary policies raises an awkward problem. It implies that the Bundesbank and the SNB really pursued inflation targets, but dressed up that strategy in monetarist clothes. Why would the two central banks have gone to the length of staging a silly window-dressing exercise?

The answer to this question is simple. It is misleading to characterize the Bundesbank and the SNB as inflation targeters in disguise. Mishkin and Bernanke-Mihov overlook an important element in the debate on monetary targeting. They seem to treat inflation and monetary targets as substitutes, that is, central banks may opt for one or the other. However, the Bundesbank and the SNB did not frame their analysis in these terms. Instead, they emphasized the role of money as an *intermediate* target variable. The monetary target was not an end in itself. It was viewed as a device helping the central bank to reach the *ultimate* objectives of monetary policy.[2] The SNB has always regarded achieving and maintaining price stability as its chief ultimate objective of monetary policy. When a conflict arose between the intermediate target and the ultimate objective, it was of course the ultimate objective that did prevail. For this reason, the SNB, from the inception of monetary targeting, stressed the *conditional and contingent nature* of its intermediate target. The Bundesbank followed the same approach.

Since both targeting frameworks imply or implied a strong commitment to price stability, I am not surprised that central banks targeting inflation display very similar behavior to those that focused on the money supply. Nevertheless, I would not go as far as to argue that the two approaches, for all practical purposes, are identical. In my view, three differences remain.

First, central banks targeting inflation insist that they should be endowed with a clear mandate to pursue price stability. Moreover, the objective of price stability should be framed in terms of a numerical inflation target known to the public. The central bank should be committed to achieving and maintaining the numerical target. Thus, inflation targeting implies a strong commitment to the ultimate objective of monetary policy. The Bundesbank and the SNB, by contrast, placed less emphasis on quantifying the ultimate objective of monetary policy because they did not express that objective in terms of a numerical inflation target. This raises the question of whether the Bundesbank and the SNB could have strengthened their commitment to price stability by quantifying the mandate conferred upon the central bank.

Second, while both approaches, albeit in different degrees, imply a strong commitment to price stability, the Bundesbank and the SNB proceeded one step further. They attempted – and this is the issue Mishkin and Bernanke-Mihov fail to understand clearly – to commit the central bank not only to the ultimate objective of price stability, but also to an operational framework for meeting that objective. The desire to commit the central bank to both the ultimate objective and the operational framework derived from the long lag between the central bank's actions and the full response in the inflation rate. In Switzerland, that lag amounts to as much as three years. Considering the length of the lag, the SNB possesses ample scope for engaging in time-inconsistent monetary policies so long as the commitment is limited to the ultimate target of price stability. Policy makers uncommitted to an operational framework and eager to embrace populist causes jeopardizing price stability in the long run need not worry too much: The day of reckoning is far away! For this reason, it may be useful to commit policy makers not only to the objective of, but also to an operational framework for, achieving and maintaining price stability. Commitment to an operational framework implies that the barriers to the pursuit of time-inconsistent monetary policies are put in place at an early stage in the transmission of monetary disturbances to the inflation rate.

Proponents of inflation targeting are of course aware of the problems posed by policy lags. Svensson (1997) argues that central banks should target a conditional inflation forecast, rather than the recorded inflation rate. The inflation forecast should assume the role of an intermediate target variable, like the money stock under monetary targeting. In this way, central banks could be committed to an operational framework even if they were to opt for an inflation target.

While commitment to a suitable operational framework is clearly desirable, it is difficult to develop and implement such a commitment technology in practice. Monetary targeting at the Bundesbank and the SNB originally was strongly influenced by Friedman and other monetarists. Friedman (e.g. 1959) advocated fixed intermediate targets for money growth in order to commit the central bank to an operational framework.

In the 1970s, various central banks adopted monetary targets in the sense of Friedman. As they gained experience with this approach, they increasingly realized that a commitment technology based on fixed intermediate targets was suboptimal. Today, even monetarists (see Meltzer 1998) reject fixed intermediate targets. Instead, they show that optimum policy strategies generally prompt the intermediate target variable (or the policy instrument) to change over time. Thus, steady money growth, as advocated by Friedman, tends to be suboptimal even if a stable relationship exists between money and the price level. This creates a dilemma for monetary targeting. A fixed target for money growth, as was employed by the Bundesbank, is simple to understand but suboptimal. A flexible target, as the SNB attempted to pursue in the 1990s, is optimal, but difficult to comprehend. This raises the question of whether a monetary target is a sensible means of committing central banks to an operational framework.

Third, it is not obvious that an inflation target provides for greater transparency and accountability of monetary policy than a monetary target. Laubach and Posen (1997), Mishkin (1999) and Bernanke et al. (1999, Chapter 4) themselves stress the efforts undertaken by the Bundesbank and the SNB to explain to the public their policy actions. Their analysis suggests that a central bank's willingness to open its books to the public depends less on the type of target pursued than on the extent of its commitment to an ultimate objective and to an operational framework. As already indicated, both inflation and monetary targeting embody strong elements of commitment.

In the following, I examine more closely the common features of, and the differences between, the two targeting approaches. Section 2 presents some evidence confirming that central banks committed to price stability tend to behave in similar ways. In Section 3, I analyse the differences between the two approaches in terms of commitment to the ultimate objective of price stability. Section 4 is devoted to the tricky issue of commitment to an operational framework. In Section 5, I present the SNB's current policy approach and I show how it attempts to deal with the issues raised in the preceding two sections. Section 6 offers a summary and conclusions.

2. SIMILARITY IN BEHAVIOR OF CENTRAL BANKS COMMITTED TO PRICE STABILITY

As indicated in Section 1, central banks committed to price stability are liable to pursue broadly similar monetary policies, regardless of the targeting procedure employed, provided they are successful in achieving and maintaining their ultimate objective. A remarkable development in the last decade has been the return to low inflation in most industrialized countries and in many countries outside the industrialized world. Considering recent successes in lowering or even eliminating inflation, I would expect central banks to display increasingly similar patterns of behavior. This should also hold for central banks that do not feature explicit inflation or monetary targets, but nevertheless successfully control inflation through an eclectic policy approach. Central banks endeavoring to achieve and maintain price stability should respond in similar ways to shocks that are likely to jeopardize their ultimate objective. Although their reaction patterns will be similar, the procedures followed for setting monetary policy may differ according to the targeting system employed.

Figures 2.1 to 2.6 shed light on the behavior patterns of six central banks. The sample includes two eclectic institutions (United States, Japan), two with inflation targets (United Kingdom, Canada) and two that operated monetary targets (Germany, Switzerland). The behavior of the central banks is analysed by comparing the actual movements in money market rates (measured by the three-month deposit rate in the Euromarket) with a hypothetical series derived from the monetary policy rule developed by Taylor (1993). He suggests that the central bank should vary the money market rate (i) according to the following formula:

$$i_t = r + \pi_t + 0.5(y - y^*)_{t-1} + 0.5(\pi - \pi^*)_t, \qquad (2.1)$$

where r stands for the real money market rate, $y - y^*$ for the output gap (logarithmic difference between actual and potential output), π for actual inflation and π^* for the inflation target.[3] The Taylor Rule is employed as a benchmark for analysing the behavior of the six central banks. It is designed to trace the movements in the money market rate required to achieve and maintain price stability in the long run. Therefore, the monetary policies of central banks successful in meeting the ultimate objective of price stability are likely to trigger

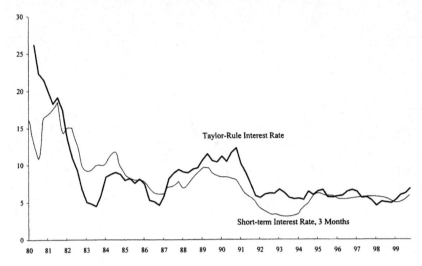

Figure 2.1 United States

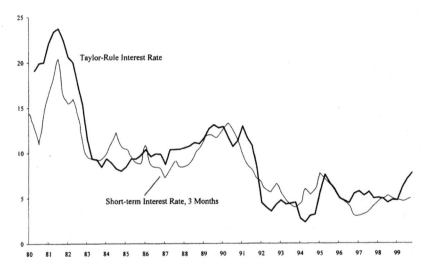

Figure 2.2 Canada

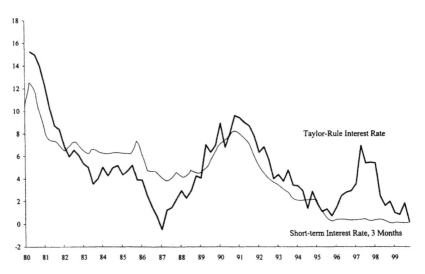

Figure 2.3 Japan

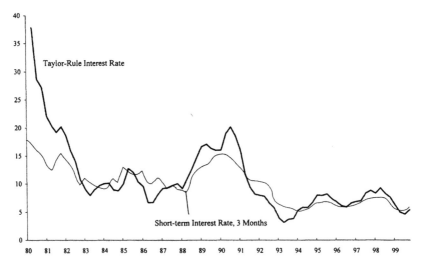

Figure 2.4 United Kingdom

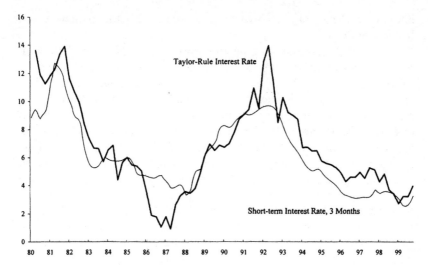

Figure 2.5 Germany

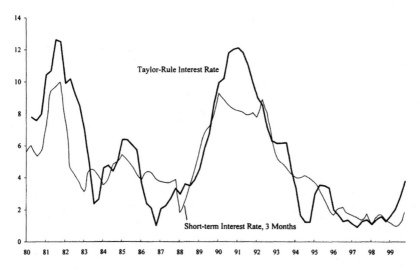

Figure 2.6 Switzerland

interest rate movements broadly consistent with the benchmark of the Taylor Rule.

Central banks pursuing an inflation target will certainly have to react to deviations in the actual inflation rate from the target, as suggested by the Taylor Rule. Considering the long lags in the effects of monetary policy, however, they should adjust the money market rate in response to discrepancies between the *anticipated* inflation rate and the target. The forward-looking elements of behavior are captured by the output gap in equation (2.1). The insertion of the output gap need not imply that the central banks pursue an output objective, in addition to the goal of price stability. The output gap may merely serve as a tool for forecasting the future inflation rate (see also Freedman 1995, p. 255). The inflation dangers normally increase during the expansion phase of the business cycle as the output gap closes. Therefore, central banks committed to price stability must react to cyclical shocks to aggregate demand, as revealed by the fluctuations in the output gap. Of course, it is unlikely that the inflation forecasts are based exclusively on the output gap since the Phillips curve, linking the future inflation rate to that gap, is often subject to considerable instability. The central banks with inflation targets are thus likely to use other information, not considered in equation (2.1), to forecast future price movements.

Central banks adhering to a monetary target base their policy decisions primarily on the signals extracted from money growth. If these signals are reliable, the central banks targeting money are prompted to counteract threats to price stability arising from cyclical shocks to aggregate demand. During the expansion phase of the business cycle, the growth in money demand tends to accelerate. As the central banks undertake to rein in supply, they cause money market rates to rise. Thus, the Taylor Rule mimics the behavior of the central banks targeting money even if they do not monitor directly the variables on the right-hand side of equation (2.1).[4] In practice, the Bundesbank and the SNB tended to watch other indicators, besides money, including those considered by the Taylor Rule.

To apply the Taylor Rule to the six countries, several assumptions must be made. Since the analysis covers the period 1980I – 1999IV, the question arises as to the numbers that should be assigned to the inflation target appearing in equation (2.1). The central banks targeting inflation did not introduce the new approach until the early 1990s. Therefore, we do not know what implicit inflation targets, if any, they pursued beforehand. The same problem arises for the eclectic central banks. The Bundesbank and the SNB, though spelling out inflation objectives underlying their monetary targets (see Section 3), were not committed to precise inflation targets either. There is little doubt that in all the countries considered, inflation was still unacceptably high at the beginning of the 1980s, but had declined to the desired low levels by the end of the sample period. Therefore, I assume somewhat arbitrarily that the 'inflation targets' equaled one-half of the average inflation rates recorded during the sample period. This procedure yields target rates of 2.5 percent for the U.S. and Canada, 1 percent for Japan, 3 percent for the U.K., and 1.5 percent for Germany and Switzerland.[5] Inflation is measured by the year-on-year rate of change in the CPI.

The output gap is approximated by the percentage deviation in real GDP from its trend, determined by applying a Hodrick-Prescott filter to the actual data.[6] The real rate of interest is calculated by deducting the average inflation rate over the sample period from the corresponding average for the nominal money market rate.

Figures 2.1 to 2.6 indicate that the movements in the money market rates in all the countries considered broadly conformed to the benchmark derived from the Taylor Rule. Moreover, except in the case of Japan (Figure 2.3), actual money market rates in the latter part of the sample period were closer to the benchmark than in the early 1980s.[7] Thus, the evidence points to great similarities in the central banks' reaction to shocks. It also suggests that the central banks have strengthened their commitment to price stability in recent years.

As I already indicated, the evidence should not be construed as implying that the central banks considered actually followed a Taylor Rule.[8] Nor do I wish to suggest that central banks in the future should follow such a rule. It is easier to apply the Taylor Rule *ex post* in order to analyse past behavior of central banks than to use it *ex ante* as a guide to policy makers. The output gap, in particular, is a highly elusive concept. As indicated by equation (2.1), central bankers applying the Taylor Rule should have reliable information about the size of the output gap in the preceding quarter. GDP data invariably get revised, often substantially, as time goes on. It should be noted that Figures 2.1 to 2.6 rely on revised data on the output gap, rather than the information that was available to central banks at the time when they took policy decisions.[9] Another problem arises from setting the optimum parameters in the reaction function (2.1). They may not match those suggested by Taylor. Moreover, the Taylor Rule is probably not sufficiently forward looking to prompt central banks to take timely action in the event of an inflation threat.[10]

Taylor (1999, pp. 675) is well aware of these problems. However, he rightly emphasizes that all forecasts are ultimately based on current and past data. Central banks cannot help reacting to current and past data even if they insist on a forward-looking approach. Therefore, the question that really matters is whether the Taylor Rule could be made more forward looking by placing less weight on the current inflation rate and by including other variables such as the money supply on the right-hand side of equation (2.1). Taylor (1999, pp. 660–1) himself recommends that central banks monitor the money supply even if they are using interest rate rules as a guideline.

3. STRENGTHENING THE COMMITMENT TO PRICE STABILITY

A key advantage of inflation targeting lies in a strong central-bank commitment to achieving and maintaining the ultimate objective of price stability, with the objective expressed as a numerical target. The public knows precisely the objective the central bank is expected to pursue and may thus monitor its behavior. Inflation targeting commonly involves three elements:

1. The political authorities assign to the central bank a clear mandate to pursue the ultimate objective of price stability.
2. The ultimate objective is framed in terms of a numerical target, which is typically specified as a target band or a point target for CPI inflation. If a target band is set, the midpoint is invariably a low but positive number, with the width of the band typically ranging from 2 to 3 percentage points. The central banks targeting inflation do not aim at perfect price stability because they are prepared to take account of the measurement bias in the CPI and of possible downward rigidities in prices and wages.[11] The targeted CPI inflation number is frequently adjusted for indirect taxes and subsidies, the interest component of the CPI, food and energy prices, as well as various administered prices. The adjusted inflation measures are called core or underlying inflation.
3. The central bank is free to choose the operational framework and the policy instruments required to meet the inflation target.

   In principle, points 1 and 3 also applied to the Bundesbank and the SNB under monetary targeting, except that in the Swiss case, the central bank does not possess a clear legal mandate to pursue price stability. Although Swiss legislation is vague about the ultimate objectives of monetary policy, the SNB already interpreted its mandate as an obligation to safeguard price stability under monetary targeting.

The main difference between inflation and monetary targeting arose from point 2. The Bundesbank and the SNB did not translate their commitment to price stability into a precise numerical target. Nevertheless, the public was aware of the ultimate monetary policy objectives. Both the Bundesbank and the SNB explained how they calculated their monetary targets, which were derived from a definition of price stability and an estimate of the economy's growth potential. Until 1999, the SNB typically defined price stability as an average annual increase in the CPI of 1 percent.[12] The SNB aimed at a modestly positive inflation rate because of the measurement bias inherent in the available data on the CPI. In Germany, the Bundesbank's monetary target was designed to accommodate an average increase in the CPI of no more than 2 percent per year.[13]

Neither the Bundesbank nor the SNB treated the definition of price stability underlying the monetary target as a binding numerical objective. In practice, the SNB allowed for an unspecified range of variation around the inflation assumption. Since the monetary target also took account of an estimate of potential growth, it had more in common with a nominal income target than with an inflation target so long as it was adjusted, if necessary, for permanent shifts in the velocity of money.

In view of these ambiguities, the question arises whether the commitment to price stability under monetary targeting could not have been strengthened by quantifying the ultimate objective of monetary policy. The European Central Bank, the institution in charge of monetary policy in the euro area since the beginning of 1999, has adopted a framework incorporating elements of inflation and monetary targeting. It explicitly defines its inflation objective as a rate of increase in the CPI (harmonized index for the euro area) of less than 2 percent. Moreover, it assigns a prominent indicator role to money (see Section 5). Let me examine the possibility of combining the two targeting regimes from a Swiss perspective.

There is little doubt that the SNB's commitment to price stability could be strengthened by an explicit mandate to this effect from the political authorities. Switzerland is currently revising the law governing the SNB's activities. As part of that revision, we intend to assign to the SNB an explicit mandate to pursue price stability as the main objective of monetary policy. More controversial is the question of whether the SNB would benefit from a numerical inflation target. As indicated earlier, central banks targeting inflation typically set a point target or a target band with a width of 2–3 percentage points. In practice, the SNB would find it difficult to keep the inflation rate continuously near a point target or within a band of 2–3 percentage points. The SNB cannot control price movements with a high degree of precision. Prices may vary as a result of non-monetary factors beyond the control of the central bank. Moreover, due to the long policy lags, forecasting the effects of the SNB's actions on the inflation rate entails a considerable margin of error. Particular difficulties arise from the importance of administered prices and prices of imported goods in the Swiss CPI. Administered prices react sluggishly or perversely[14] to shifts in monetary policy. Substantial unexpected movements in the exchange rate, spilling over to import prices and the CPI, may also weaken the SNB's ability to control inflation. Considering these difficulties, the SNB would likely engender higher than necessary fluctuations in output if it endeavored to keep the inflation rate within narrow limits.[15]

Thus, the SNB could not but tolerate temporary deviations in the inflation rate from a point or narrow-band target. It would respond to target misses only if it were confronted with the prospect of sustained deviations in the inflation rate from that objective. If the SNB opted for a narrow band, it would have to treat its objective as a 'soft-edged' target, rather than as a commitment to keep the inflation rate within the band at all times.[16] However, the public might not view a 'soft-edged' target as sufficiently transparent unless the SNB were willing to explain in advance the circumstances in which it might tolerate deviations from such an objective.

The problems arising from price movements beyond the control of the SNB could be mitigated by targeting or monitoring a measure of core inflation. This is a common practice among central banks targeting inflation. Although its target refers to headline inflation, the Bank of Canada (2001) focuses for operational purposes on core inflation, defined as the headline CPI purged of food and energy prices, and the effects of indirect taxes. The Bank of England (2001, pp. 5 and Section 6.2) is required to adhere to a target for a core concept in the form of RPIX (excluding mortgage interest payments). The Reserve Bank of New Zealand (1997, pp. 2–3; 1999, pp. 8) also follows a target for underlying inflation (excluding credit charges).[17] The Sveriges Riksbank (2001, pp. 51–2) by contrast, targets headline inflation, but found it difficult to meet its target, especially in 1996/97 and 1998/99. Therefore, monetary policy is now guided by underlying inflation, which excludes mortgage interest payments.

An unattractive solution would entail setting a wide target band of, say, 0–4 percent or even more, leaving sufficient scope for accommodating the bulk of price movements beyond the SNB's control. Such a wide band would be unlikely to provide useful additional information about the ultimate objectives of Swiss monetary policy. On the contrary, it might mislead the public into believing that the SNB was about to turn soft on controlling inflation because few Swiss would see an inflation rate of 4 percent as being equal to price stability.

Strengthening the commitment to price stability should not be taken to imply that central banks ought to disregard completely output and employment objectives.[18] Nevertheless, many people fear that central banks with a strong commitment to price stability are prone to pursue overly tight monetary policies, resulting in depressed output and high unemployment. Therefore, it is imperative for central banks to communicate to the public how they take account of output and unemployment in the setting of monetary policy.

In Switzerland, a further communication problem arises from the exchange rate. Since the adoption of a floating exchange rate in 1973, the SNB has been confronted with several bouts of excessive strength and weakness in the Swiss franc. An overly strong domestic currency tends to raise considerable concern among the Swiss public because of its impact on output and employment. In these circumstances, the SNB is frequently called upon to pay greater attention to the exchange rate or to go even further and to target the external value of the Swiss franc. For these reasons, the SNB cannot help explaining to the public how it intends to address these concerns. Its views on the role of output and the exchange rate in monetary policy may be summarized as follows:[19]

- If inflation is too high, the SNB will strive to restore price stability gradually in order to minimize the temporary output and employment loss, resulting from its restrictive monetary policy. Such losses are an unpleasant but inevitable sacrifice to be made on the way to price stability.
- Maintaining price stability implies avoidance of inflation *and* deflation. The SNB endeavors to react symmetrically to positive and negative aggregate demand shocks threatening to disturb price stability. Thus, the SNB does not bias monetary policy in favor of too much restriction. As already indicated in the preceding section, if the SNB reacts symmetrically to positive and negative aggregate demand shocks, it not only helps to preserve price stability, but also contributes to smoothing cyclical and other fluctuations in output and employment. However, monetary policy should not

be used actively to stimulate economic growth. If the SNB pays too much attention to output and employment, it is bound to pursue overly expansionary policies and to jeopardize price stability in the long run.

· In the presence of aggregate supply shocks (increases in indirect taxes or in the oil price) the SNB faces a dilemma as such shocks tend to raise prices and lower output. While the SNB will be prepared to minimize the temporary output loss by accommodating the once-and-for-all rise in the CPI, attributable directly to the supply shock, it will refuse to accept a propagation of these shocks and a resurgence of inflationary pressures in the economy.

The SNB takes account of the exchange rate in setting monetary policy, but – except in unusual circumstances – it does not target the exchange rate. A sustained unexpected increase/decrease in the external value of the Swiss franc affects output and the price level in similar ways as an unexpected decrease/increase in aggregate demand.[20] If the SNB tries to smooth the exchange rate too much, it risks disturbing price stability in the long run.[21] For this reason, the SNB refrains from targeting the exchange rate. It might consider a temporary target as a measure of last resort in the event of a very strong and harmful exchange rate shift. But it is clearly aware that by targeting the exchange rate, it may jeopardize price stability in the long run.

The need to clarify the role of output and the exchange rate in setting monetary policy derives from the commitment to price stability as the principal objective of monetary policy. It arises under both inflation and monetary targeting. Interestingly, the Bank of Canada (2001, pp. 6; Freedman 1995, pp. 254–5; Bernanke et al. 1999, Chapter 6) tends to address these issues in similar language as the SNB. Other central banks targeting inflation are less explicit, at least as far as the role of output is concerned.

An approach pioneered by the Bank of Canada is to construct and monitor a Monetary Conditions Index (MCI) in order to take account of the exchange rate. The MCI attempts to capture the combined influence of movements in an appropriate short-term interest rate and the exchange rate on aggregate demand (or inflation). While the MCI serves as a useful barometer of monetary ease or tightness, it is not an indicator easy to interpret. Whether or not the central bank should respond to changes in the MCI depends on the type of shocks hitting the economy. Suppose that a depreciation of the domestic currency, induced by portfolio shifts on the part of investors, threatens to raise aggregate demand and inflation. Clearly, the central bank should respond by increasing the interest rate in order to prevent aggregate demand from rising. Provided the central bank strives to keep the MCI stable, the size of the interest-rate increase will be such as to offset the effect of the currency depreciation on aggregate demand. However, a different response is required if the exchange rate depreciates as a result of an unexpected slump in domestic aggregate demand. Since the drop in the exchange rate helps to stabilize aggregate demand, the central bank should not raise the interest rate but allow the MCI to decline in line with the currency depreciation. Considering these difficulties, the Bank of Canada does not adjust interest rates mechanically to changes in the MCI.[22]

4. COMMITMENT TO AN OPERATIONAL FRAMEWORK

Central banks committing themselves to both an ultimate policy objective and an operational framework are trying to modify their behavior in the direction of following a *policy rule*. Bernanke and Mishkin (1997, pp. 103–8) and Mishkin (1999) are correct in arguing that inflation targeting, by itself, should not be regarded as policy rule. Instead, it constitutes a policy framework that improves the transparency and coherence of the central bank's behavior, but still leaves considerable scope for discretionary action. Bernanke and Mishkin (1997, pp. 106) and Mishkin (1999) understand inflation targeting as a policy approach based on 'constrained discretion' (quotation marks in original).[23] According to McCallum (1989), a central bank follows a rule if it commits itself to a systematic response pattern or reaction function, determining the movements in the intermediate target variable or the policy instrument.

As indicated in Section 1, monetary rules engendering optimum outcomes tend to call for substantial fluctuations in the intermediate target variable or the instrument in response to random shocks. Meltzer (1987, pp. 12–13) and McCallum (1989, Chapter 16) propose rules for varying the monetary base with a view to keeping the economy on a potential growth path with low inflation. Both rules prompt the central bank to adjust the monetary base to past changes in velocity. McCallum's rule also compels the central bank to take account of deviations in nominal output from its potential growth path. Simulations for a variety of countries suggest that the monetary base would have varied considerably if central banks had adhered to these rules. McCallum (1998) takes pains to distinguish between the 'rules vs. discretion' and the 'activist vs. non-activist' dichotomy. A rule need not be non-activist as the monetarists originally believed. On the contrary, the central bank following the rules espoused by Meltzer and McCallum behaves in an activist manner as it is prompted to adjust the monetary base systematically to destabilize shocks hitting the economy.

Swiss experience confirms the conclusion of both Meltzer and McCallum that steady expansion in the money supply is unlikely to represent an optimum policy strategy. In Switzerland (as in other countries) a strategy of steady money growth raises mainly two problems.

First, the demand for money is highly sensitive to changes in interest rates. The interest sensitivity varies from aggregate to aggregate. It tends to be relatively low for the monetary base,[24] higher for the broadly defined aggregate M3, and highest for the aggregates comprising only transactions balances and close substitutes for them. As interest rates rise, the public normally switches from money to other types of assets because the bulk of transactions balances and close substitutes for them either yield no interest or bear interest rates that are adjusted only sluggishly to changes in market rates.

A high interest sensitivity undermines the stabilizing effect of a policy strategy providing for steady money growth. To illustrate this point, suppose that the SNB faces a strong negative aggregate demand shock, threatening to generate deflation unless the central bank takes offsetting action. As a result of the shock, money demand rises less than expected or even falls. Since the money supply expands at the same steady pace as before, interest rates must go down in order to keep the money market in equilibrium. If the interest sensitivity of money demand is high, the decrease in interest rates may not be sufficiently strong to counteract the unexpected drop in aggregate demand. Should the deflationary danger persist, the SNB cannot but boost money growth in order to enhance the expansionary effect of its monetary policy.[25] In as much as aggregate demand shocks are mainly responsible for cyclical fluctuations in economic activity, a high interest sensitivity of money demand implies that the SNB should vary the money supply in a countercyclical manner, rather than keep it on a steady growth path.

A similar problem arises from fluctuations in the exchange rate, at least to the extent that these movements are not explained by economic fundamentals. An excessive appreciation of the Swiss franc, for example, may subject the economy to the same deflationary

pressures as a negative aggregate demand shock. If the interest
sensitivity of money demand is high, the SNB must stimulate money
growth in order to shield the domestic economy from the deflationary
pressures.

Second, a strategy of steady money growth is inappropriate in
the presence of serious instabilities in money demand. Swiss money
demand has been quite stable in the sense that its movements are
largely explained by changes in economic activity and interest rates.
However, not all the monetary aggregates are equally stable. The
aggregates M2 and – more recently – M3 have displayed remarkably
stable behavior. The monetary base – the SNB's intermediate target
variable until 1999 – has been a more problematic aggregate. It
has been plagued by temporary instabilities on various occasions.
Right now, the behavior of the monetary base once again puzzles
us because the growth in the circulation of large-denomination bank
notes began to accelerate unexpectedly in the latter part of 1996. For
a long time, the difficulties arising from instability in the monetary
base had not seriously hampered monetary policy. They had not
caused the SNB to feel completely at sea. Therefore, because of
its relatively low interest sensitivity, the monetary base had remained
the SNB's preferred intermediate target variable. The need to vary
the intermediate target variable in response to aggregate-demand
and exchange-rate shocks was less pronounced than if the SNB had
targeted the aggregates M2 or M3. However, the new instabilities
in the monetary base that emerged in 1996 were serious enough to
prompt the SNB to shift its attention to M3. At the end of 1999
the SNB decided to abandon monetary targeting altogether (more
below).

In the early 1990s, the complications arising from the interest
sensitivity of and the occasional instabilities in money demand had
already led the SNB to adopt a variable targeting strategy.[26] Until
that time, the SNB had fixed annual growth targets for the monetary
base that it had not changed much from year to year. In the late
1980s and early 1990s, the SNB faced a series of international shocks
(excessive Swiss franc strength in 1987, followed by an excessive
weakness in the second half of 1989 and 1990, partly due to German
reunification; stock market crash of 1987). These shocks, coupled
with temporary instabilities in base-money demand, forced the SNB
to adopt a flexible approach and to miss its annual targets for three
years in a row. Annual targeting ceased to be a credible means of
committing the SNB to an operational framework. Therefore, the
SNB decided to gradually introduce a new targeting procedure. It

fixed a multi-year growth target for the monetary base, described by a target line extending over a five-year period. The target line specified the evolution in the level of the monetary base judged to be consistent with price stability and potential real growth of 2 percent.[27] The SNB did not promise to expand the monetary base steadily along the target line. It emphasized that depending on the state of the economy, it would have to push the monetary base temporarily above or below the target line. However, it would avoid long-lasting movements away from the target line because these would likely undermine price stability in the long run.

At the beginning of the 1990s, the monetary base lay substantially below the target line (Figure 2.7). The SNB at that time was obliged to pursue a very restrictive monetary policy. In the difficult environment of the late 1980s, it had underestimated the expansionary forces at work in the Swiss economy. Therefore, inflation rose temporarily to over 6 percent in 1990 and 1991. As real growth began to slow, the SNB strove to expand the monetary base again. It intended to gradually push the monetary base up to the target line as the fight against inflation began to show the desired results. The SNB relaxed monetary policy further in 1995. A massive upvaluation of the Swiss franc, partly fueled by fears about detrimental effects on price stability of European monetary unification, choked off the cyclical recovery that had set in at the beginning of 1994.[28] The Swiss economy continued to stagnate until the end of 1996. Right now, the Swiss franc exchange rate is back at a more normal level, output is growing again and prices are stable.

As a result of the expansionary policy course, the monetary base rose above the target line in the middle of 1996 (Figure 2.7). However, the strong expansion in the monetary base overstates the extent of the easing because of the instabilities in money demand mentioned above. These instabilities prompted the SNB to turn to the aggregate M3. Figure 2.8 illustrates the relationship between the growth in M3 and the inflation rate. It is based on data smoothed by a five-quarter moving average in order to eliminate high-frequency fluctuations in the two series. For this reason, observations for the most recent past cannot be displayed in Figure 2.8. The evidence presented in Figure 2.8 suggests that the relationship between M3 growth and the inflation rate is complex. Obviously, the strong increase in M3 growth at the end of both the 1970s and 1980s, in due course, caused the inflation rate to accelerate.[29] The lesser peaks in M3 growth in 1983 and in 1994/97, by contrast, were not followed by a rise in inflation. They occurred during recessions, characterized by falling interest rates.

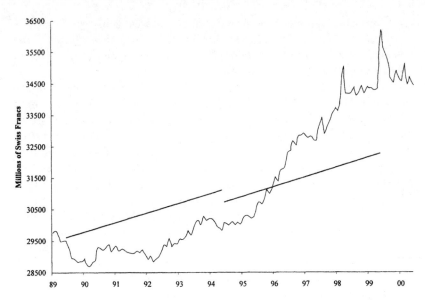

Figure 2.7 Swiss monetary base and target path

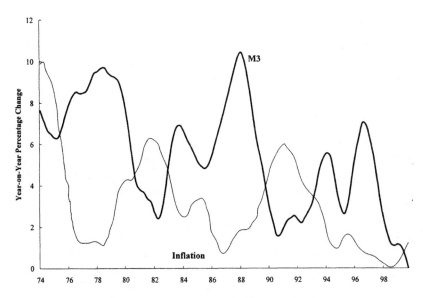

Figure 2.8 Growth in Swiss money stock M3 and inflation

As I indicated above, the growth in an interest-sensitive monetary aggregate is likely to accelerate during the contraction phase of the business cycle, without the monetary expansion raising the specter of a future surge in the inflation rate.

The patterns revealed by Figure 2.8 clearly indicate that inflation cannot be forecast by straightforward extrapolation from past data on M3 growth. An acceleration of M3 growth need not fuel future inflation in all circumstances. In particular, if it takes place during the contraction phase of the business cycle, it is likely to indicate that monetary policy is playing a stabilizing role, rather than setting the stage for a future rise in inflation. Should the SNB, by contrast, fail to curtail M3 growth during the expansion phase of the business cycle, it may undermine price stability in the long run. While Figure 2.8 points to a broadly countercyclical pattern of M3 growth, it is conceivable that the practice of setting annual monetary targets may still have led the SNB not to tighten monetary policy quickly enough as the Swiss economy moved out of recessions.[30]

Figure 2.8 leads to an additional conclusion. Recently, a number of researchers have attempted to test the stability of the relationship between economic activity and money with the help of vector autoregressions VARs involving various monetary aggregates, on the one hand, and output, prices and possibly other variables on the other. Studies applied to U.S. (Friedman and Kuttner 1996; Friedman 1997) and German (Estrella and Mishkin 1997) data generally suggest that money has little predictive power with respect to output and prices.[31] Thus, money does not appear to be stably related to economic activity, even in the case of Germany. However, this conclusion is misleading. Money demand may be stable in the sense defined above: Yet, if as in Figure 2.8 a complex relationship exists between money and economic activity, VARs may assign little predictive power to money.[32] This point becomes even more obvious if we assume that the SNB manages to keep the inflation rate constant at, say, 1 percent. To absorb the shocks threatening to disturb price stability, the SNB must vary M3 growth substantially over time. Clearly, a bivariate VAR in M3 growth and the inflation rate would lead to the false conclusion that money possesses no ability whatsoever to predict the inflation rate. Thus, these studies need not indicate that money is unstable in the sense defined above. However, they do suggest that inflation normally cannot be forecasted by straightforward extrapolation from past observations on money growth.

Since the relationship between inflation and M3 growth is likely to be complex, the question arises whether the SNB could usefully and credibly be committed to a target for such a broadly defined monetary aggregate. As indicated above, a target providing for steady expansion in M3 would be an undesirable policy strategy even if the demand for that aggregate continued to display a stable relationship to interest rates and economic activity. The SNB could not help adjusting M3 growth to aggregate-demand and exchange-rate shocks. An operational framework allowing the SNB to react appropriately to important shocks could be designed in various ways.

The SNB could adopt a feedback rule along the lines suggested by McCallum. The rule would trace out the movements in M3 growth required to achieve the SNB's ultimate policy objectives. In designing the rule, the SNB would determine the trend growth in M3, consistent with its definition of price stability and its estimate of potential growth. Moreover, the SNB would stipulate a reaction function determining the movements in M3 growth, if any, about its trend. As pointed out earlier, the SNB would have to vary M3 growth in response to at least three factors: Cyclical movements in aggregate demand, excessive swings in the exchange rate, and unexpected temporary or permanent shifts in money demand. Permanent velocity shifts would of course impinge on the required trend growth in M3.[33]

While a feedback rule of the type proposed by McCallum would imply a strong commitment to an operational framework, the SNB would run up against a number of difficulties if it decided to adopt such an approach. A major problem would arise from the fact that the SNB cannot control M3 growth with great precision. Its forecasts of M3 growth over short time horizons are particularly unreliable. For this reason, the SNB would not know with sufficient certainty how changes in its policy instruments affect M3 growth in the short run. Another problem would lie in determining the desired trend growth in M3 and the desired deviations, if any, from that trend. In practice, the SNB would find it difficult to chart the complex evolution of M3 consistent with its ultimate objective of price stability.

If the SNB were to follow such a complex feedback rule, it could never be certain that the rule would actually be helpful in attaining the stated objective of price stability. The key structural parameters of the economy impinging on the feedback rule might not remain stable over time. Moreover, they might depend on the type of shock hitting the economy and calling for a monetary policy response. Therefore, the SNB could not help forecasting inflation regularly in order to check whether the feedback rule was likely to trigger policy actions consistent with the ultimate objective of price stability.

Considering the consequences of adhering to a complex rule, the

SNB concluded that its best bet was to take a step in the direction of inflation targeting when it reviewed its policy approach in the wake of the instabilities afflicting the demand for base money. It is now setting monetary policy on the strength of inflation forecasts. To provide some commitment to an operational framework, it also attempts to identify key indicators entering into its inflation forecasts. In the following section, I discuss the SNB's current policy approach.

5. THE SNB's CURRENT POLICY APPROACH

At the end of 1999, the SNB (1999; 2000) dropped monetary targeting by modifying its policy approach in three respects:[34] First, inflation forecasts became the focal point of the internal policy debate. The SNB publishes an inflation forecast every six months, in June and December. The forecast is provided for three years ahead in order to take account of the long lags in effects of Swiss monetary policy. Moreover, the SNB reviews its forecast in March and September but does not publish a new quantitative prediction on these occasions.

Second, the SNB checks whether its forecast is in line with its main objective of price stability. To this end, the SNB specified the meaning of price stability when it modified its policy approach. For the reasons mentioned in Section 3, the SNB did not adopt an inflation target, but undertook to clarify its definition of price stability. It chose the same definition as the European Central Bank (ECB), that is, it now equates price stability with an inflation rate, measured by the headline CPI, of less than 2 percent per year. Although its definition does not feature a numerical lower bound, the SNB emphasizes that the pursuit of price stability implies avoidance of sustained inflation or deflation. The SNB is willing to tolerate temporary deviations in the inflation rate – caused by changes in the oil price, indirect taxes and similar factors – from the range of price stability. However, should the inflation forecast point to a sustained departure from the price stability range, the SNB will not hesitate to take offsetting action by adjusting short-term interest rates.

Third, the policy conclusions derived from the inflation forecast are expressed in terms of an operational target band for the three-month rate of interest for Swiss francs.[35] Since the width of the target band is one percentage point, the SNB allows for some variability in the three-month rate of interest. It has always favored procedures under which both the central bank and market participants can trigger changes in interest rates. In this way, market-induced movements in interest rates may play some role as a shock absorber in the foreign exchange market. For example, an exchange rate appreciation resulting from a portfolio shift into Swiss francs may be moderated by a market-induced decline in domestic money market rates. Furthermore, the SNB may obtain useful information on market participants' views about future changes in interest rates. For these reasons, the SNB does not directly control the three-month interest rate. Instead, it influences this rate indirectly through operations in very short-dated repos. However, if the SNB tightens or loosens monetary policy, it adjusts its operational target band. Normally, this leads to a parallel change in the three-month interest rate of the same order of magnitude.[36]

To generate its inflation forecast, the SNB relies on a variety of econometric models, including large and small structural models, vector-autoregressive models, as well as models predicting future inflation from the evolution of the aggregate M3. The model-based forecasts are supplemented by judgmental factors, including information drawn from the SNB's extensive contacts with business. The forecast, as announced to the public, takes account of any adjustment in the operational target band for the interest rate that the SNB may make upon disclosing its new forecast. Thus, the forecast, in principle, should not display anything but temporary deviations from the range of price stability unless the SNB deliberately chooses to miss its ultimate policy objective.

A key advantage of the new approach is that the inflation forecast focuses the public's attention on the main task of the SNB, that is, to preserve price stability. However, as indicated earlier, the new approach also entails a drawback: It is difficult to commit the SNB to an operational framework if policy decisions are based solely on an inflation forecast. To provide some commitment to an operational framework, the SNB attempts to identify important leading indicators of inflation that are bound to play a crucial role in its forecast of future price developments. The SNB distinguishes among two sets of indicators: Indicators of short-run and long-run movements in the inflation rate.

Over a horizon of up to 1.5 to 2 years, the inflation rate is influenced mainly by the cyclical state of the economy and the real exchange rate. For this reason, the SNB monitors various cyclical indicators, including foreign cyclical indicators bearing on the Swiss economy, estimates of the domestic output gap, and supply and demand conditions on the domestic labor market.

In the longer run, Swiss inflation is determined largely by the growth in the money supply, notably in the aggregate M3. However, as I already indicated, even though M3 contains useful information on future price developments, the relationship between money growth and inflation is complex. According to a recent study by the SNB (Jordan et al. 2001), it is possible to extract from the aggregate M3 two sets of information signaling future changes in the inflation rate. Over long horizons of 1.5 years and more, recorded growth in M3 exerts a statistically significant effect on future inflation, with the maximum impact observed after 3 to 3.5 years. Over shorter horizons, money also matters. However, it is 'excess' money, rather than recorded money growth, that influences inflation. Excess money, i.e. the error-correction term in a co-integrated demand function for M3, releases its maximum impact on inflation after 1 to 1.5 years. The best inflation forecasts are obtained if both recorded money growth and excess money are considered.

While the public is aware of the key indicators employed by Swiss policy makers, it remains to be seen to what extent the SNB can be committed to an operational framework under the new policy approach. At least, the public has a rough idea of the reaction function the SNB is likely to observe in its efforts to preserve price stability.

It should be noted that the SNB's new approach is similar, but not identical, to the policy concept adopted by the ECB. The SNB uses the same definition of price stability as the ECB. Moreover, the ECB (1999b, pp. 29–46) assigns a prominent role to money, in the form of a harmonized aggregate M3 for the euro area. However, in contrast to the ECB (1999a, pp. 47), the SNB did not adopt a two-pillar strategy, under which monetary policy decisions are based both on an inflation forecast and a reference value for the growth in the harmonized aggregate M3. The SNB was concerned that the public would be confused by such strategy and would be at a loss to understand which pillar determined monetary policy in practice. The SNB stressed that its policy decisions would be based on an inflation forecast, but that the aggregate M3 would serve as an important input into this forecast.

In conclusion, the main advantage of the SNB's new approach is that it centers the monetary policy debate on the role of the central bank as guarantor of price stability. On the whole, the shift to an approach based on inflation forecasts seems to have improved the transparency of monetary policy. The publication of inflation forecasts compels the SNB to disclose to the public its assessment of future price developments. As a result, the SNB's publications on monetary policy and economic developments have become more substantive and detailed. In this regard, the SNB has learned a great deal from the central banks targeting inflation. However, as we saw in Sections 1, 3 and 4, even before 2000 the SNB was not a secretive central bank. Pursuing a monetary target forced the SNB to explain to the public its policy actions. While the SNB's new approach appears to have enhanced transparency, I am less sure whether it features a strong commitment to an operational framework.

Regardless of the strategy followed by a central bank, explaining monetary policy to the public is not an easy task. For this reason, I am skeptical about Mishkin's (1999) contention that the public will find inflation targeting easier to comprehend than monetary targeting. The inflation target, by itself, may be easy to understand. But when we have to explain in simple language why we should not pay too much attention to output, why we use certain operating procedures but not others, or why our forecasts and intermediate targets are always conditional, all central banks face the same formidable task. Even under the SNB's new approach, communicating monetary policy will remain a challenge.

6. SUMMARY AND CONCLUSIONS

In this chapter I examined the differences between monetary and inflation targeting. Several studies comparing the two approaches to monetary policy come to the conclusion that the differences are not as large as is sometimes believed. Some authors even go so far as asserting that such central banks as the Bundesbank and the SNB that targeted money were really targeting inflation in disguise.

An analysis of the monetary policies followed by selected central banks indeed points to substantial similarities in behavior. It clearly did not make much difference whether they operated under inflation or monetary targeting regimes. These similarities also obtain for eclectic central banks such as the Federal Reserve and the Bank of Japan. The main reason for the similarity in behavior lies in the fact that the various central banks in recent years have increasingly focused their attention on price stability as the main objective of monetary policy.

Despite these similarities, there are also two important differences between inflation and monetary targeting. While the central banks under either approach are or were strongly committed to price stability, they did not employ the same commitment technology. Under the first approach, the central banks commit themselves to an inflation objective, framed in terms of a numerical target. However, they are free to select a suitable operational procedure required to meet the numerical target. The central banks that targeted money, by contrast, did not attempt to quantify precisely the ultimate objective of price stability. Instead, they endeavored to commit themselves to an operational framework designed to achieve and maintain price stability.

This chapter shows that committing the central bank to a monetary target raises various problems. Even if a stable relationship between money and the price level exists, a fixed intermediate target for money growth, as originally suggested by Milton Friedman, does not constitute an optimum operational strategy. What is required instead is a variable intermediate target for money growth. Relying on Swiss experience, I describe the issues involved in setting a variable monetary target. I show that in Switzerland money remains an important indicator of future price movements. Nevertheless, the SNB came to the conclusion that it was better to base monetary policy decisions on an inflation forecast than on a complex rule governing money growth. Under a new approach introduced at the end of 1999, the SNB now sets monetary policy on the strength of an inflation forecast, with money serving as an important input into this forecast.

Is it possible to draw more general lessons from the experiences of the central banks targeting inflation or money? In particular, is the discussion on inflation and monetary targeting relevant for the current problems of the East Asian countries? Until the outbreak of the 1997 crisis, several countries in that part of the world pegged their currencies to the U.S. dollar. Some of them still maintain a peg today. Fixed exchange rate systems do not always work properly. While a fixed exchange rate helps international trade, it severely restricts the scope of the domestic central bank for pursuing internal policy objectives such as price stability. The internal objectives must be subordinated to the goal of preserving the peg. Thus, under a fixed exchange rate, conflicts between the internal objectives of monetary policy and the desire to stabilize the external value of the currency may arise. The authorities may try to expand their room for maneuver by adjusting the exchange rate from time to time or by allowing that rate to crawl at a predetermined rate. Nevertheless, conflicts among the internal objectives and exchange rate stability are unlikely to disappear entirely even if some flexibility is built into the peg.

Should the authorities, in the event of conflicts, accord priority to the internal policy objectives, they may jeopardize the fixed exchange rate. They run the risk that the peg will lose its credibility among market participants, who may be prompted to attack the domestic currency. An unwillingness to subordinate the internal policy objectives to maintaining the exchange rate peg was probably one of several reasons for the outbreak of the Asian crisis.

In the presence of serious policy conflicts, it is understandable that the authorities are mainly concerned about the needs of the domestic economy. However, if the internal policy objectives take precedence over the external stability of the domestic currency, the authorities, in principle, should opt for a floating exchange rate and undertake to pursue an autonomous monetary policy aimed at the needs of the domestic economy.

The pursuit of an autonomous monetary policy may also run up against a number of difficulties. Market participants may not be convinced that the domestic central bank will be able and willing to achieve and maintain internal stability. The domestic central bank may lack the credibility required for pursuing an effective autonomous monetary policy aimed at internal stability. To gain the required credibility, the domestic central bank may learn from the experience of its colleagues targeting inflation or money: A clear mandate to pursue price stability, supplemented by an inflation target and, as far as possible, by a commitment to an operational framework will help the domestic central bank to acquire the urgently needed credibility.

ACKNOWLEDGEMENTS

A first draft of this chapter was presented at the 'International Conference on the Conduct of Monetary Policy', organized by the Central Bank of China and the Institute of Economics, Academia Sinica, Taipei, Taiwan, June 12–13, 1998. I am indebted to Barbara Rudolf for preparing Figures 2.1 to 2.6. I am also grateful to David Archer, Andreas Fischer, Chen-Min Hsu, Otmar Issing, Mervyn King, Allan Meltzer, Rick Mishkin, Michel Peytrignet and Anna Schwartz for very helpful suggestions and comments. I particularly benefited from Chuck Freedman's painstaking comments on an earlier version of the paper.

NOTES

1. Mishkin (1999) provides an excellent discussion of the pros and cons of exchange rate targeting. He shows convincingly that exchange rate targets are often handled in an inappropriate manner.
2. Issing (1998, pp. 9) makes a similar point.
3. Taylor (e.g. 1998) has also explored variants of equation (2.1) in which the money market rate depends on the inflation rate and the output gap, with a weight of 1.5 attached to the inflation rate and weights of 0.5 or 1 attached to the output gap.
4. After completing the first draft of my paper, I realized that Taylor (1999, pp. 661) makes the same point. If the central banks expand the money supply steadily in sympathy with the target, the size of the increase in money market rates depends on the interest elasticity of money demand (see also Section 4). Thus, the amplitude of the cyclical movements in money market rates need not match those generated by the Taylor Rule.
5. For Germany and Switzerland, the 'inflation targets' are close to the inflation assumptions underlying their monetary targets (Section 3). See note 11 for the inflation targets of the U.K and Canada.
6. Due to the effects of reunification on potential output, the HP filter cannot be applied to German GDP data in a straightforward way. For this reason, we allowed actual and potential output to shift up by 26 percent as a result of reunification. The shift was derived from a dummy variable in an econometric equation determining German GDP.
7. In the case of Canada, the Taylor Rule would have called for substantially lower interest rates between 1992 and 1995. The Bank of Canada underestimated the speed of the reduction in inflation from mid-1991, and overestimated the strength of the subsequent recovery. In an unpublished earlier version of their published paper, Freedman and Macklem (1998) describe the difficulties of setting appropriate monetary conditions in this period.
8. Clarida and Gertler (1997) draw such a misleading conclusion from their analysis of the Bundesbank's reaction function.
9. Applying the Taylor Rule to the U.S., Orphanides (1998) employs two different data sets on the output gap. First, he uses data that were available to him at the time when he conducted his study. Second, he constructs an estimate of the data that were known to policy makers at the time when they took their policy decisions. He finds that the results are very sensitive to the type of data employed for the output gap.
10. Nevertheless, the SNB for some time has monitored interest rate series derived from the Taylor Rule, besides other indicators.

11. See Bank for International Settlements (1996, pp. 62–71; 1997, Graph IV.6; 1998, pp. 65–75); Gordon Thiessen (1998). In the U.K. the target was initially set at 1–4 percent and then reduced to 1–2.5 percent. In 1997 the target band was replaced by a point target of 2.5 percent. In Canada, the first target was fixed at the end of 1992, with a range of 2–4 percent. The target was gradually reduced and set at 1–3 percent at the end of 1995. In Sweden, the target amounts to 1–3 percent, while in New Zealand it was changed from 0–2 to 0–3 percent at the end of 1996.
12. The SNB has spelled out its definition of price stability in its annual report since 1995 (SNB 1995, p. 9). Previously, it defined price stability as an inflation rate of 0–1 percent (Laubach and Posen 1997, p. 24). At the end of 1999, it adopted a new definition of price stability (see Section 5).
13. The Bundesbank used this price assumption from 1984 onward. Previously, it had argued in terms of 'unavoidable price increases' (Laubach and Posen 1997, p. 18).
14. Problems are created, above all, by housing costs, which appear in the Swiss CPI with a weight of over 20 percent. A majority of Swiss residents live in rental housing. Tenants may object to rent increases that they regard as unfair by appealing to a court. In judging on the appeal, the courts must employ a cost-based system of identifying unfair rent increases, with mortgage rates forming an important cost element. Therefore, when the SNB tightens monetary policy, housing rents, at first, rise sharply and thus react perversely to the policy change. However, in the longer run, housing rents are mainly determined by market forces.
15. Cecchetti (1998, p. 7) presents simulations for the U.S. pointing to a steep trade-off between the variability of inflation and output.
16. I am indebted to Chuck Freedman for the distinction between 'soft-edged' and 'hard-edged' targets. He views the Canadian inflation-control target as a soft-edged target.
17. In 1999, New Zealand introduced a new measure of the CPI that is similar to the core concept used previously by the Reserve Bank of New Zealand (1999, pp. 8).
18. Mishkin (1999) also emphasizes this point.
19. The SNB has expressed these views on numerous occasions. A good summary of its views is contained in a report of an expert group which was charged with preparing a proposal for revising the monetary provisions of the Swiss constitution (see Expertengruppe 1997).
20. The change in the exchange rate also affects the CPI directly through changes in import prices.
21. See Rich (1997a) for an analysis of this issue.

22. The Reserve Bank of New Zealand (2000, pp. 35) also paid considerable attention to a MCI, but dropped the MCI from the tables included in its *Monetary Policy Statement* in 2000. The SNB too monitors a MCI, but as a leading indicator of inflation, the MCI does not perform as well as the broadly defined monetary aggregates (Lengwiler 1997).
23. Laubach and Posen (1997, p. 2) talk about 'disciplined discretion'.
24. In the case of the monetary base, the interest sensitivity reflects mainly a statistically significant relationship between the demand for large-denomination bank notes and the rate on savings deposits.
25. In the 1970s the Bank of Canada faced a similar difficulty after it had adopted a target for M1. Its aim was to gradually reduce the growth in that aggregate in order to bring inflation under control. However, its gradualist approach was hampered by several problems, notably, shifts in money demand and an unexpected increase in inflation in 1978/79. The target for M1 did not trigger a sufficiently strong increase in interest rates in response to that price shock. As a result, the Bank of Canada failed to offset the additional inflationary pressures quickly (Thiessen 1983, pp. 102–3).
26. See Rich (1997a) for a more detailed discussion of the shift to flexible targeting. Bernanke et al. (1999, Chapter 4) also analyse this shift.
27. The target line implied an average annual growth rate of 1 percent in the monetary base. Due to ongoing innovations in the payments system, the trend increase in the monetary base velocity was estimated to amount to about 2 percent per year.
28. The SNB was criticized for not doing enough to counteract the upvaluation of the Swiss franc. It refused to open fully the monetary floodgates because it was concerned about the long-run consequences of its actions. With hindsight, the SNB should have avoided the renewed temporary drop in the monetary base in 1994 (Figure 2.7).
29. In 1978 the SNB relaxed monetary policy in order to counteract a strong appreciation of the Swiss franc. In 1987 and 1988 the SNB (over) reacted to another bout of Swiss franc strength and to the stock market crash (Rich 1997a).
30. Had the SNB followed a Taylor Rule, its performance would likely have been worse, rather than better. As shown by Figure 2.6, in 1986 and 1987, for example, the SNB would have pursued an even more expansionary course, whereas in 1990 it would have overreacted to the then high inflation rate. If a measure of core inflation is substituted for the headline series in Figure 2.6, the performance of the Taylor Rule improves for 1986 and 1987, but not for 1990.
31. In a study of the link between money growth and inflation in the U.S., Stein (1994) reaches a different conclusion than the authors relying on

VARs. He finds that growth in the money stock M2 is a good predictor of inflation in the long run, but not in the short run.

32. In a comment on Friedman's (1997) paper, I ran bivariate VARs in Swiss nominal GDP and the money stock M2. Money explains only a small part of the variation in nominal GDP (Rich 1997b, pp. 172–4), despite the fact that demand for M2 is about as stable as for M3 (Peytrignet and Stahel 1998). See also Meltzer (1998) on the same issue. However, multivariate VARs, including structural VARs (Kugler and Jordan 2000), attribute an important role to the monetary aggregates in forecasting Swiss inflation, especially over longer horizons.

33. Once-and-for-all and continual velocity shifts call for temporary and continual adjustments in the trend growth of M3 respectively. In the case of permanent shifts in potential growth, the trend growth of M3 must also be adjusted permanently.

34. See Rich (2000) for a more detailed discussion of the SNB's current policy approach.

35. The SNB chose the Libor rate as its operational target variable. It regards the rate on Swiss-franc deposits quoted in the London market as the most representative money market rate. Since capital can move freely in and out of Switzerland, the London market for Swiss francs, for all practical purposes, is part of the domestic money market.

36. Until the end of 1999, the SNB set operational targets for bank reserves, but strove to avoid excessive fluctuations in money market rates.

REFERENCES

Bank for International Settlements (1996), *66th Annual Report,* Basle.
Bank for International Settlements (1997), *67th Annual Report,* Basle.
Bank for International Settlements (1998), *68th Annual Report,* Basle.
Bank of Canada (2001), *Monetary Policy Report,* Ottawa, May.
Bank of England (2001), *Inflation Report,* London, February.
Bernanke, Ben S. and Ilian Mihov (1997), 'What does the Bundesbank target?', *European Economic Review,* **41** (June): 1025–53.
Bernanke, Ben S. and Frederic S. Mishkin (1997), 'Inflation targeting: a new framework for monetary policy?', *Journal of Economic Perspectives,* **11** (Spring): 97–116.
Bernanke, Ben S., Thomas Laubach, Frederic S. Mishkin and Adam S. Posen (1999), *Inflation Targeting: Lessons from the International Experience,* Princeton, NJ: Princeton University Press.
Clarida, Richard and Mark Gertler (1997), 'How the Bundesbank conducts monetary policy', in Christina D. Romer and David H. Romer (eds), *Reducing Inflation: Motivation and Strategy,* Chicago: University of Chicago Press, pp. 363–406.

Cechhetti, Stephen G. (1998) 'Policy Rules and Targets: Framing the Central Banker's Problem, FRBNY Economic Policy Review' (June) 1998 pp. 1–14.

Estrella, Arturo and Frederic S. Mishkin (1997), 'Is there a role for monetary aggregates in the conduct of monetary policy?', *Journal of Monetary Economics,* **40** (October): 279–304.

European Central Bank (1999a), *Monthly Bulletin,* Frankfurt am Main, January.

European Central Bank (1999b), *Monthly Bulletin,* Frankfurt am Main, February.

Expertengruppe 'Reform der Währungsordnung' (1997), *Der neue Geld-und Währungsartikel in der Bundesverfassung,* Berne, 24 October.

Freedman, Charles (1995), 'What operating procedures should be adopted to maintain price stability? – practical issues', *Achieving Price Stability,* Federal Reserve Bank of Kansas City, Kansas City, MO, pp. 241–85.

Freedman, Charles and Tiff Macklem (1998), 'A comment on the "the great Canadian slump" ', *Canadian Journal of Economics,* **31** (August): 646–65.

Friedman, Benjamin M. (1997), 'The rise and fall of money growth targets as guidelines for US monetary policy', in Iwao Kuroda (ed.), *Towards More Effective Monetary Policy,* Basingstoke and London: Macmillan, pp. 137–64.

Friedman, Benjamin M. and Kenneth N. Kuttner (1996), 'A price target for U.S. monetary policy? lessons from the experience with money growth targets', *Brookings Papers on Economic Activity,* **1**: 77–125.

Friedman, Milton (1959), *A Program for Monetary Stability,* New York: Fordham University Press.

Issing, Otmar (1998), 'Welche geldpolitische Strategie für die EZB?', Deutsche Bundesbank, *Aüszuge aus Presseartikeln* (excerpts from the press), Frankfurt am Main, 11 May.

Jordan, Thomas J., Michel Peytrignet and Georg Rich (2001), 'The role of M3 in the policy analysis of the Swiss National Bank', in Hans-Joachim Klöckers and Caroline Willeke (eds), *Monetary Analysis: Tools and Applications,* European Central Bank, July, pp. 47–62.

Kugler, Peter and Thomas J. Jordan (2000), 'Structural vectorauto regressions and the analysis of monetary policy interventions: the Swiss case', WWZ/University of Basel and Swiss National Bank, November.

Laubach, Thomas and Adam S. Posen (1997), 'Disciplined discretion: monetary targeting in Germany and Switzerland', *Essays in International Finance,* No. 206, Princeton, NJ: International Finance Section, Princeton University, December.

Lengwiler, Yvan (1997), 'Der "Monetary Conditions Index" für die Schweiz', *Geld, Währung und Konjunktur,* 15 (Quarterly Review of the SNB), March, pp. 61–72.

McCallum, Bennett T. (1989), *Monetary Economics,* New York: Macmillan.

McCallum, Bennett T. (1999), 'Issues in the design of monetary policy rules', in John B. Taylor and Michael Woodford (eds), *Handbook of Macroeconomics,* Vol. IC, Amsterdam: North Holland, Chapter 23, pp. 1483–530.

Meltzer, Allan H. (1987), 'Limits of short-run stabilization policy', *Economic Inquiry*, **25**: 1–14.

Meltzer, Allan H. (1998), 'Monetarism: the issues and the outcome', *Atlantic Economic Journal*, **26** (March): 8–31.

Mishkin, Frederic S. (1999), 'International experiences with different monetary policy regimes', *Journal of Monetary Economics*, **43** (June): 579–605.

Orphanides, Athanasios (1998), 'Monetary policy rules based on real-time data', paper presented at the 'NBER Conference on the Formulation of Monetary Policy', Boston, MA, December 4–5.

Peytrignet, Michel and Christof Stahel (1998), 'Stability of money demand in Switzerland: a comparison of the M2 and M3 cases', *Empirical Economics*, **23**: 437–54.

Reserve Bank of New Zealand (1997), *Monetary Policy Statement*, Wellington, December.

Reserve Bank of New Zealand (1999), *Monetary Policy Statement*, November.

Reserve Bank of New Zealand (2000), *Monetary Policy Statement*, December.

Rich, Georg (1997a), 'Monetary targets as a policy rule: lessons from the Swiss experience', *Journal of Monetary Economics*, **39** (June): 113–41.

Rich, Georg (1997b), 'Comments', in Iwoa Kuroda (ed.), *Towards More Effective Monetary Policy*, Basingstoke and London: Macmillan, pp: 171–5.

Rich, Georg (2000), 'Monetary policy without central bank money: a Swiss perspective', *International Finance*, **3** (November): 439–69.

Svensson, Lars E.O. (1997), 'Inflation forecast targeting: implementing and monitoring inflation targets', *European Economic Review*, **41**: 1111–46.

Sveriges Riksbank (2001), *Inflation Report*, Stockholm, March.

Swiss National Bank (1995), *87th Annual Report 1994* (Abridged version), Berne.

Swiss National Bank (1999), 'Monetary policy decisions of the Swiss National Bank for 2000', *Quartalsheft*, **17** (December).

Swiss National Bank (2000), *92nd Annual Report 1999*.

Stein, Jerome L. (1994), 'Can the central bank achieve price stability?', *Federal Reserve Bank of St. Louis Review*, **March/April**: 175–201.

Taylor, John B. (1993), 'Discretion versus policy rules in practice', *Carnegie-Rochester Conference Series on Public Policy*, **39** (December): 195–214.

Taylor, John B. (1998), 'Information technology and monetary policy', *Monetary and Economic Studies*, Bank of Japan, **16** (December): 19–28.

Taylor, John B. (1999), 'The robustness and efficiency of monetary policy rules as guidelines for interest setting by the European Central Bank', *Journal of Monetary Economics*, **43** (June): 655–79.

Thiessen, Gordon (1983), 'The Canadian experience with monetary targeting', in Paul Meek (ed.), *Central Bank Views on Monetary Targeting*, Federal Reserve Bank of New York, pp. 100–4.

Thiessen, Gordon (1998–1999), 'The Canadian experience with targets for inflation control', The Gibson Lecture, Queen's University, *Bank of Canada Review*, **Winter**: 89–107.

E57 E43
E31 E52

3. Historical U.S. money growth, inflation, and inflation credibility

William G. Dewald

1. INTRODUCTION

Although many forces affect individual prices in the short run, the historical record shows that in the long run changes in the general level of prices, i.e., inflation, have been linked systematically to changes in the quantity of money. The Federal Reserve uses as its principal monetary policy target an overnight inter-bank interest rate, the federal funds rate, which it manipulates by open market operations that change its portfolio of government securities, which in turn influences monetary growth. Economists both inside and outside the Federal Reserve monitor a wide range of indicators so as to judge the appropriateness of a monetary policy target relative to the goals of achieving a stable price level and sustained real growth. For many years presidents of the Federal Reserve Bank of St. Louis and many of its economists have called attention to research showing that long-term growth of monetary aggregates is among the more important of these indicators. They also have championed the preeminence of price level stability as a monetary policy goal to provide the best environment for sustained economic growth in a market economy.

The historical data reveal a consistent correlation between long-term growth rates in broad monetary aggregates, spending, and inflation in the United States, but not between such nominal variables and real output. Data from the bond market show that, despite inflation being at its lowest level in decades, the Federal Reserve Bank has not regained fully the inflation credibility that it lost in the 1960s and 1970s.

2. NOMINAL AND REAL GROWTH, AND INFLATION

The financial press and the public often seem to believe that the way to contain inflation is to pursue policies that reduce real economic growth. The view that it necessarily takes lower real growth, or even a recession, to slow inflation is an improper reading of historical data. It fails to differentiate between the short run and the long run. Sustained real output growth depends on increases in the supply of labor and capital, and increases in the productivity of such inputs. Growth in demand for output certainly influences what is produced, but fundamental scarcities limit the aggregate amount of how much can be produced on a sustained basis. Furthermore, as the level and variability of inflation increase, price signals become fuzzier and decisions are distorted, which would tend to decrease real gross domestic product (GDP). Thus, one should not expect an increase in demand growth to increase real growth on a sustained basis, but if at all, only in the short run. An examination of the historical record supports this proposition.

Figure 3.1 is a plot of percentage changes over 1959–97 in nominal GDP, real GDP, and the GDP price index. The chart includes year-over-year and 10-year moving averages. The four-quarter changes – the fine lines – remove the high frequency noise from the data. The 10-year changes – the heavy lines – remove the business cycle fluctuations as well. The gap between nominal and real GDP growth rates approximates inflation, as measured by percentage changes in the GDP price index, which are shown in the bottom panel of Figure 3.1.[1] Figure 3.1 reveals several regular patterns:

- Inflation trended up through about 1980, and down since then.
- Annual growth rates in nominal GDP and real GDP went up and down together.
- Annual growth rates in nominal and real GDP were also more volatile than annual inflation rates.
- Recessions occurred more frequently from the late 1960s through the early 1980s when inflation was high and rising than since the early 1980s when it trended down.
- Inflation typically accelerated before cyclical peaks, but then decelerated beginning in recessions and extending into the early phase of recoveries.
- In recent years, inflation has been its lowest and most stable since the late 1950s and early 1960s, and, atypically, it has continued to decelerate in the seventh year of the expansion.

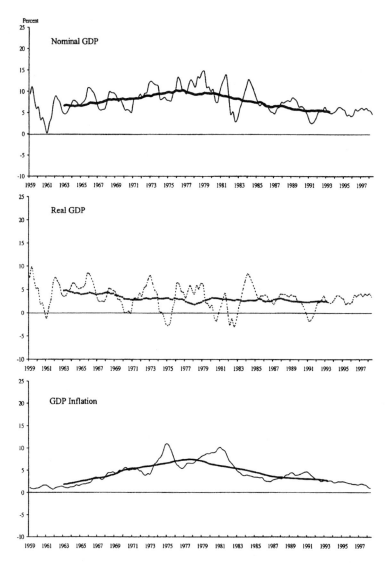

Note: The bold lines are contered 10-year moving averages of the respective scries.

Figure 3.1 Inflation and real growth (year/year and 10-year averages)

The year-over-year movements in nominal and real GDP are matched closely in the short run, an observation seemingly suggesting that policies to increase nominal GDP growth would increase real GDP growth, too. That short-run relationship, however, does not hold up in the long run. From the 1960s through the early 1980s the increase in 10-year average nominal GDP growth was associated with a matching increase in 10-year average inflation, but, if anything, a decrease in 10-year average real GDP growth. Thus, increased average nominal GDP growth in the long run was not associated with increased real GDP growth, but only with inflation.

International evidence supports this finding that inflation harms long-run growth. Studies of other countries have identified a small negative effect of even moderate inflation on real growth.[2] Small differences amount to a lot over long periods because of compounding. Thus, it may not be an accident of history that the most highly industrialized economies with the highest per capita income today have had comparatively low inflation over extended periods. With respect to countries that have experienced inflation of 40 percent a year or more, the evidence is unambiguous: High inflation reduces real growth.[3]

High inflation also has been linked to cyclical instability. There was a deep recession in 1981 and 1982. This recession was associated with a genuinely restrictive monetary policy and interest rates at unprecedented levels. The rate of unemployment built up to more than 10 percent and inflation fell far more sharply than most forecasters had expected. Despite some relapse in the late 1980s, inflation has trended down since the early 1980s, and real GDP growth has averaged somewhat less than it did in the 1960s, but this is because of lower productivity growth and not because of recessions and unemployment. In fact, the U.S. economy has performed very well relative to its potential and better than ever in terms of cyclical stability. The 29-quarter expansion from 1991:Q1 through 1998:Q2 had not yet lasted as long as the record 34-quarter expansion of the 1960s. However, as inflation decreased from the end of the recession in 1982:Q4 through 1998:Q2, there were 63 expansion quarters and only three contraction quarters, an unprecedented era of cyclical stability in U.S. history. It surpassed the record of 1961:Q1 through 1973:Q4, which included 47 positive growth quarters and four contraction quarters. The record was not too shabby in either case, but there was a difference. The 1960s and early 1970s were a period of accelerating inflation, which laid a foundation for the instabilities that followed. The 1980s and so far the 1990s have been a period of decelerating inflation, which has lain a foundation for stable price level credibility and efficient resource utilization. The next figures bring monetary growth into the picture.

3. MONETARY GROWTH AND INFLATION

M2 is a measure of money that Milton Friedman and Anna Schwartz trace in their *Monetary History of the United States*.[4] It is a broad measure made up of assets having a common characteristic: Each is either issued by the monetary authorities, for example, currency and coin, or is an obligation of a depository institution legally convertible into such standard monetary units. M2 assets can be divided into M1 and non-M1 categories. M1 components can be used to make payments directly (currency, traveler's checks, and checking accounts). Non-M1 components, which can be readily turned into M1 assets, include savings deposits, money-market mutual fund balances, and short-term time deposits. Such non-M1 components of M2 have become increasingly accessible to depositors for payments in recent years. M2, as a broad monetary aggregate, represents the essence of 'liquidity', i.e., a way station between income receipts and expenditures for both households and non-financial businesses, and, as such, a variable that would be expected to be related to total national spending in current dollar terms, i.e., nominal GDP.

Figure 3.2 plots growth rates in M2, nominal GDP, and the GDP price index. It reveals some regular short-term patterns in the year-over-year data:[5]

- M2 and nominal GDP growth rates slow before and during the initial stages of a recession.
- M2 growth turned down many more times than the number of cyclical peaks.
- M2 growth turned up during each recession and early recovery except during the most recent instance when it continued to slow.
- M2 and nominal GDP have been growing at similar rates between 1995 and 1998.

This figure reveals the major reason why M2 has been discredited as an indicator of the stance of monetary policy in recent years – in the short run, movements in the monetary aggregates, nominal GDP, and inflation sometimes appear to be unrelated. For example, whereas M2 growth slowed dramatically between 1992 and 1994, nominal GDP growth accelerated. That discrepancy produced the largest and most

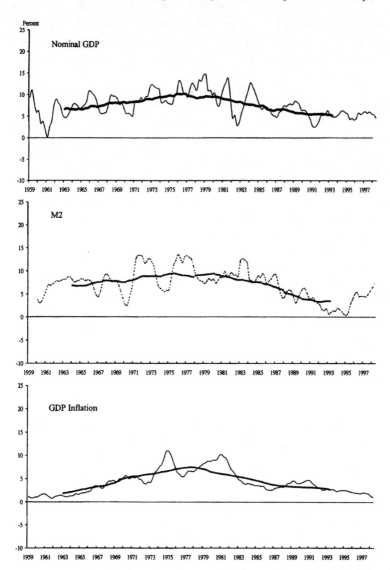

Note: The bold lines are contered 10-year moving averages of the respective scries.

Figure 3.2 M2 and nominal GDP growth, and inflation (year/year and 10-year averages)

persistent deviation between the growth rates in M2 and nominal GDP in many years. This deviation has led the Federal Open Market Committee (FOMC) and the public to place less emphasis on the money supply targets.

Nevertheless, giving up on the aggregates might be a mistake. The reason is that there has been a close *long-term* fit between M2 growth and nominal GDP growth and, in turn, inflation. Figure 3.2 shows the general upward trend in 10-year average M2 growth, nominal GDP growth, and inflation during the 1960s and 1970s, and the general downward trend in these 10-year averages during the 1980s and so far in the 1990s. Such a longer-term historical relationship is presumably a reason why M2 is one of the monetary variables for which the Federal Reserve continues to announce a target range in the Congressional Humphrey-Hawkins hearings twice a year. In his Humphrey Hawkins testimony in February 1998, and again in July, Chairman Alan Greenspan noted that M2 growth might be back on track as an indicator of nominal GDP growth and inflation, after it appeared to have been off track earlier in the expansion.

Observations about M2, nominal GDP growth, and inflation over the long run support Milton Friedman's dictum that 'inflation is always and everywhere a monetary phenomenon'. The looseness of the short-term association supports his dictum that 'lags are long and variable'. Figures 3.3 and 3.4 makes these points with data going back to 1875.

Figure 3.3 shows that short-run, year-over-year changes in these historical series are very noisy. Yet, even on a year-over-year basis, the association of large movements in M2 with large movements in nominal gross national product (GNP) and inflation is apparent, (for example, the contraction of monetary growth and nominal GDP growth in the early 1930s and the associated deflation). In less turbulent times such as recent decades, however, there is no clearly discernable systematic short-run association between broad money growth, nominal GNP growth, and inflation. Of course, a change in the price level over a year or two is not really what is meant by inflation unless it is substantial enough to change the price level a lot.

Figure 3.4 shows that over the past 35 years the long upward and downward cycle in M2 and nominal GNP growth rates and inflation is only one of a series of comparable long cycles in U.S. history. Following a period of low M2 growth and deflation in the 1870s and 1880s, there have been four long inflation–disinflation cycles. They are marked on the figure by troughs in centered 10-year average inflation in 1893, 1909, 1928, and 1962. In 1998, it is not known yet

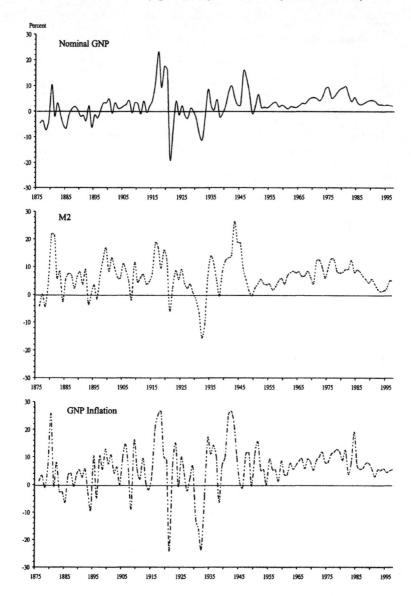

Figure 3.3 M2, nominal GNP growth, and inflation (annually)

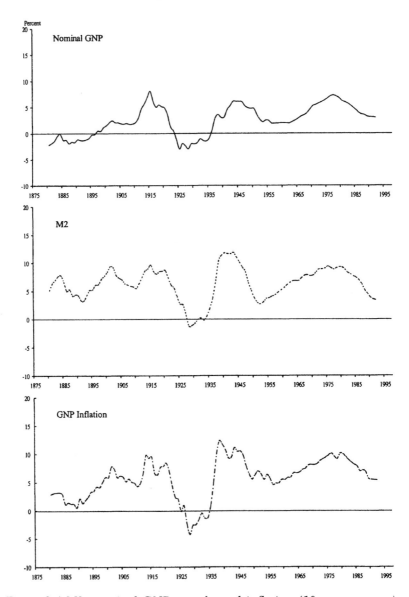

Figure 3.4 M2, nominal GNP growth, and inflation (10-year averages)

whether the last 10-year average plotted was a trough.

Because M2 growth tracks all previous inflation–disinflation cycles, it goes a long way to avert the suspicion that the relationship between monetary growth and inflation is spurious. Monetary historians such as Milton Friedman and Anna Schwartz have recognized that the mere association of monetary growth with inflation does not establish the direction of causality. To confirm that monetary growth causes inflation, they cite the evidence that the long-term relationship between monetary growth and inflation has remained much the same throughout history, including periods when we know that monetary growth resulted from supply-side factors. For example, when monetary growth accelerated in the 1890s, as engineering advances increased gold output, there was an associated inflation. Gold was then a standard into which currencies could be converted. When monetary growth collapsed in the early 1930s because of bank failures, there was an associated deflation.

The historical record also includes episodes when demand pressures led the Federal Reserve Bank to support monetary increases. In both World Wars I and II, Federal Reserve Bank policies to help the government finance its debt stimulated monetary growth. What followed were substantial increases in inflation. Nevertheless, even in wartime, there is reason to think that the Federal Reserve Bank could have kept a damper on inflation. When federal deficits rose in the 1980s, but the rate of monetary growth fell, inflation did not rise. It fell. The historical evidence is that when the Federal Reserve Bank has held interest rates down in the face of demand pressures by stimulating monetary growth, inflation has accelerated. However, in periods such as the 1980s, when monetary growth has not accelerated, inflation has not accelerated.

Every major acceleration in M2 growth has been associated with a major acceleration in inflation. Likewise, every major deceleration in M2 growth has been associated with a major deceleration in inflation. Accordingly, policy makers might be making a serious mistake if the noisy short-term movements in M2 and inflation persuaded them that money does not matter anymore. At a minimum, policy makers and the public might be wise to monitor monetary growth, mindful that inflationary demand pressures do not cause money growth unless the monetary authorities passively allow that to happen. Since the long run consists of an accumulation of short runs, it follows that sustained shifts in M2 growth are worth noting when formulating monetary policy. Keeping longer-term average M2 growth and nominal GDP growth in the neighborhood of longer-term real growth remains a practical guide for achieving a stable price level environment.

4. INFLATION AND INTEREST RATES

Readers might be surprised that monetary policy has been discussed
to this point without much reference to interest rates. This approach
was not an oversight.

Interest rates compensate lenders for giving up current purchasing power and taking some risk. One risk is that borrowers
might default. Another is that what they pay back might have less
purchasing power than what was lent.

Despite the conventional wisdom to the contrary, interest rates
often have not been a good measure of the thrust of monetary policy
on demand growth and inflation.[6] Because increases in expected
inflation would tend to raise rates, rising nominal interest rates do
not necessarily signal an anti-inflationary (tighter) monetary policy.
Correspondingly, falling nominal interest rates are not necessarily a
measure of a more inflationary (easier) monetary policy.

Nominal interest rates are highly sensitive to inflation and inflationary expectations. High inflation expectations lead lenders to
demand compensation for the expected depreciation in the purchasing
power of the money they lend, and borrowers are forced to add an
inflation premium to the interest rates they pay.

Apart from default and inflation risk premiums, real (inflation
adjusted) interest rates depend largely on underlying real factors
such as domestic saving and investment and international capital
flows, not on monetary growth and inflation. Thus, regardless of
monetary growth and inflation, higher real interest rates generally
reflect increased investment opportunities or decreased saving. That
real interest rates reflect underlying real factors is another reason why
interest rates are not a reliable measure of the stance of monetary
policy.

In this regard, technological change in the 1990s, coupled with the
long expansion, may have increased the return to capital investment
in the U.S. economy, and hence the demand for capital relative
to historical experience, which would tend to increase real interest
rates. In such circumstances, there is a monetary policy risk in
underestimating the upward pressures on real interest rates that
result from an increase in real investment demand. Any attempt to
attenuate such pressures by stimulating monetary growth would risk
a build up of inflationary pressures.

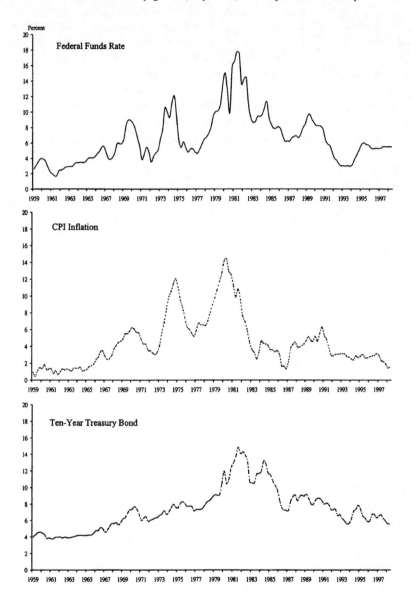

Figure 3.5 Inflation and selected interest rates

Fundamentally, monetary policy is tighter or easier not in terms of whether nominal or real interest rates are rising or falling, but in terms of whether inflationary pressures are falling or rising. As the historical figures have demonstrated, inflation in a longer-term sense is associated with high monetary growth. Figure 3.5 shows that increases and decreases in inflation trends are reflected in major increases and decreases in nominal interest rate levels.

Figure 3.5 plots the federal funds rate, the 10-year Treasury bond rate, and annual changes in the Consumer Price Index. When inflation held in the range of 1.5 to 2 percent during the late 1950s and early 1960s, 10-year Treasury bonds yielded about 4 percent. From the mid-1960s through the early 1980s, inflation trended up and so did both short- and long-term nominal interest rates. Since then, inflation has trended down and so have both short- and long-term nominal interest rates. Thus, the events of recent decades tend to confirm that high inflation is associated with high nominal interest rates and low inflation with low nominal interest rates. As a corollary, Federal Reserve policies that increase the growth of the monetary aggregates, and thereby inflation, would in due course also increase nominal interest rates, despite the myopic view that expansionary monetary policies lower nominal interest rates. Federal Reserve policies cannot lower nominal interest rates permanently except by actions that lower inflation.

5. INFLATION CREDIBILITY AND INTEREST RATES

Given the propensity to save, average real (inflation-adjusted) interest rates would tend to rise with an increase in trend real GDP growth. The reason is that measured real GDP growth is associated with increased real rates of return on investment. Average nominal interest rates tend to deviate from the real rate of return on investment by an amount that reflects expectations of inflation and inflation risks. The greater the gap between nominal interest rates and real rates of return, the lower the Fed's credibility is for keeping inflation low. Thus, the difference between nominal interest rates and trend real growth provides a crude measure of inflation expectations in the bond market, i.e., inflation credibility.[7]

Real GDP growth (averaged over 10 years to remove business cycle movements) drifted down from about 4 percent during the 1950s and early 1960s to about 2 percent during the late 1970s and early 1980s. It then rose back up to about 3.5 percent so far during

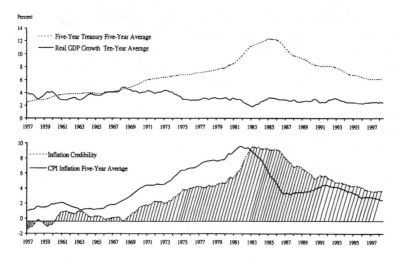

Figure 3.6 Long-term yields, real growth, and bond market inflation credibility

the 1990s. Five-year average inflation drifted up from about 1 to 2 percent during the 1950s and early 1960s to nearly 10 percent in 1980, then back down to about 3 percent during the 1990s. The five-year average of the five-year Treasury security yield rose from 2 percent during the 1950s to 12 percent during the early 1980s; but it then fell back to about 6 percent in the 1990s. Since bond yields rose when inflation accelerated, but real GDP growth slowed, the influence of inflation outweighed the influence of real GDP growth on bond yields. Correspondingly, when inflation decelerated, bond yields fell even though real GDP remained stable.

The difference between the five-year average of the five-year Treasury security yield and the 10-year average of real GDP growth is an estimate of the bond market's five-year inflation forecast, adjusted for inflation risk. It is the height of the shaded area in the lower panel of Figure 3.6. This measure of inflation credibility roughly lagged inflation, indicating that bond yields have not been very forward looking in forecasting inflation. The measure of inflation credibility hovered close to zero during the 1950s and early 1960s, which was credibly a zero-inflation-expectations period. It under-forecast inflation from the late 1960s until the early 1980s when inflation was rising. It over-forecast inflation in the 1980s and so far in the 1990s as inflation has fallen. It peaked at about 10 percent in the early 1980s, but fell to about 4 percent in recent years.

The bond market inflation forecast (or inflation premium) over the past five years represents a substantial gain in credibility compared with the early 1980s, but a substantial loss compared with the 1950s and early 1960s. In that earlier period, actual inflation was about 2 percent, but the bond market forecast a rate close to zero. In recent years, inflation has averaged about 3 percent, but the bond market has forecast about 4 percent inflation inclusive of an inflation risk premium. Thus, despite recent inflation being the lowest and most stable in decades, bond markets have seemingly not yet been convinced that inflation is down to stay. If the inflation premium were eliminated, bond yields could fall to match trend real growth, as was the pattern in the 1950s and early 1960s. That is about 3 percent, which is considerably lower than the approximately 5 to 5.5 percent bond yields observed in mid-1998.

Double-digit inflation and inflationary expectations are what explain the all-time peak in security yields in October 1981 as plotted in Figure 3.7. Since then, the entire yield curve has shifted down by roughly 10 percentage points, undoubtedly a reflection of the decline in inflation and inflationary expectations. Although markets do not expect double-digit inflation today, they do not expect price stability either. During the 1950s and early 1960s inflation was low and generally expected to stay low, a condition that was reflected in long-term rates hovering in the 3 to 4 percent range as represented by the January 3, 1959, yield curve on the figure. Despite the historical record of an unstable price level in the short run, there really was widespread expectation of longer-term price stability until inflation took off in the mid-1960s. In fact, never before the 1960s had the U.S. federal government borrowed long term at more than a 4.5 percent rate.

During the expansion that began in 1991, the yield curve touched a cyclical low on October 15, 1993. It then shifted up to a cyclical peak on November 7, 1994. Three-month bill rates had increased from 3 percent to 5.4 percent and 30-year bond rates, from 5.8 to 8.2 percent. The latter was presumably an illustration of increases in long-term interest rates indicative of rising inflationary expectations in the bond market. Although inflation, in fact, did not increase much during the 1990s expansion, bond markets may well have been anticipating a repeat of the experience of inflation accelerating as had typically occurred in the past. Historically, monetary policy often has lagged behind market interest rates in expansions and thereby added to, rather than damped, inflationary pressures. By comparison, the record during the 1990s expansion has been very good: An extended

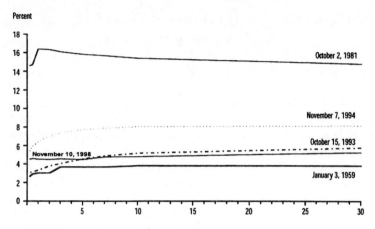

Figure 3.7 Government securities yield curve

period of positive real growth with inflation held in check. Yet, with bond rates still above the real growth trend, the bond markets seemingly continue to reflect the fear that inflation will rise again.

6. HOW TO GET AND KEEP INFLATION CREDIBILITY

What could the Federal Reserve do to enhance its inflation credibility, and thereby allow long-term interest rates to stay low and prospectively fall further? Most important, the Federal Reserve Bank should continue to keep inflation low by limiting the rate of monetary growth. A practical goal would be to get back to the low inflation and low interest rates of the late 1950s and early 1960s. One way to persuade markets that low inflation is here to stay is for the FOMC to focus more sharply on the desired outcome for inflation by following several other countries that have legislated specific low inflation targets for their central banks. This list includes Australia, Canada, New Zealand, and the United Kingdom, as well as Portugal, Spain, and Sweden. Whether or not such efforts are directly responsible, the fact is that these countries have had considerable success in bringing inflation down and keeping it down.

A second proposal comes from economists who have argued that credibility would be enhanced if there were an announced policy rule (with respect to the federal funds rate or monetary growth) and the Federal Reserve Bank acted on the basis of that rule. The advantage of a rule is that markets would know in advance how the

Federal Reserve Bank would react to deviations of nominal spending, inflation, or other variables from specified targets.

A third proposal made by Dewald (1988) is that federal budget offices base their budget projections over a 5- to 10-year horizon not on their own inflation assumptions, but on longer-term inflation forecasts from the Federal Reserve. Since the Federal Reserve Bank has the power to influence inflation over the long term, why not relieve the budget offices of the responsibility for making an independent assessment of future inflation as they make their budget projections? Not only could the budget offices benefit, but also every business, state and local government, and household could benefit from having confidence that the Federal Reserve Bank would act to keep inflation as low as it had forecast. Lars Svensson (1996) has proposed that the Federal Reserve Bank make its own announced inflation forecasts an explicit policy target. By using a forecast as a guide to policy, the Federal Reserve Bank would be focused on this objective, but not blind to other things going on in the economy that influence inflation.

An environment of credible price stability has a high payoff in a market economy. The historical evidence examined in this chapter supports the conclusion that risks of starting another costly inflation–disinflation cycle could be avoided by monitoring M2 monetary growth and maintaining a sufficiently tight monetary policy to keep a damper on inflation. Having achieved the lowest and most stable inflation environment in many decades, the Federal Reserve has an unusual opportunity to persuade markets that it will continue to keep inflation low and, in principle, eliminate it. An environment of credible price stability would allow the economy to function unfettered by inflationary distortions – which is all that can be reasonably expected of monetary policy, but precisely what should be expected of it.

ACKNOWLEDGEMENT

Reprinted from 'Historical U.S. Money Growth, Inflation, and Inflation Credibility', *Federal Reserve Bank of St. Louis Review*, Vol. 80, No. 6 (November/December 1998), pp. 13–23. Earlier versions of this chapter were presented at the Morgan Stanley Dean Witter Interest Rate Conference, Little Rock, Arkansas, May 6, 1998; the Conference on the Conduct of Monetary Policy, Institute of Economics, Academia Sinica, Taipei, Taiwan, June 12, 1998; and the Institute of Developing Economies, Tokyo, Japan, June 17, 1998.

NOTES

1. With chain-weights, price indexes and quantity indexes are calculated separately for components of GDP and therefore the difference between nominal GDP and real GDP growth is only approximately equal to the change in the GDP price index. With fixed-weights, the GDP deflator is defined as the ratio of nominal to real GDP and hence the gap between nominal and real GDP growth rates is precisely equal to the growth rate in the GDP deflator.
2. See Barro (1996) and Eijffinger et al. (1998).
3. See Bruno and Easterly (1996).
4. See Friedman and Schwartz (1963).
5. Despite M2's imperfections as a cyclical indicator, the Conference Board's monthly Leading Indicators Index includes M2 relative to the price level as one of its 10 components.
6. The faultiness of interest rates as measures of monetary policy in a non-inflationary environment was evaluated in Dewald (1963).
7. The analysis rests on the assumption that the real rate of interest equals the rate of growth of real GDP, when both series are averaged over a moderately long period of time. This condition arises in theoretical models in which consumers are Ricardian and the rate of time preference is zero. The condition that the real interest rate is equal to the real output growth rate arises in theory since real GDP growth is acting as a proxy for an equilibrium rate of return on investment. It would be appropriately expressed in per capita terms. Per capita GDP growth has slowed more than overall GDP growth over the period plotted on Figure 3.6. Therefore, current inflation credibility would have fallen even more relative to its level in the late 1950s and early 1960s than indicated on Figure 3.6, if per capita real GDP growth had been used to proxy the equilibrium rate of return on investment.

REFERENCES

Barro, Robert (1996), 'Inflation and growth', *Federal Reserve Bank of St. Louis Review*, **78** (May/June): 153–69.
Bruno, Michael and William Easterly (1996), 'Inflation and growth: in search of a stable relationship', *Federal Reserve Bank of St. Louis Review*, **78** (May/June): 139–46.
Dewald, William G. (1963), 'Free reserves, total reserves, and monetary control', *The Journal of Political Economy*, **LXXI**(2): 141–53.
Dewald, William G. (1988), 'Monetarism is dead; long live the quantity theory', *Federal Reserve Bank of St. Louis Review*, **70** (July/August): 3–18.

Eijffinger, Sylvester, Eric Schaling and Marco Hoeberichts (1998), 'Central bank independence: a sensitivity analysis', *European Journal of Political Economy*, **14**: 73–88.

Friedman, Milton and Anna J. Schwartz (1963), *A Monetary History of the United States*, 1867–1960, Princeton University Press.

Svensson, Lars (1996), 'Commentary: how should monetary policy respond to shocks while maintaining long-run price stability? – conceptual issues', *Achieving Price Stability, A Symposium Sponsored By the Federal Reserve Bank of Kansas City*, August 29–31, 1996, pp. 209–27.

E31 E43
E51
E52

4. Money growth and inflation in the United States

Gerald P. Dwyer, Jr.

1. INTRODUCTION

In this chapter, I examine whether the current neglect of monetary aggregates in formulating monetary policy is consistent with the data. Monetary aggregates play little or no role in the formulation of monetary policy in the United States. Is this neglect justified? Inflation in the United States has fallen from 8 to 9 percent per year from 1979 to 1981 to roughly 2 percent in 2000 as measured by the GDP deflator. If it is hard to argue with success, then whether justified or not, perhaps the neglect is low cost if not justified. Some recent papers have examined this issue with differing conclusions (Friedman and Kuttner 1992; Estrella and Mishkin 1997; Thoma and Gray 1998; Den Haan 2000). Partly related papers have examined the relationship between monetary aggregates and nominal and real income (Feldstein and Stock 1996; Swanson 1998). In this chapter, I examine a facet of this question: Is a monetary aggregate a useful indicator of United States inflation? If so, then completely ignoring the behavior of monetary aggregates may be an unwise way to conduct monetary policy.

This narrow focus means that I will not examine other possible uses of monetary aggregates in formulating and implementing monetary policy. I take it for granted that values of monetary aggregates are nonsensical goals for monetary policy. Inflation and possibly real income growth are tenable goal variables; monetary aggregates are not. Monetary aggregates may be useful intermediate targets for achieving these goals, but I do not examine the implications of using monetary aggregates as intermediate targets. Monetary aggregates currently are used in Switzerland and have been used by other countries (Gomme 1998). A precondition for using monetary aggregates as an intermediate target for inflation is the aggregate's usefulness for predicting inflation or real income growth, so the analysis in this chapter does have implications for the likely usefulness of money as an intermediate target.

The analysis in this chapter is limited to inflation and generally ignores real income growth. This limitation is due to a number of factors, but perhaps the most telling is that recessions are hard to predict by any set of variables or methods. The desirability of using a monetary aggregate as in McCallum's proposed rule for monetary policy (McCallum 1988) or an interest rate as in Taylor's proposed rule (Taylor 1993), also depends on the closeness of the relationship between the monetary aggregates and the goals. Hence, this seemingly narrow focus is not really all that narrow. Money's usefulness as an indicator of inflation is a necessary condition for other possible uses of money in conducting monetary policy.

2. MONEY AND PRICES

It is conventional wisdom that 'inflation is always and everywhere a monetary phenomena' [*sic*], an epigram due to Friedman that has been repeated by him and others many times (Friedman 1992). There seems to be widespread agreement about this observation in the theoretical literature, and the empirical relevance of the observation is taken for granted by many. Figure 4.1 uses quarterly data on money, real income and the price level for 1953 though 1997 to show why money's empirical relevance is taken for granted.[1] In Figure 4.1, higher prices are associated with higher quantities of money relative to income, both in terms of the overall trend and changes in trend. There is one startling deviation: money per unit of output fell from 1992 to 1997 but the price level did not. This graph suggests that the relationship between money per unit of output and the price level since 1992 is looser than for the previous thirty-five years. This deviation in the 1990s is larger in absolute and relative terms than earlier deviations. There is some suggestion that the deviation was a permanent downward shift in money per unit of output. The slope of the line for the price level and money per unit of output is most dramatically different for 1992 to 1995 and is more nearly the same for 1995 to 1997.

While it is natural to focus on this recent period, the current period is not as atypical as examination of Figure 4.1 by itself would suggest. Figure 4.2 shows the relationship between money and prices in the United States for the twentieth century. The deviation of money per unit of output from the price level in the 1990s still is

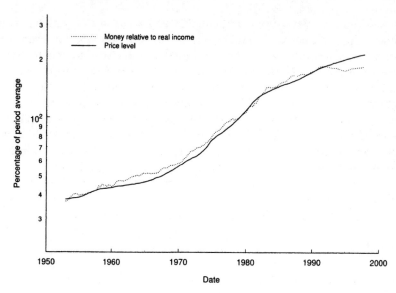

Figure 4.1 United States price level and money relative to real income – quarterly, 1953 to 1997

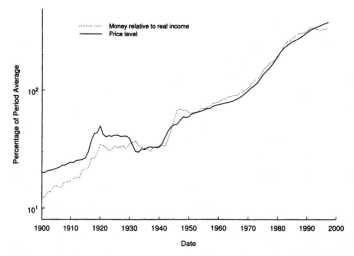

Figure 4.2 United States price level and money relative to real income – quarterly 1900 to 1997

visible but this deviation is not as large as some prior deviations. Just before the Treasury–Federal Reserve Accord in 1953, for example, there was a substantial increase in money relative to income and then a decrease. In the earlier years of the twentieth century, money relative to income increased more than prices until the 1930s. The graph shows money relative to income and prices as a percent of the period average. As a result, changes in the mean can affect the size of the deviations. Still, the recent deviations are relatively large and hardly are comforting about the usefulness of the relationship between money growth and inflation for predicting inflation.

The figures above are abundantly clear about two things: money is indeed related to inflation when allowance is made for the behavior of real income; the relationship is not an exact linear one. This message is similar to that delivered by graphs presented by Milton Friedman in many places for some years, for example (Friedman 1992).

The quantity theory is a basis for thinking about these graphs. The quantity theory is

$$MV = Py, \qquad (4.1)$$

where M is the nominal quantity of money, V is income velocity, P is the price level and y is real income. The figures show the relationship between money per unit of output, M/y, and P, which would be identical lines if velocity were constant. Hence, one interpretation of the figures is that changes in velocity are important.

These figures are not the only possible way of summarizing the relationship between money and the price level. The relationship between money and nominal income $(Y = Py)$ is another way of summarizing the relationship between money and inflation that also allows for the growth of real income. Yet another way of summarizing equation (4.1) is in terms of the relationship between money growth and inflation directly. The relationship between money growth and inflation is rough over shorter time periods and closer over longer time periods (Dwyer and Hafer 1988; McCandless and Weber 1995). Dwyer and Hafer (1999) use the growth of money per unit of output and inflation to illustrate the relationship between money growth and inflation. In this chapter, I use money growth, nominal income and inflation to examine the relationship between money and the price level.

Table 4.1   United States: Correlations of money, income and the price level (I/1953 to IV/1997)

	Growth Rate of Money	Growth Rate of Nominal Income	Growth Rate of Real Income	Inflation Rate
Quarterly				
Growth Rate of Money	1.000			
Growth Rate of Nominal Income	0.346	1.000		
Growth Rate of Real Income	0.223	0.818	1.000	
Inflation Rate	0.223	0.365	−0.238	1.000
Annual Average				
Growth Rate of Money	1.000			
Growth Rate of Nominal Income	0.594	1.000		
Growth Rate of Real Income	0.307	0.584	1.000	
Inflation Rate	0.376	0.565	−0.339	1.000
Two-Year Annual Average				
Growth Rate of Money	1.000			
Growth Rate of Nominal Income	0.692	1.000		
Growth Rate of Real Income	0.303	0.362	1.000	
Inflation Rate	0.456	0.715	−0.392	1.000
Three-Year Annual Average				
Growth Rate of Money	1.000			
Growth Rate of Nominal Income	0.754	1.000		
Growth Rate of Real Income	0.275	0.257	1.000	
Inflation Rate	0.543	0.789	−0.391	1.000
Four-Year Annual Average				
Growth Rate of Money	1.000			
Growth Rate of Nominal Income	0.790	1.000		
Growth Rate of Real Income	0.209	0.178	1.000	
Inflation Rate	0.614	0.827	−0.407	1.000
Five-Year Annual Average				
Growth Rate of Money	1.000			
Growth Rate of Nominal Income	0.824	1.000		
Growth Rate of Real Income	0.177	0.102	1.000	
Inflation Rate	0.661	0.861	−0.419	1.000

Table 4.1 shows simple correlations of money growth, nominal and real income growth and inflation for data averaged over different time periods. The time periods spanned by the changes of the variables used in the correlations range from quarters to five years. The quarterly correlations are correlations of quarterly growth rates of nominal GDP, real GDP and the GDP price index with money growth. The correlations for one or more years are correlations of growth rates of annual average data for the same variables for the number of years indicated.[2] Several things are apparent in the table.

First, the quarterly correlations are quite low. The correlation of quarterly money growth with inflation is 0.223, which is the same as the correlation of quarterly money growth with real income growth. The correlation of money growth with nominal income growth is 0.346, which is higher than the correlation with inflation although not spectacularly so. Figure 4.3 indicates why these correlations appear as they do. The plots of quarterly money growth and nominal income are broadly similar, while quarterly inflation is much smoother than either money growth or nominal income. Money growth and inflation only agree in terms of relatively long-term movements.

Second, the correlation of money growth with inflation changes systematically as the data are averaged over longer periods. Averaging

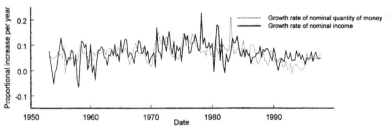

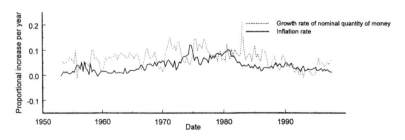

Figure 4.3 United States growth rate of money, the growth rate of nominal income and the inflation rate quarterly (1953 to 1997)

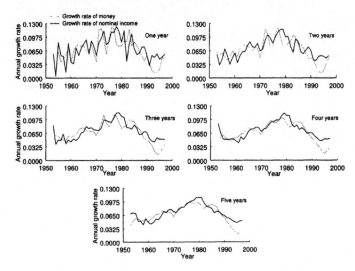

Figure 4.4 United States growth rates of money and nominal income averaged over different periods (1953 to 1997)

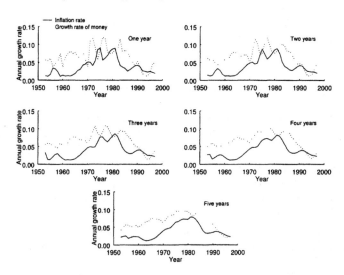

Figure 4.5 United States growth rates of money and the inflation rate averaged over different periods (1953 to 1997)

over longer periods has little effect on the correlation of money growth with nominal income growth. On the other hand, averaging over longer periods increases the correlation of money growth with inflation and decreases the correlation of money growth with real income growth.

Figure 4.4 shows why the time period over which nominal income growth is calculated makes relatively little difference. Figure 4.4 shows nominal income growth and money growth averaged over intervals of one to five years. The averaging tends to increase the smoothness of both series similarly. It is apparent that the averaging smooths out many wiggles in both series, some of which are idiosyncratic and some of which are common.

Figure 4.5 shows why the averaging matters for inflation. The averaging has relatively less of an effect on the behavior of inflation than on money growth. Inflation is smooth even on an annual basis (actually even on a quarterly basis), but money growth is substantially smoother with changes over four or five years than over just one year.

There are various ways of interpreting these figures, but it is hard to quarrel with the observation that money growth and inflation are positively correlated and this correlation is greater over longer periods of time. Still, is this correlation useful for formulating monetary policy?

I assume that an association between monetary growth and inflation is a useful *indicator* for formulating monetary policy if money growth is helpful for predicting inflation. Is it?

3. A VECTOR AUTOREGRESSION

In order to estimate whether money growth is helpful for predicting inflation, it is necessary to have an empirical model of the behavior of the economy rather than just figures and simple correlations. It would require substantially more knowledge than is currently available to specify a structural econometric model of the economy. Instead, I estimate a small vector autoregression (VAR) using quarterly data from 1953 to 1997 for four variables: the logarithm of nominal income; the logarithm of the price level; the interest rate on 3-month Treasury bills; and the logarithm of the money stock measured by M2.

The Johansen test for cointegration among the four series indicates that they are not cointegrated. Table 4.2 provides the test statistics. These are consistent with the null hypothesis of there being no cointegrating vector between these variables for 1953 through 1997. Given the data in Figure 4.1, this is not entirely surprising. The divergence after 1991 of the price level and money relative to real income suggests that these series are not likely to be cointegrated

Table 4.2   *Test statistics for one or more cointegrating vectors in the estimated vector autoregression (United States, I/1953 to IV/1997)*

Rank	Test Statistic	Critical Value 95 percent
0	31.185	54.11
1	17.509	34.56
2	10.737	18.15
3	0.877	3.84

Note: The critical values are from Johansen (1995, pp. 216). The results for a vector autoregression with no trend are similar.

Table 4.3   *Summary statistics for the estimated vector autoregression, (United States, I/1953 to IV/1997)*

Statistic	First Difference of			
	Nominal Income (logarithm)	Price Level (logarithm)	Interest Rate on Treasury bills	Money Stock (logarithm)
Std. Dev. Variable	1.004	0.601	0.029	0.972
Std. Dev. First Differenced Variable	0.042	0.025	0.008	0.037
Std. Dev. Residuals	0.033	0.011	0.006	0.026
R^2	0.483	0.846	0.461	0.580
LaGrange Multiplier Test for ARCH	0.036 (0.849)*	4.218 (0.040)	5.030 (0.025)	3.802 (0.051)
Skewness of Residuals	0.305	0.303	−0.480	0.974
Kurtosis of Residuals	1.248	0.350	4.928	4.940
Sign Test	−5 (0.502)	−2 (0.823)	2 (0.823)	4 (0.602)
Sign Rank	−197 (0.779)	−200 (0.776)	349 (0.619)	−220 (0.754)
Shapiro-Wilk	0.983 (0.588)	0.987 (0.799)	0.949 $(< 10^{-3})$	0.960 (0.001)

Note: * The p-values of test statistics are in parentheses.

by themselves, and the behavior of the interest rate apparently does not explain that deviation in the levels.[3]

Table 4.3 provides summary information about the VAR. Preliminary F-tests are consistent with reducing each estimated autoregression from twelve to eight lags but are not consistent with reducing the lag lengths of the nominal income or interest rate regressions to four lags. All regressions are based on eight lags of the first differences of all of the variables.[4] The first rows of Table 4.3 present unconditional standard deviations of the variables and R^2s, the fractions of variation explained, of the regressions in the VAR. The R^2s are reasonably high. The table indicates that the inflation rate has a smaller standard deviation than either the growth of nominal income or the money stock, and the R^2 for the inflation-rate regression is substantially higher than the other R^2s.[5]

The other statistics in the table provide some evidence about the adequacy of the estimates and a normal approximation for the residuals. With the exception of nominal income growth, the results suggest that there are problems with assuming a normal distribution. The test for autoregressive conditional heteroskedasticity (ARCH) in the residuals indicates that all series other than nominal income have serially correlated squared residuals.[6] The non-zero values of the skewness and kurtosis statistics suggest that the distributions may be skewed and have 'fat tails' but do not provide a statistical test. The next rows of Table 4.3 provide some evidence concerning the adequacy of symmetric or normally distributed error approximations. The sign test is a test whether the median residual equals the mean and the signed-rank test is a test whether the distribution is symmetric conditional on the median equals the mean. Test statistics as large or larger in magnitude than those in the table are quite likely, which indicates that these test statistics provide no evidence inconsistent with the hypothesis of symmetry. The Shapiro-Wilk test statistics, though, suggest that a normal distribution is inconsistent with the residuals for both the interest rate and the money stock. Overall, the serial correlation of squared residuals is the strongest evidence inconsistent with using a time-invariant normal distribution for the residuals. Evidence in Barnhart and Dwyer (1999) indicates that this evidence of ARCH is due to the assumption of linearity of the autoregressions rather than to an error concerning the distribution of the errors. Pursuing this aspect of the data is beyond the scope of this chapter and I continue to use linear regressions to summarize the data.

Table 4.4 summarizes the test results concerning whether the variables help to predict each other. The F-ratios in Table 4.4 are test statistics for testing null hypotheses that the coefficients of each variable are zero in each of the four equations. At usual significance levels, the money stock is quite helpful for predicting nominal income, as are the inflation rate and the change in the interest rate. The inflation rate is unrelated to all of the other variables even at the ten percent significance level. If the requisite significance level were raised to 17 percent or higher, the money stock would be 'statistically significant' but the interest rate would not. The interest rate has a p-value of 43 percent in the inflation regression. Given the serial correlation evident in Figure 4.3, it is not surprising that money growth is less important than lagged values of the inflation rate itself for predicting future inflation. Overall, I conclude that money growth is important for helping to predict the future evolution of nominal income and more important than the other variables for predicting the inflation rate.

Table 4.4   Tests of restrictions on estimated equations in the vector autoregression (United States, I/1953 to IV/1997)

Test*	Variable			
	Nominal Income (logarithm)	*Price Level (logarithm)*	*Interest Rate on Treasury Bills*	*Money Stock (logarithm)*
No lagged income	2.492 (0.015)	0.542 (0.823)	1.82 (0.078)	0.735 (0.661)
No lagged price level	2.605 (0.011)	27.646 ($< 10^{-3}$)	1.141 (0.196)	4.218 ($< 10^{-3}$)
No lagged interest rate	2.584 (0.011)	1.005 (0.435)	8.708 ($< 10^{-3}$)	3.466 (0.001)
No lagged money stock	4.219 ($< 10^{-3}$)	1.419 (0.168)	1.219 (0.292)	7.171 ($< 10^{-3}$)

Note: * The test statistics are F-ratios for testing the null hypothesis that all coefficients on the lagged values of the variable are zero in each regression. The degrees of freedom of the F-ratios are 8 and 147. The p-value are provided in parentheses.

Figures 4.6 through 4.9 are plots of actual and predicted values as well as residuals from the vector autoregression. All variables are plotted as quarterly changes, and the quarterly changes in the logarithms of nominal income, the price level and the money stock are annual growth rates as are the residuals. The vertical scales of axes in the figures are not the same; as a result, sizes of movements are not comparable across figures. For all variables, a solid line indicates the actual values and the dashed line indicates the predicted values. The graphs of actual and predicted values include a horizontal reference line at the mean and the graphs of residuals include a horizontal reference line at their mean of zero.

Despite the prominence of the deviation of the price level from money per unit of output from 1992 to 1995 in Figure 4.1, errors predicting inflation do not appear to be out of line with earlier prediction errors. Figure 4.10 focuses directly on this issue. The upper panel in Figure 4.10 shows actual deviations of money per unit from the price level and those predicted one quarter ahead by the VAR. These deviations also can be interpreted as the ratio of money to nominal income – the inverse of velocity.[7] Because the differences between actual and predicted values of the ratio of money to income are so small that they are not easy to see, the bottom panel of Figure 4.10 shows the residuals.

It is striking that the estimated vector autoregression is quite capable of predicting the deviation of money per unit of output from the price level. The deviations that are not predicted actually are small relative to those for most of the last forty-five years. In general, disentangling the source of the prediction is tenuous and I do not attempt to do that here.[8] Even so, the source of the deviation between money per unit of output and the price level in Figure 4.1 appears to be predictable by the vector autoregression.

Of course, the vector autoregression is estimated over data for the whole period and it is quite possible that the VAR estimated over data that ends in 1991 would not have predicted the deviation. Would the decrease in money relative to income have been predicted by a VAR estimated through the end of 1991? For this purpose, I use coefficients estimated through the end of 1991 and compute one-step-ahead predictions for each quarter. Figure 4.11 shows the one-step-ahead predictions for 1992 through 1997 of the deviations of money relative to income. The upper part of the figure indicates that the fall in money relative to income is predicted by this VAR. This VAR predicts the fall even though the fall is beyond the range of past ratios of money relative to income. The VAR does underpredict the fall and does not recover from that error until 1997, but it does predict most of it. This implies that the fall of the ratio of money

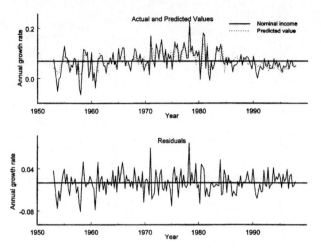

Figure 4.6 Actual and predicted values of the growth rate of nominal income (United States, 1953 to 1997)

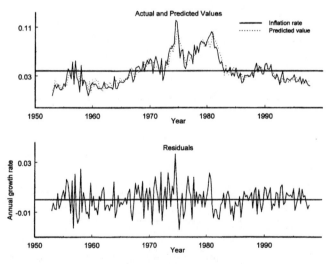

Figure 4.7 Actual and predicted values of the inflation rate (United States, 1953 to 1997)

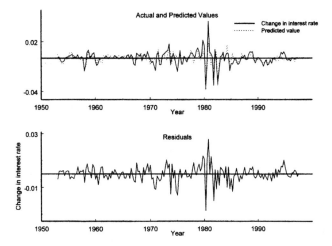

Figure 4.8 Actual and predicted values of the change in the interest rate (in proportional terms, United States, 1953 to 1997)

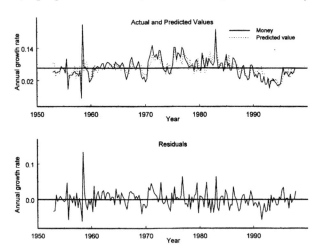

Figure 4.9 Actual and predicted values of the growth rate of money (United States, 1953 to 1997)

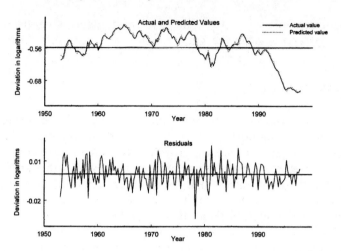

Figure 4.10 Actual and predicted values of deviations of money relative to income from the price level (United States, 1953 to 1997)

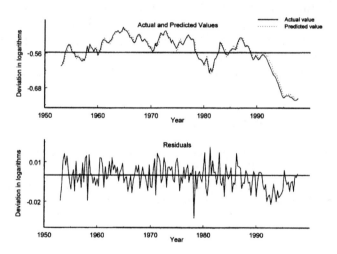

Figure 4.11 Actual and predicted values of deviations of money relative to income from the price level – regressions through 1991– (United States, 1953 to 1997)

to income, while beyond the range of prior data, is consistent with prior coefficients given the data.[9]

4. CONCLUSION

It would be hard to interpret the evidence in this chapter as suggesting that money is uninformative as an indicator of inflation. Nominal income is related to money growth. It follows that real income growth, inflation or both are related to money growth. Virtually all economic theories suggest that the eventual effect of money growth on real income growth is small to none. Money growth is more useful for forecasting inflation than other variables besides past inflation.

The alleged uselessness of money for monetary policy is based in part on recent inexplicable deviations of the money stock from its prior relationships with other series. Such an interpretation of the data is not consistent with the statistical analysis. While the results in this chapter are far from an explanation of the recent deviations, they do suggest that part of the explanation is consistent with patterns in the coefficients estimated before the deviations. While there is a large decrease in money relative to nominal income from 1992 to 1995, this decrease appears to be consistent with prior regressions.

ACKNOWLEDGEMENT

I thank R. W. Hafer for helpful discussions, J. L. Lin for helpful comments and Shalini Patel for research assistance. Any views are the author's views and not necessarily those of the Federal Reserve Bank of Atlanta or the Federal Reserve System.

NOTES

1. The sources of the data are discussed in the Data Appendix.
2. Rather than arbitrarily select periods over which to compute non-overlapping intervals for the longer changes, I use observations for all of the years. This means that the variables have induced serial correlation, which would be problematic for standard tests of zero correlation but is not for examining how a non-zero correlation changes as the averaging interval increases. The correlations, of course, are based on fewer independent observations than the number of observations used in the correlations.

3. A test for cointegration up to 1991 yields a different result: the series appear to be cointegrated. A related paper (Dwyer 1998) provides an analysis of the data in levels.
4. Preliminary F-tests are consistent with reducing the lag length from twelve to eight lags but not from eight to four.
5. As the next table indicates, this reflects the much higher serial correlation of the inflation rate.
6. The test is Engle's (1982) test based on the number of observations and the squared correlation of the squared residual this period and last.
7. These deviations are computed using the logarithms of the variables for simplicity because the equations are estimated using the logarithms of the variables. Let $\ln X$ denotes the logarithm of X. The quantity equation is $MV = Py = Y$, where Y is nominal income. In logarithms, the deviation of money per unit of ouput from the price level can be written $\ln M - \ln P - \ln y = -\ln V$. Hence, the plot of the deviations is a plot of the logarithm of the inverse of velocity.
8. Gordon and Leeper (1994) is an excellent example of an attempt to identify money demand and supply that nicely illustrates how difficult it is to identify them.
9. This may not be so surprising for a VAR estimated using first differences but a VAR estimated using the levels of the series yields the same conclusion (Dwyer 1998).

DATA APPENDIX

Monthly data on seasonally adjusted values of M2 for 1948 through 1958 are from Robert Rasche at http://www.msu.edu/~rasche/research/money.htm on April 23, 1998. Monthly data on seasonally adjusted values of M2 for 1959 through 1997 are from the Federal Reserve Bank of St. Louis at http://www.stls.frb.org/fred/dataindx.html on April 7, 1998. These data are converted to a quarterly frequency by averaging the monthly averages of daily values. I do not use M1 because M1 in recent years is distorted by sweep accounts.

Quarterly data on Gross Domestic Product for 1947 through 1997 are from the Department of Commerce at http://www.stat-usa.gov/BEN/bea2/national/nipahist.html on April 16, 1998.

The annual data on the money stock are from Friedman and Schwartz (1982, Table 4.8, pp. 122–29) for 1900 through 1947 and are annual averages of the data from Robert Rasche and the Federal Reserve Bank of St. Louis thereafter. The definition of M2 has changed since the compilation by Friedman and Schwartz and the data based on the new definition of M2 are spliced to their data by the ratio in 1948. In 1948, the primary difference between Friedman and Schwartz's measure of M2 (and an earlier measure constructed by the Board of Governors) is the inclusion in the current version of M2 of saving deposits and small time deposits held in thrift institutions. An examination of the data suggests no reason that the choice of a year other than 1948 to splice the data would have affected the data materially.

The annual data on income are from Friedman and Schwartz (1982, Table 4.8, pp. 122–29) for 1900 through 1959 and from the United States Department of Commerce at http://www.stat-usa.gov/BEN/bea2/national/nipahist.html on April 22, 1998 for 1960 through 1997. Friedman and Schwartz's data on nominal and real income are nominal and real net national product in 1948 and later years. The data for later years are net national product in current dollars and real net national product in chained 1992 dollars. These data are spliced by their ratio in 1959, the first year in which net national product currently is readily available.

REFERENCES

Barnhart, Cora and Gerald P. Dwyer, Jr. (1999), 'Nonlinearity and business cycles', unpublished paper, Florida Atlantic University.

Den Haan, Wouter J. (2000), 'The comovement between output and prices', *Journal of Monetary Economics*, **46** (August): 3–30.

Dwyer, Gerald P. (1998), 'Is money growth a useful leading indicator of inflation?', unpublished paper, Federal Reserve Bank of Atlanta.

Dwyer, Gerald P. and R.W. Hafer (1988), 'Is money irrelevant?', *Federal Reserve Bank of St. Louis Review*, **70** (May/June): 1–17.

Dwyer, Gerald P. and R.W. Hafer (1999), 'Are inflation and money growth still related?', *Economic Review*, Federal Reserve Bank of Atlanta, **84** (Second Quarter): 32–43.

Engle, Robert F. (1982), 'Autoregressive conditional heteroskedasticity with estimates of the variance of U.K. inflation', *Econometrica*, **50** (July): 987–1007.

Estrella, Arturo and Frederic S. Mishkin (1997), 'Is there a role for monetary aggregates in the conduct of monetary policy?', *Journal of Monetary Economics*, **40** (October): 279–304.

Feldstein, Martin and James H. Stock (1996), 'Measuring money growth when financial markets are changing', *Journal of Monetary Economics*, **37** (February): 3–27.

Friedman, Benjamin M. and Kenneth N. Kuttner (1992), 'Money, income, prices and interest rates', *American Economic Review*, **82** (June): 472–91.

Friedman, Milton (1992), *Money Mischief,* New York: Harcourt Brace Jovanovich.

Friedman, Milton and Anna J. Schwartz (1982), *Monetary Trends in the United States and the United Kingdom*, Chicago: University of Chicago Press.

Gomme, Paul (1998), 'Canada's money targeting experience', *Economic Commentary*, Federal Reserve Bank of Cleveland, February 1.

Gordon, David B. and Eric M. Leeper (1994), 'The dynamic impacts of monetary policy: an exercise in tentative identification', *Journal of Political Economy*, **102** (December): 1228–47.

Johansen, Søren (1995), *Likelihood-based Inference in Cointegrated Vector Autoregressive Models*, Oxford: Oxford University Press.

McCallum, Bennett T. (1988), 'Robustness properties of a rule for monetary policy', *Carnegie-Rochester Conference Series on Public Policy*, **29**: 173–203.

McCandless, Jr., George T. and Warren E. Weber (1995), 'Some monetary facts', *Quarterly Review*, Federal Reserve Bank of Minneapolis, **19** (Summer), 2–11.

Swanson, Norman (1998), 'Money and output viewed through a rolling window', *Journal of Monetary Economics*, **41** (June): 455–73.

Taylor, John B. (1993), 'Discretion versus policy rules in practice', *Carnegie-Rochester Conference Series on Public Policy*, **39**: 195–214.

Thoma, Mark A. and Jo Anna Gray (1998), 'Financial market variables do not predict real activity', *Economic Inquiry*, **36** (October): 522–39.

|UK| £31   £52
               £37

5. Inflation targeting and inflation forecasting: two sides of the same coin?

DeAnne Julius

1. INTRODUCTION

A new Bank of England Act, amending that of 1946, received its Royal Assent towards the end of April and came into force on the first of June 1998. It gives statutory force to the creation of a Monetary Policy Committee (MPC), a committee of the Bank, with the responsibility for setting monetary policy in order to meet an inflation target specified by government. In fact, on an interim basis, the MPC was established shortly after the new Labour government was elected in May 1997. The committee had its first formal meeting in June 1997 and thus has at the time of writing just completed its first year of operation.

The structure and workings of the MPC reflect a mixture of lessons learned from other countries, recent developments in the economic literature on monetary policy arrangements and the particular characteristics of the British political system. The central feature of the new system is the explicit inflation target set by government to define price stability. There is a large and growing literature on inflation targeting and the role of rules and forecasts in its operation. This chapter provides a practitioner's perspective on the role and usefulness of inflation forecasts in an inflation targeting regime.[1] It focuses on the political economy contribution that forecasts make to the quality of decision-making (rather than their strictly technical merit), and it identifies six issues that arise in the linkage between an inflation forecast and a monetary policy decision.

2. DISTINCTIVE FEATURES OF THE UK MONETARY POLICY REGIME

Prior to the most recent change of government in the UK, interest rate decisions were taken by the Chancellor after consultation with the Governor of the Bank of England. When the two did not agree, it was the Chancellor's view that prevailed, and he carried the political responsibility for the decision and its consequences. Under the new arrangements, the Chancellor retains responsibility for setting the objectives of monetary policy in terms of inflation and other macroeconomic variables, but the tactical and operational decisions on interest rates are vested in the Monetary Policy Committee.

This combination of instrument independence with goal dependence is similar to the New Zealand model, but quite different from the goal and instrument independence of the German Bundesbank or the US Federal Reserve Board. The latter two central banks operate within federal systems of government where checks and balances have been deliberately created to apportion democratic power and accountability. Thus monetary and fiscal authorities are institutionally separated and individually powerful. Their independence and the check they provide over each other is a strength of the system as a whole. The risk of such independence is that economic policy can become grid-locked in a clearly sub-optimal combination if the budgetary authorities and central bank each feel that the other should change its policy stance in order to remedy the overall policy mix.[2] The policy-making bodies of the US and German central banks both contain regional as well as central representatives, embodying another dimension of federal political systems. This has implications for the size of the policy-making body which, as discussed below, is relevant to the use of an inflation forecast.

In a unitary state such as the UK, democratic power resides in the elected Parliament with cabinet ministers acting as the main executive agents. Thus the legitimacy of central bank independence in a parliamentary system of government is enhanced when its target (or objective function) is set by elected representatives of the people. But this too carries risks. During periods of political or economic turmoil or, conceivably, election campaigns with populist or economically naive candidates, the inflation target could became a point of dispute between the parties. It is unlikely that the subtleties of the short-run versus long-run Philips curve could be quickly communicated to the opposition MPs or the voting public. A sudden change of target, which might seem small to much of the population in a country with an inflation-prone history (say, from 2.5 percent to 5 percent), could have quick and disastrous consequences in the financial markets. Such a catastrophe is unlikely – or at least unlikely to happen more than once! In the case of the UK, it is also questionable whether a target of 5 percent would be consistent with the objective of price stability as laid down in the Act. The risk of such a politically motivated target change needs to be balanced against the risk of popular opposition to full central bank independence in a system of parliamentary sovereignty.

Britain's Monetary Policy Committee is composed of nine members, including the Governor as its chair, four senior Bank officials and four members appointed from outside the Bank. Decisions on interest rates are taken by majority vote, with a quorum of six and the Governor having a second casting vote in the event of a tie. The MPC meets monthly and publishes the minutes of each meeting within six weeks; i.e., a week after the subsequent meeting.[3] The minutes provide a full (but unattributed) description of the areas discussed, the arguments made and the points of agreement and disagreement. They also record the votes of individual members.

Unlike the arrangements in New Zealand, where the Governor alone is held accountable for achieving the government's inflation objective, each member of the UK Monetary Policy Committee is individually accountable for his/her votes. The Treasury Select Committee of the House of Commons can question any or all of them on their views and reasons for voting as they did.[4] This questioning generally takes place soon after the quarterly publication of the MPC's *Inflation Report* which contains its inflation forecast. Thus it is important that each member of the MPC can support the published forecast, or that dissensions or alternative forecasts are also published. The Forecast itself is presented as a 'fan chart' representing the probability distribution around the most likely (modal) path for inflation over the coming two years. Not every MPC member will agree with every assumption, but the 'fan chart' that results from the Committee's work on the forecast will generally encompass the views of all members.

The final distinctive feature of the UK arrangements that is relevant for the use of an inflation forecast is the nature of the objective given to the Bank. It is currently defined as a point target for inflation, set at 2.5 per cent per year increase in the Retail Price Index excluding mortgage interest payments (RPIX). Subject to maintaining price stability (as defined by this target, but without an explicit time horizon), the MPC is charged to 'support the economic policy of the government including its objectives for growth and employment' (Bank of England Act 1998).

If the RPIX should deviate by more than one percent on either side of the target, then the Governor must write an open letter to the Chancellor to explain why and to set out the actions that the MPC is planning to take to bring inflation back to the target over a particular time horizon. Because the MPC is expected to give some weight to the government's growth and employment objectives, the expectation is that the open letter would be based on an inflation forecast that would show how inflation would be gradually returned to target (following some shock) over a period long enough to avoid excessive output volatility. It has been suggested that this form of remit should be considered an 'incomplete contract' in that it leaves scope for judgement about the short term trade-off between output and inflation volatility.[5]

3. THE ROLE OF THE INFLATION FORECAST

The inflation forecast probably plays a more prominent part in the deliberations of the MPC than it does in the policy-making bodies of most other independent central banks. This is partly because of the legal parameters in the new Act which require the Monetary Policy Committee to approve and publish a quarterly report (unless an alternative frequency is agreed between the Treasury and the MPC). Both the publication and the endorsement by the MPC are important. In the United States, a forecast is prepared by Federal Reserve Board staff for the use of the FOMC, but it is not necessarily approved by them, nor is it published until five years later in any detail.[6] In the case of the Bank of England, the quarterly *Inflation Report* (which contains the forecast) is presented at a press conference, receives close scrutiny and widespread publicity from financial journalists, and is the basis for questioning of individual MPC members by the Treasury Select Committee, usually in the week after its publication.[7]

In addition to the contribution it makes to transparency and accountability, the inflation forecast serves two other functions. First, it provides a forward-looking and internally consistent framework for MPC discussions. During the month before each *Inflation Report* is published, the MPC hold a number of additional meetings with Bank staff to discuss and agree the assumptions that go into the forecast and any changes they wish to make in the model properties.

These meetings provide the opportunity for the MPC to debate some of the underlying fundamentals of the economy's changing structure (e.g. its long-term potential growth rate after a decade of structural reform, the propensity to consume out of household wealth as share ownership becomes more widespread), and to reflect their views – sometimes divergent – in the central assumptions and skews that go into the forecast equations. The complexity of the issues and the sheer logistics of arranging numerous meetings of the full committee to discuss them imply that such a process would become less feasible if the size or professional diversity of the policy-making committee were greater.

Second, during the months between *Inflation Reports,* the most recent forecast serves as a jointly agreed calibration device against which to assess new data. At the monthly MPC meetings, members frequently compare the latest output or wages figures, for example, with what was projected for those variables in the forecast. This helps to avoid over-reactions to monthly statistics that may differ significantly from the previous month's reading, but are in line with medium-term expectations. Having invested the time in debating and agreeing the forecast previously, the MPC reaps the benefits during subsequent months of having a common starting point for its discussions.

4. LINKING FORECASTS TO MONETARY POLICY DECISIONS

It might seem, from this discussion of the prominent role of the inflation forecast in the UK monetary policy regime, that decisions on interest rates should follow the forecast mechanistically: if the two-year ahead forecast shows inflation below (above) the target, then interest rates today should be lowered (raised) sufficiently to close the gap between the forecast and the target. Indeed, some of the academic literature on inflation targeting claims (or assumes) that the inflation forecast is the intermediate target or feedback variable for monetary policy (Svensson 1997; Haldane 1997a), although there is also a recognition by most authors that considerable discretion or judgement is involved in applying forward-looking (forecast based) policy rules. This section classifies the main issues that, in practice, complicate the linkage between the inflation forecast and the monetary policy decision.

4.1 Forecast Horizon and Transmission Lags

Ever since the 'long and variable lags' between a change in monetary policy and its effect on inflation were famously highlighted by Milton Friedman (1959), it has been recognised that forward looking inflation targeting carries the risk of destabilising both output and inflation if the time horizon is inappropriate. At the Bank of England we currently use an eight-quarter horizon for the published forecast, while recognising that the full effect of a change in monetary policy is likely to extend beyond two years. Longer term forecasts, however, are subject to greater uncertainty and much of the effect of an interest rate change will fall within the two-year period, especially when the exchange rate is part of the transmission mechanism.

As noted above, the UK inflation target is to be met over the medium term; it does not have a specified date. When (as now) underlying inflation is close to target, a two-year forecast can easily produce a projected path for inflation that lies partly above and partly below the target. If the policy transmission lag were known with certainty it would be possible to fine-tune policy over the full period with a series of interest rate steps that would enable inflation to track the target exactly in the future. But when the lag is highly uncertain and variable, it is important to give some weight to the full projected path of future inflation in setting policy, and not to focus unduly on the quarterly inflation estimate at the forecast horizon.

4.2 Output versus Inflation Volatility

Much has been written about the implications for optimal monetary policy of central bank objective functions that give weight both to output volatility and price stability. The general conclusion is that giving more weight to output implies a longer optimal horizon over which policy should be set to return inflation to target following a shock.[8] For example, Svensson (1997) has shown that so-called 'strict' inflation-forecast-targeting, whereby policy is set to bring the inflation forecast back to target after two years, will be optimal (under the rather specific conditions of his model) when the authorities care only about inflation. When output volatility is also a concern, then the central bank should set interest rates to close the gap between forecast inflation and the inflation target over a longer period (so-called 'flexible' inflation-forecast-targeting).

There are at least two difficulties with applying such rules in practice. The first, and most significant, relates back to the previous issue of the uncertainty around the real length of the lag. If the transmission lag is already thought to be long, then lengthening the policy horizon even further to accommodate output objectives risks damaging the credibility of the authorities' commitment to price stability.   On the other hand, some researchers have found that shorter time horizons and frequent interest rate changes can lead to greater output volatility including secondary (overlapping) fluctuations (Amano et al. 1998).

The second complication is that the relative weights given to output volatility and inflation by a government or central bank are unlikely to be decided explicitly or, even if they were, to be time-invariant over the economic cycle. The *level* of inflation (or unemployment) at any point may well influence the macroeconomic gain to be derived from its prompt reduction. It might be possible to construct a set of equations to describe time varying patterns of output/inflation weights, but that would add a new level of complexity to forecast models that assume their exogeneity.

4.3   Uncertainties about the Present (Data)

A more mundane, but nonetheless important, problem in making monetary policy decisions is the general unreliability of data especially near turning points in the economic cycle.   A forecast is heavily dependent on its starting point, and much of the time of policy-making committees is spent reviewing the latest month's statistics in an attempt to understand just where the economy is at the moment.

There have been periods in recent UK history when quarterly GDP estimates were subsequently revised by as much as one percentage point on an annual basis. For this reason, there is actually more uncertainty around the early quarters of a forecast than is usually appreciated. Such uncertainty magnifies the variance around the future inflation path, especially when the economy is operating close to capacity.   When it is not clear whether the output gap is positive or negative at the starting point of the forecast, then unless growth is expected to be clearly above or below its trend rate in the near future, the policy judgement will be finely balanced and may be more dependent on views about current GDP than on the precise projection of future inflation.

4.4 Uncertainties about the Future (Shocks)

A forecast is built upon a set of assumptions about exogenous variables such as commodity prices, exchange rates and external demand growth. These assumptions are usually in the form of a central estimate with an assumed normal distribution. At the Bank of England we also build in a skew around an assumption that the MPC feels contains more risk on one side than the other. An example from recent forecasts was the treatment of the sterling effective exchange rate index. The central (i.e. modal) assumption in the May 1998 *Report* was for a gradual depreciation in line with uncovered interest parities as implied by the market at the time the forecast was made. Assuming unchanged UK interest rates, this would bring the index down from its starting point of 106 to about 103 over a two-year period. However the MPC took the view that there was an asymmetric risk of the exchange rate depreciating more than in the central case as some of the uncertainties surrounding the introduction of the euro were resolved. This was reflected in the mean, or expected value, of the exchange rate index at the end of the forecast period, which stood at around 96, seven per cent lower than in the central case (the mode).

While such skews are a statistical way of accommodating rather tame, well-behaved and predictable 'shocks', few would claim they were adequate to incorporate the low probability/high impact events that, in the past, have been responsible for major bouts of world inflation and periods of serious recession. The oil shocks of the 1970s, the sustained dollar overshoot of the mid-1980s, the burst of the Japanese asset price bubble in the late-1980s, the Gulf War of the early 1990s and the Asian financial crisis of last year were all episodes that conventional forecasting techniques failed to anticipate. To the extent that the shocks of the future are different from those of the past (which is almost a tautology), it is wrong to claim that standard errors around historically calibrated equations encompass the true range of future uncertainties.

Scenario planning techniques are better suited to the analysis of low probability/high impact events or developments.[9] Scenario planning is, in some ways, the reverse of conventional forecasting. It starts by identifying the type of event that could have a very significant impact on the target variable. Then, working backwards from that event, the planner constructs an internally consistent path of economic and often political or social developments whose seeds can be seen in the current conjuncture. The resulting scenario is not assigned a probability which, because it would be low, tends to invite complacency in the decision maker. Rather the scenario is used, first, to develop a contingency plan for hitting the target variable *if* that event should occur and, second, to highlight those aspects of the current conjuncture (not only economic ones) that bear especially close monitoring.

4.5   Uncertainties about the Model

Any economic forecasting model is, by definition, a simplified representation of how the economy actually works. Few practitioners would claim that forecasting is an exact science, although that is often the impression given by the statistical jargon that is the vernacular of forecasters. Debates rage within the profession about the benefits of large versus small models, the relevance of output gap models (or rules) when the estimation of the gap is so prone to error, the role of nominal money variables in economic models based on real variables to predict inflation, the treatment of the business cycle in models that tend towards equilibrium, etc.

The role of an economic advisor (or the research staff of a central bank) is to build and defend the best possible forecast; but the role of an economic decision maker is to weigh the balance of all relevant evidence and advice in reaching a decision. Anyone who has worked with different models or followed the predictions of a range of forecasters over time is well aware of the pitfalls of placing all one's faith in a single forecast model.

4.6   Tactics

Finally, there are sometimes tactical considerations associated with the state of the financial markets or the timing of other announcements or events that could cause policy makers to delay or phase in the interest rate change that is implied by their forecast. The forecast itself does not dictate the particular path of interest rate changes needed to meet the target.

Tactical considerations were important in the UK during the early summer of 1997. The MPC minutes reveal that the committee decided to raise rates in a series of small steps, rather than all at once, in order to moderate the effect on sterling which was already thought to be stronger than could be explained by the economic fundamentals.

5. CONCLUSION

The current fashion for independent central banks is spreading to more countries, propelled both by its apparent success in bringing down inflation without greater output volatility in those countries adopting inflation targeting (Haldane 1997b) and by the sudden foreign exchange difficulties and problems of policy credibility in pegged exchange rate regimes. The long-term durability and success of central bank independence, however, will depend as much on the political support of the public as on the economic judgement of the central bankers. An inflation forecast can contribute to both.

A published inflation forecast can serve as a tool of accountability by making transparent the assumptions used by the policy makers. It can help educate the commentators and, through them, the public at large about the long lags between changes in interest rates and changes in growth and inflation. It can demonstrate the complexity of forces that spur or hold back inflationary pressures at some particular point in the economic cycle. Perhaps most important, it can reinforce (low) inflationary expectations by frequent references to the inflation target and the policy moves that may be needed to bring the inflation forecast into line with it. These explanations will be especially important to central bank credibility and legitimacy when interest rates need to rise to pre-empt future inflation at a time when the economy is still operating below capacity.

The role of a forecast in the policy judgement itself is more complex. On the one hand, taking any decision today to influence a variable in the future requires at least an implicit model that connects the two. Where the decision is taken by a committee, it must be helpful to share an underlying model or, failing that, to use a comprehensive modeling framework to explore where the key differences lie. On the other hand, the very real complexities in the monetary policy transmission process and the inherent uncertainties surrounding the data, future shocks and the appropriate structure of any economic model argue against a mechanistic link between an inflation forecast and a policy decision. Indeed, too close a linkage would introduce two additional risks. It could encourage manipulation of the model's assumptions to produce a forecast that fits a policy judgement, rather than vice versa. And secondly, belief in a single model could blind the policy maker to a gradual accumulation of news that points in another direction – or to a low probability/high impact event – thereby delaying necessary action or 'fighting the last war' when the world has moved on. In the final analysis, consistently good decisions require carefully balanced judgements by the decision makers and depend on their ability to assimilate new information and recognise novel developments before they become firmly established trends. An inflation forecasting model can help with both, but it cannot substitute for either.

NOTES

1. This perspective should be considered provisional, given the brief history and still evolving nature of the arrangements in the UK, as well as the author's short period of membership on the MPC. I am grateful to Len Berkowitz, Andrew Haldane, Neal Hatch, Paul Tucker, John Vickers, Caroline Webb, Mr Fa-Ching Liang and other participants in the June 1998 International Conference on the Conduct of Monetary Policy for comments on earlier drafts. The views expressed do not necessarily represent those of other MPC members or the Bank of England.
2. Examples include the early 1980s in Germany when the Bundesbank faced a coalition government that was itself deeply divided over its high fiscal deficit but united in demanding lower interest rates despite inflation at 5.5 percent (Kennedy 1991).
3. This procedure has subsequently been changed. The minutes are now published two weeks after the MPC meeting rather than six.
4. This is also different from the practice in the United States where only the Chairman of the Federal Reserve Board provides testimony to Congressional committees.
5. Professor C. Bean has argued this before the Treasury Select Committee (Bean 1998), but gone on to show that because the optimal policy frontier for the UK is close to rectangular, the incompleteness of the remit need not be a cause for concern and may lead to a more satisfactory outcome than the fuller prescription implied by the New Zealand model.
6. The Federal Reserve Bank forecast is published only after a lag of five years in the 'Green Book' alongside the full minutes of the relevant FOMC meeting.
7. The Act does not specify that the report must contain an inflation forecast, nor that the MPC must endorse one. But publication is expected since there is a five-year history of *Inflation Reports* containing the Bank's forecast. The key difference is that the forecast is now that of the MPC rather than the Bank and that MPC members are individually, rather than collectively, accountable for their views.
8. For a discussion of how this could work in practice in a UK context see M.A. King (1997).

9. For a general reference see P. Schwartz (1996). For a case study on how Royal Dutch Shell planners used scenario techniques to 'predict' and prepare for the 1973 oil price shock see P. Wack (1985).

REFERENCES

Amano, R., D. Coletti and T. Macklem (1998), 'Monetary rules when economic behaviour changes', Bank of Canada paper for conference on Central Bank Inflation Targeting, Stanford University and Federal Reserve Bank of San Francisco, March.
Bank of England (1998), *Inflation Report,* May.
Bean, C. (1998), 'The new UK monetary arrangements: a view form the literature', *Economics Journal.* November, 1998.
Friedman, M. (1959), *A Program for Monetary Stability,* New York: MacMillan.
Haldane, A.G. (1997a), 'Designing inflation targets', in P. Lowe (ed.), *Monetary Policy and Inflation Targeting,* Sydney Reserve Bank of Australia.
Haldane, A.G. (1997b), 'Some issues in inflation targeting', Bank of England Working Paper Series NO. 74, December.
Kennedy, E. (1991), *The Bundesbank: Germany's Central Bank in the International Monetary System,* The Royal Institute of International Affairs and The Council on Foreign Relations.
King, M.A. (1997), 'The inflation target five years on', *Bank of England Quarterly Bulletin,* November.
Schwartz, P. (1996), *The Art of the Long View; Planning for the Future in an Uncertain World,* New York: Doubleday Books.
Svensson, L.E.O. (1997), 'Inflation-forecast-targeting: implementing and monitoring inflation targets', *European Economic Review,* **41**: 1111–46.
Wack, P. (1985), 'Scenarios: uncharted waters ahead' and 'Scenarios: shooting the rapids', *Harvard Business Review,* September/October and November/December.

6. Monetary policy and the Asian crisis: the role of dollar exchange rate targets

Philip Turner

1. INTRODUCTION

Were there any lessons for monetary policy in the recent crisis? Although issues related to the process of financial intermediation (domestic and foreign) lay at the root of this crisis, monetary policy was not quite blameless. During the first half of the 1990s, capital inflows were very heavy and monetary policy was in effect constrained by the objective of resisting nominal exchange rate appreciation, usually by intervening to keep an implicit exchange rate target or band. Many central banks were at that time well aware that domestic economic conditions (notably the rapid growth of bank credit, sizable increases in property prices and other signs of inflationary pressure) required higher interest rates; but they were reluctant to raise rates for fear of attracting further (unwanted) inflows.[1] They were also worried about the latent weaknesses of their financial systems. For these reasons, monetary policy was in general too lax in the first half of the 1990s. In addition, when capital flows reversed (putting downward pressure on foreign exchange reserves), the authorities in many countries failed to respond quickly or strongly enough to counter downward pressure on the currency. In the end, exchange rate targets proved to be rather 'soft'.

The chapter is organised as follows. The first section considers evidence about the 'hardness' or 'softness' of the exchange rate commitment historically. It turns out that many countries in Asia have tended to preserve dollar pegs only when the dollar was itself weakening. Moreover, 'hard' exchange rate policies have virtually never been used during disinflationary periods. The second section assesses the stance of monetary policy from the perspective of monetary conditions indices: by this measure, monetary policy in the 1990s appears to have been much easier than it was in the early to mid-

1980s. And inflation performance has been distinctly uneven. The third section finds a marked reluctance to tighten monetary policy in the early stages of the crisis – and this probably prolonged the crisis. The fourth section argues that, once exchange rate pegs or bands had been abandoned, the authorities found it very difficult to judge the stance of monetary policy: the markets realised this not least because of well-publicised disagreements among the many actors.

2. EXCHANGE RATE TARGETS

Monetary policy in most of Asia (outside Japan), until the recent crisis forced the widespread adoption of floating exchange rates, was apparently geared to sustaining a nominal exchange rate peg or band (usually largely against the dollar).[2] Yet, with the notable exception of Hong Kong, such exchange rate pegs generally went unannounced. Although the authorities in many cases went to some lengths to maintain the exchange rate, they were not in general publicly committed to a particular rate or band (Table 6.1).

Table 6.1   Summary of currency regimes at end-1996

China	Managed floating; daily movements against US dollar limited to 0.3%.
Hong Kong	Pegged to US dollar since 1983, with local currency issue backed by dollar holdings.
Korea	Managed floating; band for daily fluctuations against the dollar of ± 2.25%.
Singapore	Managed floating; broad band.
Taiwan	Managed floating
Indonesia	Managed floating; intervention band widened from less than 3% to 5% in June 1996 and to about 8% in September 1996.
Malaysia	Managed floating.
Philippines	Independent floating.
Thailand	Pegged to a basket of currencies.

Table 6.2   Changes in exchange rates against the US dollar[1]
             (annual rates)

	Oct 78 – Feb 85	Feb 85 – Apr 95	Apr 95 – Apr 98	Memo: Volatility[2] of the exchange rate 1990–96
Hong Kong	−7.6	0.1	−0.1	0.1
Korea	−8.3	0.9	−17.9	0.7
Singapore	−0.6	4.8	−4.4	0.9
Taiwan	−1.4	4.4	−8.3	1.0
Indonesia	−14.1	−6.8	−35.1	0.3
Malaysia	−2.3	0.3	−12.7	1.1
Philippines	−13.4	−3.4	−12.3	1.7
Thailand	−5.0	1.3	−14.7	0.4
Average of above[3]	−6.6	0.2	−13.2	0.8
Memo: Japan	−5.3	11.8	−14.1	2.9
Australia	−6.9	−0.1	−3.9	1.7

Notes:

As explained in the text, these periods were chosen as periods of dollar strengthening, dollar weakening and renewed dollar strengthening respectively.

[1] Defined as US$ per local currency.

[2] Standard deviation of monthly percentage changes.

[3] Simple average.

One simple indication of the *de facto* firmness of an exchange rate target is the volatility of the exchange rate. This is shown in the final column of Table 6.2 (where volatility is measured by the variance of month-to-month movements). The low volatility of the exchange rates of their currencies suggests that Indonesia and Thailand had relatively rigid exchange rate objectives. Although the other countries had somewhat more volatility, none came even close to the volatility of the Japanese yen. With the exception of the Philippine peso, all currencies were also significantly less volatile than the Australian dollar. However, the observed volatility of the exchange rate may reflect the different magnitude of shocks that countries are subjected to, and not the different response functions of the authorities. A comparison between interest and exchange rate volatility can in part allow for such differences. To maintain a targeted exchange rate with an open capital account, the central bank will, other things equal, have to accept more volatile interest rates. On the other hand, if the main target of monetary policy is a short-term interest rate (determined by the needs of the domestic economy), then the exchange rate is likely to be more volatile.

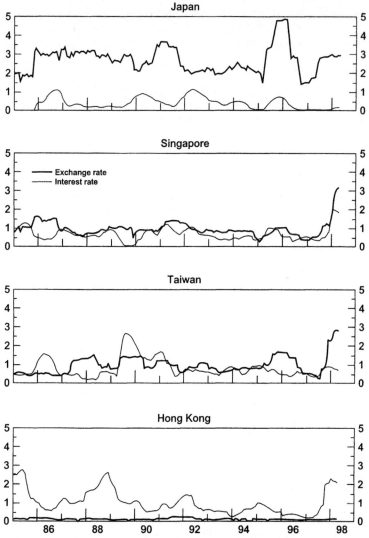

Note: Volatility defined as 12-month moving standard deviation of 3-month interest rates and monthly % changes in the exchange rate.

Figure 6.1 The volatilities of exchange rates and interest rates compared

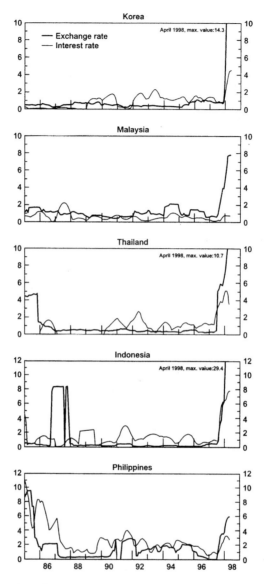

Figure 6.1 continued

The volatilities of interest rates and exchange rates for several Asian economies over the period 1985–98 are compared in Figure 6.1. Only in the case of Japan does the exchange rate volatility exceed the interest rate volatility for the whole of the period: the implication is that interest rates are set for domestic objectives and not to stabilise the exchange rate. The pattern of relative volatilities is similar in the case of Singapore, although the difference between the volatility of the exchange rate and that of interest rates is much smaller. In the case of Taiwan, the relative magnitudes of volatilities has varied over time: in 1986 and 1989, for example, a certain amount of interest rate volatility was accepted, apparently in order to stabilise the exchange rate. At the other extreme, the Hong Kong dollar has been virtually fixed, and a significant amount of interest rate volatility accepted. Similar exchange rate stability prevailed in Indonesia between 1988 and mid-1997, the Philippines between 1987 and 1990 and in Thailand between 1987 and mid-1997. Keeping the volatility of the exchange rate unusually low doubtless nurtured a misperception of exchange rate risk that led Asian borrowers to become over-exposed to foreign currency debts. With a flexible exchange rate, and frequent movements in both directions, firms and households learn from their daily experience to take account of exchange rate risk. But when many years of artificially low volatility is followed by a large, discrete shift, the danger that private agents will be caught unprepared is much greater.

The evidence from historical volatility is that several countries clearly oriented monetary policy towards stability of their exchange rate without publicly declaring that they were doing so. Operating bands (or pegs) that were in effect kept confidential (or at least not published) had the advantage of giving the authorities flexibility both in the day-to-day intervention operations by the central bank and in shifting policy when necessary. But it may also have signalled to financial markets a lower level of commitment to the exchange rate than, for example, Hong Kong's much more explicit dollar peg. In this sense, exchange rate commitments may have been rather 'soft' constraints for monetary policy.

A cursory examination of exchange rate movements against the dollar over the last twenty years appears to confirm this impression of 'softness' – at least for many countries. Several countries in Asia tended to preserve dollar pegs only when the dollar was itself weakening against other major international currencies (notably the yen). Sticking with the dollar in such circumstances served in effect to maintain or improve competitiveness; but it did not necessarily lead to lower inflation. Table 6.2 shows movements in the dollar exchange rate over one long period of dollar weakening (from February 1985 to April 1995) and two periods of dollar strengthening (October 1978 to February 1985 and April 1995 to April 1998). During the first period of dollar strengthening, the average rate of depreciation against the dollar for currencies of the countries shown in the table was 6.5% a year, slightly above the rate of depreciation of the yen over the same period. During the second period of dollar strengthening, the average rate of depreciation was about 13%, again remarkably close to the rate of depreciation of the yen. An oversimplification of these trends might be that Asian currencies have on average followed the yen down when it is depreciating against the dollar and followed the dollar down when it is depreciating against the yen, suggesting that the objective of maintaining or improving competitiveness took precedence over the objective of lowering the rate of inflation.

Two notable exceptions to this oversimplification are Singapore and Taiwan. Their currencies depreciated by much less than other currencies during the first period of dollar weakness and, equally significantly, actually appreciated significantly against the dollar when it was weakening. And during the recent crisis both currencies held up relatively well.

A second question is whether Asian countries have used 'hard' exchange rates to 'break' inflation in the way that Latin American countries and countries in transition have done. To explore this, five episodes of high inflation identified in a recent study were examined (Table 6.3). In each case cited in this study, inflation was brought down from around 20% a year or higher to below 5%. But a 'hard' exchange rate policy apparently played no part in any of these five disinflationary episodes. In three cases, the exchange rate actually depreciated in real effective terms;[3] and the appreciation in the other two instances was marginal. Hence disinflation in Asia after a surge of inflation has tended to be home-grown, and not exchange rate based.

This pattern is consistent with other evidence that inflation in Asia is less sensitive in the short run to the level of the real exchange rate (relative to the sensitivity to domestic economic activity) than is the case in Latin America (where movement in the real exchange rate has often appeared to dominate short-term inflation developments).[4] Figure 6.2 summarises some recent BIS evidence that while inflation in Latin America has tended to be dominated by the real exchange rate, inflation in Asia has been much less sensitive to the level of the

Table 6.3   Breaking inflation momentum: historical episodes in Asia

Country	Stabilisation period	Inflation		Monetary policy framework	Change in real effective exchange rate during stabilisation (%)
		Initial	Final		
Korea	1980–83	28.7	3.4	Short-term intermediate targets	+2.9
Malaysia	1974–75	17.3	4.5	Discretion	−4.4
Philippines	1984–86	50.3	0.8	Discretion	−14.8
Singapore	1974–75	22.4	2.6	Discretion	−5.2
Thailand	1980–83	19.7	3.7	Exchange rate peg with capital controls	+2.9

Note: classification based on announced policy targets.
Source: This table is based on Carlo Cottarelli and Curzio Giannini 'Credibility without rules? Monetary frameworks in the post-Bretton Woods era.' Bank of Italy. Discussion papers No. 312 (August 1997).

real exchange rate. Given the great openness to (and dependence on) trade in Asia, this is perhaps a somewhat surprising finding. It reflects the fact that the exchange rate has not typically been used to 'break' inflation in Asia, probably because Latin American-style hyperinflation (which typically forced the exchange rate to the centre of disinflation) has not occurred in Asia. Rather, inflation has been determined by variations in the level of domestic economic activity. (As discussed further below, this result has been confirmed by recent experience: very large real depreciation had surprisingly little impact on inflation: see the comparison between Asia recently and Mexico in 1994 in Table 6.8.)

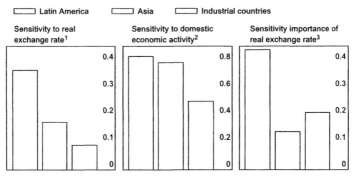

Figure 6.2 Estimated sensitivity of inflation in major world regions

3. MONETARY CONDITIONS INDEX

Even if exchange rate targets have not been central to anti-inflation policy in Asia, the exchange rate still influences inflation. Hence the exchange rate developments may need to influence monetary policy decisions even in countries with floating exchange rates, although exactly how this influence is to be exerted remains a matter of controversy.

Some have tried to formalise the issue by developing a so-called 'monetary conditions index'. This index (MCI for short) is simply a short-hand way of capturing the impact of the exchange rate in the monetary transmission mechanism. It is a weighted average of changes in a shorthand interest rate and an effective exchange rate; it can be defined in both nominal and real terms. Although the indicator has many defects,[5] it can provide a convenient first approximation to broad trends. (An important qualification is that the equilibrium real exchange rate can change over time – a point discussed further below.) Figure 6.3 incorporates real monetary conditions indices for several Asian countries, using the following definitions:

• the real interest rate (r) is a three-month market rate deflated by the year-on-year rise in the CPI;

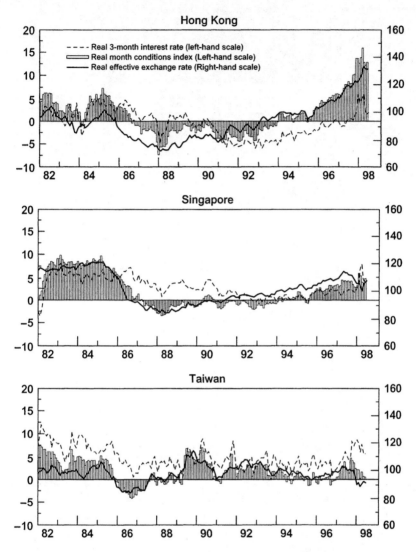

Note: For definitions see test. A positive MCI indicates relative restrictiveness. An expanded graph covering 1997 and 1998 is Graph 5.

Figure 6.3 Monetary conditions in selected Asian countries

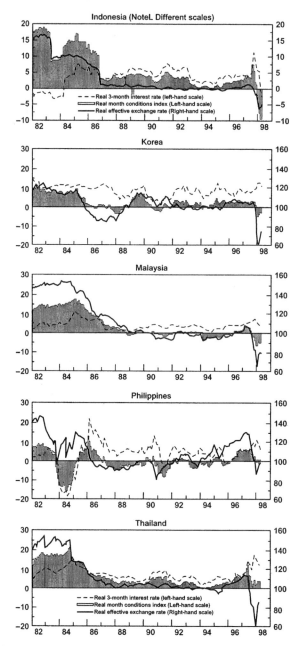

Figure 6.3 continued

- the real effective exchange rate (*rer*) is based on consumer prices (Dec. 1993 = 100);
- the MCI was defined in a way analogous to the definition used in the BIS's 67th Annual Report, viz.:

$$\frac{3}{4}(r - \bar{r}) + \frac{1}{4}(rer - \overline{rer})$$

where $\bar{r}, \overline{rer}$ indicate the values of these series in December 1993.

This choice of weights is of course somewhat arbitrary but was chosen to capture the relative importance of the interest rate and the exchange rate channels in the monetary transmission process in industrialised countries. (The choice of December 1993 is also arbitrary but does not alter *movements* in the index.)

What do these MCIs say about monetary policy in Asia? The observed patterns over time in the MCIs for the countries shown have two striking common features. The first is that monetary conditions were *relatively tight in the early to mid-1980s*: the only exception is the Philippines, particularly in 1984 when inflation rose sharply (leading to a subsequent stabilisation programme). According to this measure, policy was particularly tight in Indonesia, Korea, Malaysia and Thailand; in all cases, the measured degree of tightness reflected mainly the level of real effective exchange rates rather than the level of real interest rates. The second common feature is that *monetary conditions were relatively slack in the first half of the 1990s*, when growth was exceptionally strong and when bank credit expanded sharply. The degree of easing from the early 1980s to the mid-1990s was greatest in Indonesia, Malaysia and Thailand. For these three countries the pre-crisis year in which monetary policy was most slack was 1994: between then and the end of 1996, conditions tightened somewhat (the real interest rate and the real effective exchange rate both rose). But in each case policy remained significantly slacker than it had been in the 1980s.

The main potential weakness of this comparison of MCIs between two distinct periods is that the equilibrium real exchange rate may have changed between the two periods. In the case of the comparison made above, however, the probable direction of change in the equilibrium real exchange rate appears to strengthen rather than weaken the argument. The real exchange rate measure used is based on consumer prices, largely because of the absence of reliable and comprehensive data on unit labour costs. Given the more rapid relative growth

Table 6.4　Inflation measured by the implicit GDP price deflator (%)

	Average 1979–81	Average 1989–91	Average 1994–96
Hong Kong	14.1	9.7	4.9
Korea	20.2	8.4	4.8
Singapore	7.8	4.4	3.1
Taiwan	13.2	3.6	2.2
Indonesia	26.6	10.7	8.7
Malaysia	6.6	3.8	5.2
Philippines	10.8	12.9	8.8
Thailand	10.0	5.9	5.1
Simple average	13.7	7.4	5.4
Memorandum			
Japan	4.1	2.3	−0.3
United States	9.1	4.2	2.4
Australia	10.2	4.7	1.9

Source: IMF *International Financial Statistics* and national data.

of productivity in the manufacturing sector, the real exchange rate defined using consumer prices (which includes a high proportion of non-tradables where productivity growth is typically lower) would probably have had to appreciate to maintain constant competitiveness in the tradable sector.

The apparent difference in monetary conditions between the late 1980s and the early 1990s was, for most countries, reflected in a faster rate of disinflation during the 1980s than during the first half of the 1990s (Table 6.4). At the beginning of the decade, the average rate of inflation for the eight economies shown in the table was almost 14%: by the end of the decade, it had fallen to a little over 7%, a significant decline that mirrored the decline in the major industrial economies. Moreover, the decline in inflation was broadly based, with virtually each country (the only exception being the Philippines) registering a sizable drop in inflation. The experience of the first half of the 1990s was rather different: disinflation was, on average, less marked and rather more variable across countries (with the inflation in the more recently industrialised countries remaining relatively high). Nevertheless, inflation remained rather moderate in most dynamic Asian economies – particularly as rapid structural change would itself be associated with larger changes in relative prices, and higher inflation, than in more slowly growing economies.

By the mid-1990s, inflation could be described as low only in Singapore and Taiwan, whose currencies had both tended to appreciate against the dollar when it was weakening. Both economies had a rate of inflation of 2 to 3%, similar to that in most industrial countries. Elsewhere annual inflation was around 5% or higher.

Could monetary policy in much of Asia have been much tighter in the 1990s? The most commonly cited constraint on raising interest rates at that time was that higher rates would have encouraged local borrowers to denominate their borrowing in yen or in dollars. Indeed, the main problem for many countries in the early 1990s was excessive inflows, a large part of which was foreign currency borrowing from international banks. Probably the only effective way in which monetary policy could have limited inflows would have been to allow the exchange rate to appreciate, perhaps significantly, so that the risk of subsequent depreciation could have served to deter or limit inflows.[6] But Asian monetary authorities were reluctant to accept such an appreciation. One reason for such reluctance may have been uncertainty about how far the exchange rate would have to appreciate: while they might have accepted an appreciation of, say, 10%, they would have been reluctant to accept one of 30%, or higher. The experience of many industrial countries has been that once an appreciation begins, extrapolative expectations take over and attract still further inflows. The exchange rate may then rise to uncompetitive levels.

4. MONETARY POLICY RESPONSES TO THE CRISIS

The comparative laxity of monetary policy in the years before the crisis did not change as the crisis approached. Indeed, there was considerable reluctance to tighten monetary policy in most Asian countries in the early stages of the crisis. The main reason was that pressure on exchange rates typically arose at a time when a marked slowdown in exports and in domestic demand had already set in (and asset prices in some centres were under heavy downward pressure). Reluctance to raise interest rates in such circumstances was reinforced by a financial structure in which debt was predominantly short-term (or contracted at floating rates). This meant that higher rates would immediately hit borrowers hard and – even worse – would threaten

Monetary policy and Taiwan's economy

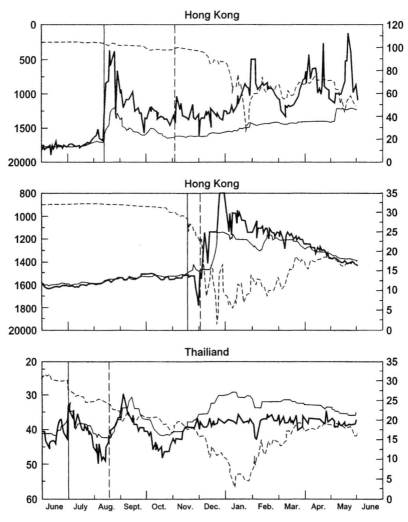

Note: Volatility defined as 12-month moving standard deviation of 3-month interest
rates and monthly % changes in the exchange rate.

Figure 6.4 Interest rates and exchange rates during the crisis

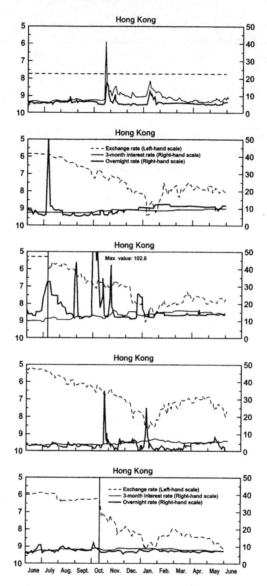

Figure 6.4 continued

the viability of banks.   Since foreign exchange market participants knew that the authorities were thus constrained, many central banks found it difficult to defend their currency in ways that those in financial markets found credible. In some instances, credibility was further undermined by uncertainties about political leadership, which created doubts about the government's ability to pursue any coherent economic policy.

Figure 6.4 charts the movements of interest rates in each country during the crisis. Two key dates are highlighted: the date when the currency was in effect floated (shown by a continuous vertical line) and the date when the IMF standby credit was formally approved (a dotted vertical line). With the exception of the Philippines (which was already under an IMF programme), the IMF was called in only after forced floating.

Although the exact pattern of events differed somewhat from country to country, two generalisations can be made:

• interest rates were higher after floating than before (the only exception was Taiwan, where interest rates peaked before the de facto floating of the New Taiwan dollar). If a robust defence of the currency had been made, one would normally have expected interest rates to be higher before floating than afterwards;

• interest rates did not peak until several weeks *after* the formal approval of IMF standby credits. As initial monetary policy prescriptions could be put in place quickly (with the IMF presumably requiring substantial immediate increases in interest rates), this suggests that the IMF did *not* (as some have suggested) go for 'overkill' by requiring that interest rates go to levels from which they could only decline.

The main reason interest rate responses were (with hindsight) initially inadequate was probably that almost everybody underestimated how far exchange rates could fall. The 'good' fundamentals of many countries (low budget deficits or even surpluses; moderate rates of inflation; flexible labour markets, etc.) and a formidable capacity to increase exports meant that most observers did not expect the Asian currencies to collapse. Rather they expected an adjustment of moderate size that would not undermine financial and monetary stability. Experience of exchange rate movements since 1970 seemed to support this optimism. Exchange rates in previous crises had not in general fallen by more than 20%, and often much less: only in the major crises in Indonesia and in the Philippines in the 1970s did the exchange rate fall exceed 30%. The depth of the declines

Table 6.5 *Exchange rate declines compared*

	Change from June 1997 to January 1998 (%)	Previous largest decline* % change	Previous largest decline* Dates
Indonesia	−75	−34	Oct 78 – May 79
Korea	−48	−20	Dec 79 – July 80
Malaysia	−43	−13	May 74 – Dec 75
Philippines	−38	−37	Jun 69 – Aug 70
Singapore	−19	−10	May 74 – Dec 75
Taiwan	−18	− 7	Apr 94 – Nov 95
Thailand	−52	−18	Aug 84 – Mar 85

Note:

*Since 1970.

The exchange rate is defined as US dollars per unit of foreign currency.

Change over seven months in all cases.

Table 6.6 *Interest rates and exchange rates during the crisis*

	Interest rates Overnight rate Peak	Interest rates Overnight rate Date	Interest rates Three-month rate 1st half 1997	Interest rates Three-month rate Peak	Interest rates Three-month rate Date	Exchange rate Low[1] between July 1997 and March 1998 Depreciation[2]	Exchange rate Low[1] between July 1997 and March 1998 Date
Hong Kong	100.0	23.10	5.8	25.0	23.10	0	–
Taiwan	11.5	7.10	6.1	9.8	7.10	−19.3	12.1.98
Indonesia	300.0	25.8	13.7	27.7	31.10	−84.3	23.1.98
Korea	27.2	30.12	12.7	25.0[3]	23.12	−54.6	23.12
Malaysia	50.0	10.7	7.2	8.8	20.11	−46.3	8.1.98
Philippines	102.6	6.10	14.0	85.0	8.10	−41.8	7.1.98
Singapore	50.0	23.10	3.6	10.3	19.12	−21.0	12.1.98
Thailand	27.4	5.9	13.1	26.0	25.12	−55.0	12.1.98

Notes: Dates refer to 1997 unless otherwise indicated.

[1] Closing rate.

[2] Percentage change in the US dollar/local currency exchange rate since June 1997.

[3] Not unique.

in exchange rates in this crisis surpassed by far earlier experience – doubtless because of the much greater integration of capital markets and very large short-term external debts (Table 6.5).

The main consequence of delay was that countries suffered the worst of both worlds. They got both an over-depreciated currency (which aggravated the difficulties of those with large foreign currency debts) *and*, eventually, very high real interest rates. The textbook trade-off between lower exchange rate *or* higher interest rates was not available in the way that previous experience might have suggested because the loss of confidence in the currency was too severe. The whole curve shifted against them by a magnitude that few at the time realised.

The *Thai baht* had been under periodic pressure for many months before the final crisis and at least two major attacks had earlier been successfully repelled by central bank intervention in the foreign exchange markets. When pressure intensified in mid-1997, the central bank intervened massively in both the spot and forward markets but resisted upward pressure on interest rates. The authorities also introduced measures to separate the onshore and offshore markets for the baht. In June – the month before the floating of the exchange rate – overnight rates had to rise sharply in the face of intense pressure. But in the second half of the month overnight rates were allowed to fall well below three-month rates, probably because the authorities were all too anxious to prevent rates rising very far (Figure 6.4). Although overnight rates had been allowed to rise to 20% during the crisis, they had, by early August, fallen back to 10%. This was allowed to happen even though the exchange rate was weakening. The adoption of an IMF programme in August (dotted line in Figure 6.4) forced a sharp increase in overnight and three-month rates to levels significantly above those reached at the climax of the July crisis. Yet again the authorities apparently relaxed too soon: the sharp decline in rates from early September to mid-October had to be largely reversed when the baht came under renewed downward pressure. From November to the time when this chapter was written (May 1988), however, the authorities persevered with a high interest-rate policy (although overnight rates remained below three-month rates).

Unlike Thailand, *Malaysia* opted to preserve its foreign exchange reserves by allowing the exchange rate to fall when pressure mounted on the foreign exchange markets. Even before the crisis, the Malaysian ringgit had not been rigidly fixed (exchange rate volatility, shown in Table 6.2, tended to be significantly higher in Malaysia than in either Indonesia or Thailand). Interest rates in Malaysia did rise sharply in the days surrounding the floating of the Thai baht, but only very briefly. Overnight rates remained at or below 10% for much of the crisis despite almost continuous downward pressure on the exchange rate. Moreover, special measures were taken to limit the pass-through to three-month rates.

The *Philippines* kept overnight rates high in the period immediately after the outbreak of the crisis for longer than either Malaysia or Thailand. Moreover, the central bank allowed sharp increases in overnight rates on at least three separate occasions. The 'spikes' in the graph of overnight rates for the Philippines resemble those seen in Hong Kong and Singapore, where the authorities have acquired a reputation for firm action in defence of the exchange rate.

Indonesia raised overnight interest rates to 300% when the rupiah floated in August (intraday hence not shown on the graph which shows end-of-day rates). Three-month interest rates rose more sharply than in other countries. However, this failed to stabilise the exchange rate because of doubts about other domestic policies and because of the provision of liquidity support (at lower rates) for weak banks. Thereafter there was considerable instability, monetary and otherwise.

Both overnight and three-month rates in *Korea* moved upwards only slowly from July until November. Pressure on the won did not lead to sharp increases in rates before the currency was floated (when intervention was very heavy). Interest rates rose substantially only after an IMF programme had in effect specified higher interest rates: three-month interest rates rose to 25% by the end of December and remained above 20% during the months that followed (see Figure 6.4). It was only the combination of a much higher level of interest rates and the conclusion of an agreement extending the maturity of massive short-term foreign currency debt that eventually halted, and then reversed, the depreciation of the won.

In summary, interest rates generally reached peaks only in the later stages of the crisis and exchange rates did not touch bottom until January 1998. Initial increases in interest rates early in the crisis usually proved inadequate, and only subsequent bouts of renewed downward pressure on the exchange rate forced substantial increases in interest rates, often in the context of an IMF programme.

One notable exception to this pattern of interest rate policy was of course Hong Kong, where there were sharp and sustained increases. Interest rates rose along the maturity spectrum (with three-month rates reaching 25% at one point). This served to successfully defend the dollar peg, in the face of steep declines in asset prices.

5. JUDGING THE STANCE OF MONETARY POLICY

As the crisis unfolded it became clear that, once exchange rate pegs or bands had been abandoned, neither the authorities nor the markets had any widely agreed way of judging the stance of monetary policy. This uncertainty may well have widened risk premia. The difficult dilemma the authorities faced was that confidence in the currency could be restored only by high interest rates that would worsen recessionary tendencies that were already undermining corporate viability and add to serious banking sector problems. There were at least three distinct issues involved:

• How effective are higher interest rates in limiting currency depreciation?
• How should 'real' interest rates be measured when the rate of inflation is unstable?
• What should be the relative weights attached to interest rates and to the exchange rate in measuring monetary conditions?

These issues are considered in turn.

How effective is raising interest rates in limiting currency depreciation?   The link between interest rates and the exchange rate is complex because it depends crucially on expectations. It could be argued that only substantial increases in interest rates can effectively support a currency under pressure. Increases in interest rates that are only moderate run the risk that the market will expect further increases; investors might then delay moving into domestic currency assets until they believe that interest rates have peaked and that the likely future direction will be downwards. On this view, the reluctance in several Asian countries to raise interest rates in the early stages of the crisis, and to keep them up for long enough to rebuild reserves, created unfavourable expectations and thus weakened policy-makers' credibility. Brazil's experience with its sudden doubling of interest rates seems to support this interpretation: the reflow of funds into real-denominated assets, at first rather modest, gathered strength only when interest rates began to drift down and the market came to expect further falls. The Brazilian central bank took pains to slow down the decline in interest rates, taking advantage of inflows to substantially increase foreign exchange reserves. It did not allow interest rates to fall back to pre-crisis levels as soon as the immediate pressure subsided.[7] Even Hong Kong, with its very large foreign exchange reserves, raised interest rates sharply when its currency came under pressure.

However, unrealistic increases in interest rates that the market judges to be unsustainable have in some cases given the markets the impression of desperation on the part of the authorities. Excessively high interest rates can damage the creditworthiness of viable companies and thus not only weaken future prospects for growth but also accentuate reversed capital inflows (e.g. as foreign banks cut credit lines to borrowers perceived as less creditworthy). In these circumstances, the effect on the exchange rate could be the opposite to that intended. Sweden's doomed attempt to save its currency by increasing interest rates to 500% has become a lesson to all.

How to define the 'real' interest rate? The measure of the level of real interest rates depends on the definition of the rate of inflation used to deflate nominal rates. A common definition, of the rate of consumer price inflation over the previous twelve months, suggests that real short-term interest rates in the countries most affected by the crisis rose steeply towards the end of 1997 and into early 1998 (see the left-hand side of Table 6.7). It also suggests that real rates remained significantly lower in economies which maintained their exchange rate peg (China and Hong Kong). However, inflation rates have changed sharply as a result of recent exchange rate movements. Deflating by the rate of inflation over the previous three months shows a quite different picture (see the right-hand side of the table). Real interest rates thus measured were significantly negative in Indonesia and somewhat below zero in Korea and Malaysia. Note, incidentally, how high real rates went in Brazil to defend its currency.

In contrast, real interest rates in China, Hong Kong and Singapore (where inflation has fallen in recent months) appear somewhat higher than on the first measure. High real interest rates, if maintained beyond the immediate crisis period, would be a significant change for all three economies, where real rates in the past have been very low or even negative. The change is most marked in the case of Hong Kong, where real short-term rates have risen to 5%, compared with minus 3.5% in 1990–95. Other things equal, a shift of this size should have a major effect on economic activity and on asset prices.

The choice of deflator depends in part on trends in underlying inflation, and, in particular, how inflation responds to exchange rate shocks. In the case of Mexico, the exchange rate depreciated by over 100%[8] and the rate of inflation rose by 45 percentage points (from 7.1% to 52% as shown in Table 6.8). Hence inflation accelerated by fully two-fifths of the rate of depreciation. In Asia, however, the domestic inflation response to depreciation has proved much more

Table 6.7   Short-term interest rates[1] in real terms: alternative deflators

Deflated by:	(a) year-on-year inflation[2]						(b) quarterly inflation[3]			
	1990–95	1996	| 1997			1998	1997			1998
			Q2	Q3	Q4	Q1	Q2	Q3	Q4	Q1
	annual rates of interest									
India	2.7	4.8	0.8	3.1	2.6	1.9	3.6	2.2	0.3	−0.4
China	−2.4	0.7	4.4	5.2	4.6	5.6	9.3	−2.0	10.7	8.9
Hong Kong	−3.4	−0.5	0.6	1.2	4.8	3.8	0.6	0.3	7.2	4.7
Taiwan	3.2	2.3	5.4	6.4	7.4	5.5	3.7	2.5	12.0	4.0
Indonesia	8.1	7.3	8.5	17.3	12.4	2.1	9.9	16.4	1.8	−36.6
Korea	6.9	7.3	8.2	8.3	10.0	12.6	8.1	8.3	9.1	−0.1
Malaysia	2.7	3.5	4.8	5.2	5.9	4.1	6.7	5.7	4.2	−1.8
Philippines	4.7	3.6	5.7	8.6	10.0	10.8	5.4	6.7	9.9	8.1
Singapore	1.1	1.6	1.9	1.8	4.0	5.2	1.6	0.6	4.9	9.2
Thailand	5.1	4.7	10.4	12.3	12.4	14.5	10.5	6.5	9.2	14.2
Brazil	13.1	10.1	13.3	15.7	29.9	27.3	14.7	18.5	32.0	24.0
Other Latin America[4]	−1.2	4.9	4.6	4.6	5.6	6.7	6.0	6.1	7.7	4.6

Notes: [1] Rates on three-month paper with the following exceptions: China, the one-year deposit rate; Taiwan, the overnight rate and, before November 1994, a weighted average of six money market rates with maturities ranging from overnight to six months; Brazil, the overnight rate.
[2] Short-term rates deflated by the year-on-year change in the CPI.
[3] Short-term rates deflated by the change in the CPI over three months (annualised).
[4] Unweighted average of Argentina, Chile, Colombia, Mexico and Peru.

Source: IMF International Financial Statistics, national data and BIS estimates.

modest (leaving aside the special case of Indonesia). Korean inflation rose by 7 percentage points, Malaysia by 5 percentage points and Thai by 2 to 3 percentage points – much less than the share of imports in final expenditure would have implied. This suggests that the initial depreciation shock has been absorbed by lower real wages or profits. The more smoothly inflation shocks are absorbed the less restrictive monetary policy needs to be.

Table 6.8 Depreciation and inflation: Asia and Mexico compared

	Exchange rate[1]	Wholesale prices[2]	Consumer prices[2]	Imports as a % of total expenditure[3]
	Percentage changes			
Indonesia				
July 96 – July 97	7.3	5.9	5.7	
July 97 – March 98	282.8	94.84[4]	70.4	27.3
Korea				
July 96 – July 97	9.6	2.7	4.0	
July 97 – March 98	67.3	27.4	11.5	34.0
Malaysia				
July 96 – July 97	3.4	–	2.4	
July 97 – March 98	45.0	–	7.3	95.6
Thailand				
July 96 – July 97	19.6	5.7	6.6	
July 97 – March 98	36.0	18.5	9.1	45.8
Memorandum items:				
Mexico				
Nov. 93 – Nov. 94	9.1	7.8	7.1	
Nov. 94 – Nov. 95	122.5	58.1	52.0	28.7
Italy, Spain and Sweden[4]				
Aug. 91 – Aug. 92	1.7	0.1	4.3	
Aug. 92 – Aug. 93	27.5	5.4	4.3	22.9

Notes: [1] Change in local currency per US dollar; for Italy, Spain and Sweden, against the Deutsche Mark.
[2] Led by one month; at an annual rate.
[3] Imports defined as imports of goods and services in 1995; for Italy, Spain and Sweden 1993.
[4] December 1997.

A further complication affecting the choice of deflator is that the consumer price index may not be an appropriate deflator for interest rates when asset prices are changing rapidly. In any event, such wide discrepancies in the different measures of real interest rates create considerable additional uncertainty for investment decisions and may depress investment even if, ex post, the level of real interest rates turns out to be moderate.

How to define the relative weights of interest rates and the exchange rate? There is of course no simple answer to this question. However, it is of interest to apply the same (admittedly arbitrary) definition of the monetary conditions indices that were applied above. According

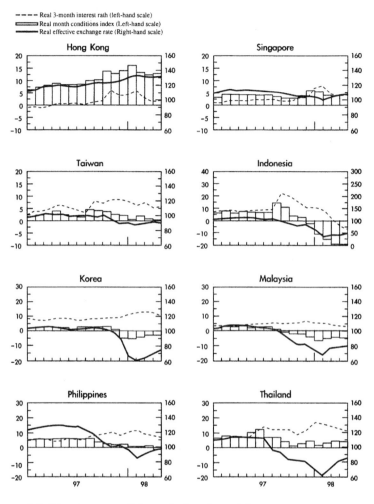

Figure 6.5 Monetary conditions during the crisis

to this, monetary conditions tightened only in Hong Kong (significantly) and in Singapore (where the change was much more modest (see Figure 6.5)). Elsewhere monetary conditions as defined in this admittedly arbitrary way have eased.

How this should be interpreted is open to question. It could be argued that a depreciation in the real effective exchange rate is an inevitable concomitant of a major weakening in external demand (declining prices for electronic goods, very weak demand in Japan, etc.). If so, a weak exchange rate cannot be interpreted as necessary evidence of easy monetary conditions. A second line of argument is that the sharp falls of many exchange rates in December and January reflected an overshooting that could not have been prevented by higher interest rates alone. The subsequent simultaneous recovery of exchange rates and easing of interest rates in the months that followed supports this interpretation.

6. CONCLUSION

In most Asian countries, exchange rates are now floating. Because monetary policy in the past was frequently exchange-rate oriented, the question of which domestic variables should guide monetary policy did not in the past receive the attention it needed. Partly because of this, but partly too because the exchange rate target was rather 'soft', monetary policy in several Asian countries did not have a sufficiently strong or convincing anti-inflation orientation. Correcting this poses policy makers with two formidable types of challenge: to find suitable domestic anchors for policy and to find a way of allowing for changes in exchange rates when framing monetary policy.

There are several ways to develop a mechanism for gearing monetary policy more closely to domestic economic conditions. One way could be to opt for a *rule-based approach*. This could include focusing on a single (or several) explicit domestically-based nominal anchor or target. Possibilities include monetary aggregates, nominal GDP, real interest rates and inflation targets. An explicit anchor would have the advantage of giving financial markets (domestic and international) some guidance about the authorities' policy intentions. Uncertainty about such intentions appears to have accentuated the recent crisis for several countries. An alternative way could be to allow central banks to exercise *discretion*. Because all mechanistic rules have serious failings, there is much in principle to be said for discretion. But discretion only works if markets can trust the central bank to take appropriate decisions. Here independence for central banks may have an important role to play, that of persuading markets that central banks can take the necessary action to ensure low inflation. Several Asian countries have begun to contemplate movement in such a direction.

The second challenge is to find an appropriate way of allowing for the exchange rate when framing monetary policy. One lesson of the recent crisis is that dollar-based exchange rate pegs demanded a monetary policy commitment that most countries were not prepared to give. (Hong Kong is of course the exception because there was and is a clear commitment of monetary policy to the fixed exchange rate.) When the dollar pegs or bands came under heavy pressure, monetary and other policies were not in general subordinated to the exchange rate. Hence the exchange rate was often, in effect, a 'soft' constraint, to be abandoned in case of difficulty. Given the intensity of pressure on present-day capital markets, this is perhaps understandable.

But recognition that simple, dollar-based pegs are not sustainable does not mean that the exchange rate will not again play a major role in monetary policy in Asia. Asian countries have periodically chosen an exchange rate peg or band because it served two valuable functions in addition to that of an anchor for monetary policy. These functions are likely to continue to be important.

The first and perhaps most important function was that it acted as a *guide to an export-led process of rapid industrialisation*. The sheer scale and speed of the radical economic transformation of several Asian countries may have made it difficult to trust the market to find the 'right' exchange rate. While it is generally accepted that faster-than-average growth of productivity in the tradable sector has to be reflected in real appreciation, it is more difficult to know *how far and how fast* to appreciate. Two conflicting considerations need to be balanced. On the one hand, an excessive or too rapid real appreciation would delay or disrupt the rapid industrialisation that was the object of policy in many countries. On the other hand, resisting appreciation for too long can simply increase inflation, with the necessary real appreciation taking the form of an increase in the price level as wages and the prices of non-tradable goods rise. This chapter suggests that some Asian countries worried too much about maintaining competitiveness and too little about preventing inflation. Many should have tightened monetary policy during the 1990s boom and allowed exchange rates to rise. Singapore perhaps set an example here.

Such tightening would of course have exposed at an earlier stage the financial system weaknesses that became fully manifest only after the crisis. In an ideal world, the supervisory framework should have been tightened before to ensure the financial system was robust enough to cope with monetary tightening. In the real world, important but politically controversial issues often get tackled only after a crisis.

The second function – important for very open small economies – was that a stable exchange rate helped to *develop local financial and banking systems*. When the exchange rate is very unstable, inflows of foreign investment will tend to be denominated in foreign currencies.

By contrast, flows into local currency financial investments (money markets, bond markets) will tend to be inhibited by high risk premia and this may in turn inhibit the development of these markets. Marked instability in the exchange rate can also limit the development of a local banking system. The extensive development of local banking systems in so much of Asia probably owes something to the stability of exchange rates (although a history of low inflation may have been a more potent factor).

One possible response could be to modify the terms of pegging or banding. One possible modification would be to adopt a *reference exchange rate* that gives greater weight to currencies other than the dollar. How to define the currency basket against which a currency is to be fixed is not a trivial question. The composition of *foreign trade* has often been used to derive basket weights and this does indeed have the advantage of minimising the effects on trade of changes in the cross-rates of currencies selected. However, the currency of denomination of trade (notably of imports) does not closely mirror the origin of trade: many non-US goods are priced in dollars in world markets so that the weight of the dollar may need to be greater than trade weights would suggest. An alternative approach is to allow for the *currency composition of capital flows*. For instance, the high proportion of Indonesia's external debt denominated in yen was a significant factor behind the weight of the yen in the country's previous currency basket. It has been argued that a *simple* basket is essential if the exchange rate is to provide an effective anchor. This may explain the preference for dollar pegs, and the reluctance in Asia to incorporate European currencies in the peg. This may change with the projected introduction of the euro, given the weight of the European economy and the depth of European financial markets.

A second modification could be wider bands around the reference exchange rate. The greatest advantage of wider bands is that they can have a particularly large effect on short-term flows, when the investment horizon is such that even rather modest movement in the spot exchange rate has a major impact on annualised expected returns. The same applies to residents' short-term borrowing in foreign currency – which was a major problem in Asia in the run-up to the crisis. An important lesson is the need to maintain significant short-term volatility even within the band.

An alternative response would be to avoid explicit exchange rate commitments but instead systematically offset *part* of the impact of excessive exchange rate changes by adjusting domestic interest rates. This chapter examined recent Asian experience in the light of

Monetary Conditions Indices that have helped to guide policies in certain industrial countries with floating exchange rates. The greater the weight in such indices of the exchange rate, and the smaller the weight of the level of domestic interest rates, the closer will policy guided by an MCI be to the policy of an exchange rate peg. In practice, of course, policy is rarely determined by such mechanistic concepts as MCIs.

Whatever the precise response ultimately adopted, it will be very important to find some way of convincing financial markets that central banks care about the exchange rate (if only because of the implications for inflation) and are prepared to tighten policies to counteract excessive depreciation. In the years that followed its crisis, Mexico sought to do this by allowing domestic liquidity conditions to tighten whenever there was downward pressure on the peso. Asian economies have found out that they are not immune from overshooting exchange rates and that excessive exchange rate depreciation can do great damage. All this is to some extent unavoidable in the new world of large-scale volatile capital flows. Monetary policy needs to avoid making matters worse.

ACKNOWLEDGEMENT

Prepared for an International Conference on the Conduct of Monetary Policy organised by the Central Bank of China and the Institute of Economics, Academia Sinica, Taipei on 12–13 June 1998. The author is grateful to Ib Madsen for very efficient research assistance and helpful comments on an earlier draft. Thanks are also due to helpful comments from Stefan Gerlach, Pablo Graf, Bob McCauley, Zenta Nakajima and Bill White. The views expressed are those of the author and not necessarily the views of the BIS. This paper was written in May 1998 and has not been revised to take account of developments since that date.

NOTES

1. The BIS *Annual Report* published in June 1996 – echoing many contemporary assessments – noted marked excess demand pressure in Indonesia, Malaysia and Thailand and drew attention to the rapid credit expansion.
2. The main exception was Indonesia, where the weight of the yen in the exchange rate basket was significant.

3. However, the Philippines peso did appreciate somewhat in real terms in 1985 before depreciating sharply in 1986.

4. See BIS: *The transmission of monetary policy in emerging market economies.* BIS Policy Papers, No. 3 (1998), especially pp. 59–62.

5. Important qualifications include: (a) a terms-of-trade shock can cause the equilibrium real exchange rate to change (this cannot be interpreted as a change in monetary conditions); (b) the exchange rate affects primarily the traded sector of the economy while it is the level of interest rates that affects the non-traded sector (hence quite different effects are being aggregated); (c) differences in the speed of impact on the economy of interest and exchange rate changes.

6. However, much of the problem of excessive inflows was unrelated to monetary policy, but reflected poor prudential limits of banks' gross (not only net) foreign currency lending to residents.

7. It should be noted, however, that such a sharp interest rate response was more feasible in Brazil than in many other countries because of certain impediments that limited the passthrough of policy-determined rates to the whole interest rate spectrum and because of the relative low degree of financial deepening (after so many years of hyperinflation).

8. This is of course based on the local currency price of foreign currency – the relevant measure for consideration of inflation impacts. The depreciation defined in the more conventional terms of foreign currency per unit of local currency was −55%.

7. Capital flows and exchange rates in Taiwan

Chung-Shu Wu

1. INTRODUCTION

Since July 1997, the world economy has been overshadowed by the Asian financial crisis. The causes are many, with high short-term debt being a crucial importance factor. Those who suffered most, such as Thailand, Malaysia, Indonesia, the Philippines and Korea, all displayed a high short-term debt ratio. In light of this fact, economists have gradually adjusted their views on the role of capital flows in developing countries, especially with regard to exchange rate determination. Though the importance of capital flows on the determination of exchange rates is hardly disputed, Agenor and Hoffmaister (1996) point out the impacts that various capital components may have on exchange rates. Without going into detail, they state that 'the impact of capital inflows on the real exchange rate relates to the composition of these flows, and their effects on the composition of aggregate demand'.

By simulating a small macroeconometric model, Fry (1998) demonstrates that foreign direct investments generate an appreciation in the real exchange rate, while portfolio investments depreciate the real exchange rate in the long run. In recent years, Taiwan has experienced active foreign direct investments and portfolio investments and it is interesting to investigate the impacts of these two different capital flows on exchange rates. In order to avoid possible spurious regression results, we will adopt Johansen's (1988, 1992a, b) maximum likelihood cointegration analysis to verify our model. Moreover, a central bank's intervention in the foreign exchange market usually has a significant impact on exchange rate movements. Without taking this into account, we might run into model misspecification problems. Therefore, the main purpose of this chapter is to investigate the impacts of foreign direct investments and portfolio investments on

128

nominal and real exchange rates by considering the central bank's intervention.

Before we go into further discussion, let us review recent developments of foreign direct investments and portfolio investments in Taiwan. Table 7.1 shows that due to bubbling real estate prices, hiking wage rates and sharp appreciation of the NT dollar, foreign direct investments have continuously flowed out since 1988, reaching a record high in 1989. On the other hand, encouraged by the liberalization of Taiwan's financial markets, portfolio investments have flowed in since 1990, except for the last two years. In terms of absolute value, the ratio of portfolio investments has also exhibited a tendency to increase.

Figure 7.1 notes that foreign direct investments and portfolio investments have displayed divergent historical patterns. This might

Table 7.1   *Foreign direct investments, portfolio investments, and NT$/US$ exchange rate (1984–97)*

YEAR	FDI	POF	SUM	RFDI	RPOF	PX
1984	127	−50	77	71.75	28.25	39.60
1985	263	−46	217	85.11	14.89	39.83
1986	261	71	332	78.61	21.39	37.84
1987	10	−372	−362	2.62	97.38	31.74
1988	−3160	−1712	−4872	64.86	35.14	28.59
1989	−5347	−902	−6249	85.57	14.43	26.41
1990	−3913	−1006	−4919	79.55	20.45	26.89
1991	−784	45	−739	94.57	5.43	26.82
1992	−1088	444	−644	71.02	28.98	25.16
1993	−1694	1067	−627	61.35	38.65	26.39
1994	−1265	905	−360	58.29	41.71	26.46
1995	−1424	493	−931	74.28	25.72	26.48
1996	−1979	−1112	−3091	64.02	35.98	27.46
1997	−2974	−8283	−11257	26.42	73.58	28.70

Notes:

FDI: Foreign Direct Investments.

POF: Portfolio Investments.

SUM: Foreign Direct Investments + Portfolio Investments.

RFDI: $|FDI|/(|FDI| + |POF|) * 100\%$.

RPOF: $|POF|/(|FDI| + |POF|) * 100\%$.

PX: NT$ /US$ exchange rate.

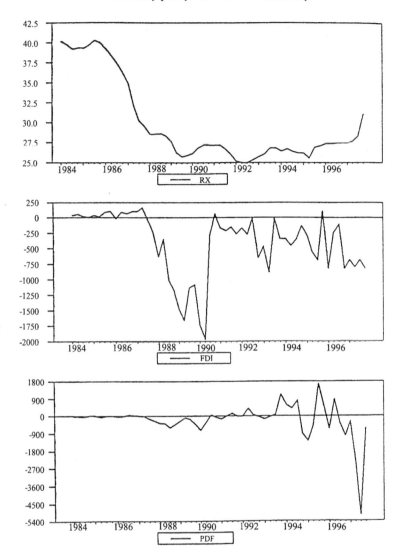

Figure 7.1 Historical trends of foreign direct investments (FDI), portfolio investments (PDF), and exchange rate (RX) (1984–97)

imply that they have different impacts on the economy. Foreign direct investments have mainly flowed into the investment sector and improved production technology and management efficiency. In contrast, portfolio investments have mainly flowed into money and stock markets. Though these investments have also had a positive impact on private consumption and investment, the effects are limited to the demand side.

As regards to exchange rate determination, the impact of the supply side is different from that of the factor coming from the demand side. Moreover, Dornbusch (1976) argues that the different paces of adjustment between the real sector and financial sector causes excessive fluctuations in exchange rates. Thus, foreign direct investments and portfolio investments may have very different impacts on real and financial markets. Therefore, it is interesting to investigate whether and how the two types of investments have different impacts on exchange rate determinates.

This paper is organized as follows. In section 2 we provide a simple model to illustrate the relationship between exchange rates and the two different capital flows. Section 3 discusses the empirical procedure and the statistical method used to analyse the cointegration system. Section 4 offers some data descriptions and empirical results. Section 5 presents concluding remarks.

2. CAPITAL FLOWS AND EXCHANGE RATES

This section utilizes an empirical model to connect capital flows and nominal and real exchange rates. According to the balance of payment equilibrium condition, under a freely-floating exchange rate system, the exchange rate moves to equilibrate the sum of the current and capital accounts in the balance of payment, while leaving official reserves unchanged. The equilibrium condition can be formulated as follows:

$$CA_t + CAP_t = \triangle OR_t = 0, \qquad (7.1)$$

where CA is the current account balance, CAP is the capital account balance and $\triangle OR_t$ is the change in official reserves. Since the central bank's intervention affects official reserves, we can include it in equation (7.1) and rewrite the equation as

$$CA_t + CAP_t + ITV_t = 0, \qquad (7.2)$$

where ITV is the central bank intervention. Moreover, we can divide the current account balance into net exports (NX) and net interest income (IK).

$$CA_t = NX_t + IR_t. \qquad (7.3)$$

We assume net exports are a function of the real exchange rate ($\frac{S_t P_t^*}{P_t}$) and other factors (Z). For the purpose of illustration, we assume that a country's competitiveness comprises a function of an overall price index, such as the CPI, which includes both traded and non-traded goods.[1]

$$NX_t = f\left(\frac{S_t P_t^*}{P_t}, Z_t\right), \qquad (7.4)$$

where S is the NT\$/US\$ exchange rate, and P_t^* and P denote U.S. and Taiwan price indexes, respectively. The Z variable is an exogenous term which encompasses some other effects such as the effects of government and private expenditures and the differences of productivity between Taiwan and the United States in the manufacturing of traded goods.[2]

As for the interest income, it can be regarded as a function of net foreign assets (NA).

$$IR_t = g(NA_t). \qquad (7.5)$$

Substituting equations (7.2)–(7.5) into equation (7.1), we can express nominal exchange rate as a function of the relative price ratio (RP), capital movements, the central bank's intervention, and net foreign assets.

$$S_t = s(RP_t, CAP_t, ITV_t, NA_t). \qquad (7.6)$$

As already mentioned in the previous section, different capital flows may have different impacts on the exchange rate. We separate the net foreign direct investment (NFI) and foreign net portfolio investment (NPI), and the equation can be re-rewritten as follows:[3]

$$S_t = s(RP_t, NFI_t, NPI_t, ITV_t, NA_t). \qquad (7.7)$$

Equation (7.7) can also be expressed in the form of a real exchange rate (REX) function.

$$REX_t = r(RP_t, NFI_t, NPI_t, ITV_t, NA_t). \qquad (7.8)$$

The reason why we retain the relative price in the real exchange rate function form is that if the purchasing power parity is not sustained, then the relative price will have no unit effect on the real exchange rate. Furthermore, Edwards (1991) argues that the terms of trade are an important factor in the determination of the real exchange rate and that the relative price can be regarded as a proxy variable in the terms of trade.

There are two main reasons for using equations (7.7) and (7.8) as the focal point of our discussion. First, they provide simple and clear frameworks to illustrate the relationship between the exchange rate and the two types of capital flows. Second, many scholars such as Abuaf and Jorion (1990), Cheung and Lai (1993), Glen (1992) and Whitt (1992) have focused their discussions of exchange rate determination on the purchasing power parity. Our model can also readily serve to verify whether the absolute purchasing power parity holds or not.

3. THE EMPIRICAL ANALYSIS PROCEDURE AND METHOD

The traditional least square regression analysis usually encounters the problem of non-stationarity of the time series. Phillips (1986) shows that in least square regressions with non-stationary regressors, coefficient estimates may not converge in probability as the sample size increases, while the distribution of t-statistics may diverge. Therefore, this chapter adopts Johansen's maximum likelihood cointegration analysis to discuss the relationship between nominal or real exchange rates, the central bank's intervention, relative prices, and two types of capital flows in Taiwan.

In examining the relationship between exchange rates and capital mobility, traditional economic theory suggests that F- or chi-square tests be applied to the restrictions of parameters in equations (7.7) and (7.8). This would be right if all variables under investigation had no unit root. However, if the regressors, regressands and residuals all have unit roots, then regressing for the level variables will result in *'spurious regression'*. All variables must be differentiated for valid statistical inference and if both the regressors and regressands have unit roots but the residuals do not, then differentiating all variables will introduce unit roots of the *MA* type to the residuals. In other words, it creates an over-differentiating problem. Moreover, the least square estimates of the level variables, when properly normalized, no longer converge into normal distribution and the traditional chi-square and F-tests no longer hold. The limiting distribution specifically comprises three components: nuisance parameters, the unit root distribution, and the mixed Gaussian distribution. The first term arises due to the existence of correlation for residuals that could be removed by adding lagged terms to whiten the residuals. The unit root distribution is caused by correlation between regressors and residuals, which in turn arise due to the existence of unit roots. This endogeneity problem can be tackled by using the system analysis. The final component can be transformed into chi-square distribution when the proper convariance matrix is taken into account.

Two types of cointegration analyses have been proposed, both of which can properly solve the problems mentioned above. They are the maximum likelihood analysis (Johansen 1988, 1991) and fully-modified *VAR* (Phillips 1995). The former utilizes an eigen value analysis, whereas the latter revises the least square estimates for residual correlation and endogeneity. This chapter adopts the former, because of the clarity it displays in testing a long-term economic hypothesis.

The Johansen methods start with a p-dimension $VAR(k)$ model:

$$X_t = \Pi_1 X_{t-1} + \cdots + \Pi_k X_{t-k} + \mu + \phi D_t + \varepsilon_t,$$

where $\quad \Delta X_t = \sum^{k-1} \Gamma_i \Delta X_{t-i} + \Pi X_{t-k} + \mu + \phi D_t + \varepsilon_t.$

A simple rearrangement will lead to the error correction model:

$$\Gamma_t = -I + \Pi_1 + \cdots + \Pi_t \ (i = 1, 2, 3, \cdots k - 1),$$

where $\quad \Pi = -I + \Pi_1 + \cdots + \Pi_k.$

The rank of the long-term impact matrix, Π, determines the long-term properties of X_t.

Testing the cointegration is equivalent to testing the rank of Π. Johansen derives the maximum likelihood estimate of all parameters under the null of cointegration and the resulting likelihood ratio statistics. One can then test the rank by either using the λ-max or the trace test statistics, both of which make limiting distributions function of Brownian motion. Johansen goes one step further by proving that the likelihood ratio test for restrictions on cointegration vector β and/or loadings α converge to the standard chi-square when properly normalized.

It is worth noting that if β is the cointegratin vector, then for any non-singular matrix r by r matrix A, $\tilde{\beta} = \beta A$ is also another cointegration matrix. Thus, the cointegration vector is identified only up to a non-singular multiplicative factor. A consequence of this is that the rank of the cointegration is no economic interpretation of the cointegration vector. One needs prior information to identify the cointegration vector (Wickens 1996). However, this does not affect testing the restriction on β, since $R'\tilde{\beta} = (R'\beta)A = 0$ is true if and only if $R'\beta = 0$.

The procedure for the cointegration analysis is as follows:

1. test unit roots for individual time series,
2. select lag order k to whiten the residual,
3. determine the cointegration rank,
4. perform the likelihood ratio test of restrictions as implied by economic theory.

4. DATA DESCRIPTIONS AND EMPIRICAL RESULTS

4.1 Data Descriptions

Since data before 1984 are unavailable, we base our models on quarterly data over the period 1984(Q1)–1997(Q4). Two kinds of capital flows are employed: total net foreign direct investments (direct investments abroad + direct investments in Taiwan, R.O.C.) and total net portfolio investments (portfolio investment assets + portfolio investment liabilities). The capital flow data and the NT$/US$ exchange rate are obtained from *Financial Statistics* published by the Central Bank of China. Data concerning the central bank's intervention are provided by the Economic Research Department of the Central Bank of China. Other data are downloaded from the AREMOS data bank in the computer center of the Education Department of Taiwan. As to the real exchange rate, we just multiply the NT$/US$ nominal exchange rate by the U.S.-to-Taiwan relative prices.

4.2   Unit Root Tests

Granger and Newbold (1974) point out that the traditional least square estimation method may run into a spurious regression problem when the time series display a non-stationary property. Therefore, prior to

Table 7.2   Unit-root tests

	$ADF(\tau_t)$	PP	$Sims(p\text{-}value)$
REX	−0.13	−1.70	0.65
S	−0.13	−2.06	0.36
RP	−2.64	−3.17	0.10
ITV	−5.25*	−4.71*	0.00*
NFI	−3.20	−3.13	0.01*
NPI	−4.84*	−4.79*	0.00*
NA	−0.91	−2.49	0.13
*REX**	−0.62	−1.65	0.71
*RP**	−0.54	−3.17	0.48

Notes:
REX: Real Exchange Rate.
S: Nominal Exchange Rate.
RP: Relative Price.
ITV: Central Bank's Intervention.
NFI: Net Foreign Direct Investments.
NPI: Net Portfolio Investments.
NA: Net Foreign Assets.
*REX**: Real Exchange Rate Deflated by *WPL*.
*RP**: Relative *WPI* price ratio.
* represents significantly rejecting unit root null hypothesis at 5%
  significant level.

any further estimation procedure, we use augmented unit root test methods suggested by Dickey and Fuller (1981)(ADF), Phillips and Perron (1988) and Sims (1988) to examine the integrated order. In Table 7.2, the results of unit root tests show that with the exception of ITV and NPI, which may not have unit roots, other variables are non-stationary.[4] Therefore, it is inappropriate to adopt the traditional least square method to estimate and test our model.

4.3 The Cointegration Analysis

Unit root tests suggest that most variables in our model possess a non-stationary property. In order to solve the non-stationary problem, many scholars put forward different methods to estimate models. By using a simulation comparison, Gonzalo (1994) finds that the maximum likelihood estimation method suggested by Johansen (1988, 1992a, b) and Johansen and Juselius (1990, 1992) is most efficient if the model is correctly specified. It should be noted that the Johansen maximum estimation method does not require variables to follow the same integrated order.

According to the theoretical model established in section 2, we may discuss the relationship between the nominal (S) or real exchange rate (REX), relative prices (RP), the central bank's intervention (ITV), net foreign direct investments (NFI), net portfolio investments (NPI) and net foreign assets (NA). Tests for cointegration are presented in Table 7.3. The maximum eigenvalue statistics, λ_{max}, are used to determine the number of cointegrating vectors r. The null hypothesis tested shows that there can be r cointegrating vectors among our model's variables. It is known that an inappropriate lag structure in the VAR estimation generates a biased estimation.

We take the suggestion of Johansen and Juselius (1990), who chose the appropriate model by examining the property of estimation errors. The table demonstrates that a stable and strong long-term relationship is established between the nominal real exchange rate and the group of system variables. However, cointegration tests indicate the existence of more than one cointegration vector, which in term indicate that the system under investigation is stationary in more than one direction and also more stable (Dickey et al. 1994). Wickens (1996) argues that one needs prior information to identify an appropriate cointegration vector. Accordingly, we chose those that have the largest eigenvalue to represent our models as shown in Table 7.4.

Table 7.3   Cointegration rank test for nominal exchange rate (without seasonal dummy, deflated by CPI)

$$S \cdot RP \cdot ITV \cdot NFI \cdot NPI \cdot NA$$

Eigenv.	L-max	Trace	$H_0 : r$	L-max90	Trace90
0.5709	45.69	128.24	0	24.63	89.37
0.4861	35.95	82.55	1	20.90	64.74
0.3668	24.68	46.60	2	17.15	43.84
0.2482	15.40	21.92	3	13.39	26.70
0.1137	6.52	6.52	4	10.60	13.31
0.0000	0.00	0.00	5	2.71	2.71
LM(1)=43.853		P-val=0.17,	LM(4)=43.740	P-val=0.18	

Note: Eigenv. is eigenvalue; L-max and Trace denote L-max Test and Trace Test statistic, respectively; L-max90 and Trace90 are 90% critical value; LM(1) and LM(4) represent 1st order and 4th order Lagrange multiplier test for serial correlation, respectively.

Table 7.4   Cointegration vectors and their significance hypothesis testing (deflated by CPI)

Normalization variable	RP	ITV	NFI	NPI	NA	χ^2 Test
			other variables			
S	1.670**	2.000***	−2.328**	2.824***	0.196	10.82***
REX	1.227**	1.905***	−2.227**	2.596***	0.127	10.65***
S^*	2.262***	1.867***	−2.570***	2.910***	0.587***	27.69***
REX^*	1.391***	1.071***	−1.427***	1.510***	0.157***	26.48***

Notes:
Rows in S and REX are estimates with seasonal factors while rows in S^* and REX^* are estimates without seasonal factors.
$\chi^2 Test$ represents the hypothesis testing of same coefficients between NFI and NPI.
*, **, *** denote rejection of the null hypothesis at 10%, 5%, and 1% significance level, respectively.

Table 7.5   Cointegration vectors and their significance hypothesis (deflated by WPI)

Normalization variable	other variables					
	RP	*ITV*	*NFI*	*NPI*	*NA*	$\chi^2 Test$
S	0.586***	0.374***	−0.202***	0.468***	0.147***	13.15***
REX	0.226***	0.312***	−0.149***	0.369***	0.103***	13.48***
S*	0.605***	0.373***	−0.183***	0.480***	0.161***	13.18***
REX*	0.245***	0.317***	−0.142***	0.389***	0.118***	13.19***

Note: see Table 7.3.

From Tables 7.4 and 7.5, we notice that relative prices have significant positive effects on both nominal and real exchange rates. In addition, most factors significantly vary from zero. It should be noted that although controversy exists over identifying the cointegration vector, hypothesis testing results as in Johansen and Juselius (1992) are still valid. The above empirical results imply that the absolute purchasing power parity does not hold in the long run.

As expected, the central bank's intervention displays a positive relationship with the nominal or real exchange rate. If the central bank buys U.S. dollars, the NT$/US$ exchange rate is expected to rise, and vice versa. As to capital flows, most economists, such as Abuaf and Jorion (1990), MacDonald (1995) and Agenor and Hoffmaister (1996), regard capital flows as having a negative impact on exchange rates; i.e., capital inflow causes an appreciation of the domestic currency while capital outflow causes a depreciation. However, according to our empirical results, this argument only holds in the case of foreign direct investments.

Portfolio investments, on the other hand, have a negative impact on nominal and real exchange rates. An inflow of portfolio investments will not cause an appreciation of NT dollars. Instead, it will cause an increase in the NT$/US$ exchange rate in the long run. Though this result differs from existing economic theories, it matches quite well the finding of Fry (1998).[5]

Why does the impact of foreign direct investments on nominal or real exchange rates differ so widely from that of portfolio investments? Though Fry (1998) already provides an interesting simulation to support our findings, we will try an alternative way of interpretation. By looking at the essence of these two different types of capital flows, we may get important clues to solve the puzzle. Foreign direct investments are usually long-term investments, and they can improve the production technology and management efficiency of the destination countries, especially that of developing countries. They are beneficial to the increase of aggregate supply. In the long run they induce a lower rate of inflation in an economy. On the other hand, portfolio investments normally represent short-term investments and most of them are for speculative purposes. Booming stock, financial, and real estate markets indeed have stimulating effects on private consumption and investment (Lin et al., 1997), however, they mainly affect the demand side, and can easily bring higher inflation rates in the long run. Therefore, in line with the relative purchasing power parity, it is understandable that foreign direct investments appreciate while portfolio investments depreciate exchange rates.

5. CONCLUDING REMARKS

Most of the existing literature advocates that capital flows have appreciating effects on destination countries. Our empirical results show that foreign direct investments indeed bear a negative relationship to the nominal and real NT$/US$ exchange rates. However, portfolio investments have a positive relationship on NT$/US$ exchange rates; i.e., inflow of portfolio investments to Taiwan might not appreciate the NT dollar in the long run, and might even cause it to depreciate. Since 1989, many Taiwanese entrepreneurs have invested in mainland China, Southeast Asia, and the United States, etc. Stimulated by the liberalization and internationalization policies of Taiwan's government, foreign portfolio investments have continuously flowed into Taiwan since 1990, except for a few times during various political crises. Our empirical results provide one of the important explanations for why the trade surplus and the NT$/US$ exchange rate have both been increasing since 1992.

Observing the different stages of economic development in Asian countries, we find that in the early stages of development, foreign direct investments did help Asian countries move from low growth rates to high growth rates. However, as the development of the economies reached a bottleneck and economic growth rates started declining, speculative portfolio investments still continuously flowed into these countries. As argued by Agenor and Hoffmaister (1996), portfolio capital flows might stimulate private consumption, not investment, but according to our finding, this might add a depreciation factor to future economic development. Therefore, when Taiwan's government plans the capital liberalization policy, it had better keep a close watch on the different impacts of different capital flow components on the economy's composition. Otherwise, it runs the risk of establishing an inappropriate long-term monetary and exchange rate policy, which may result in improper resource allocation and hence deteriorate the welfare of the economy.

ACKNOWLEDGEMENTS

We want to express our sincere thanks to Mr J.N. Liaw for providing us with the data we needed.

NOTES

1. In order to have a more general result, we use both consumer price indexes and wholesale price indexes to examine and modify our models.
2. Since we only have quarterly data, which make the sample period relatively short, many potential factors, such as domestic and foreign outputs, government expenditure, and productivity are omitted.
3. For capital flow components, aside from foreign direct investments and portfolio investments, there is another component called 'other capital flows'. However, it is hard to incorporate items in this component into the two major capital flow categories. Moreover, we also have the degree of freedom problem. Therefore, in this chapter we do not discuss this component.
4. Over certain sample periods, the NPI cannot reject an existing unit root null hypothesis.
5. It can be seen from tables in the appendix that our empirical result will not be affected by different price deflators or seasonal factors.

APPENDIX

Table 7A.1 *Cointegration rank test for real exchange rate (with seasonal dummy, deflated by CPI)*

Eigenv.	L-max	Trace	$H_0 : r$	L-max90	Trace90
0.5729	45.94	129.03	0	24.63	89.37
0.4838	35.71	83.09	1	20.90	64.74
0.3766	25.52	47.39	2	17.15	43.84
0.2455	15.21	21.87	3	13.39	26.70
0.1160	6.66	6.66	4	10.60	13.31
0.0000	0.00	0.00	5	2.71	2.71
LM(1) = 43.262 P-val = 0.19, LM(4) = 44.387 P-val = 0.16					

Note: Eigenv. is eigenvalue; L-max and Trace denote L-max Test and Trace Test statistic, respectively; L-max90 and Trace90 are 90% critical value; LM(1) and LM(4) represent 1st order and 4th order Lagrange multiplier test for serial correlation, respectively.

Table 7A.2 *Cointegration rank test for nominal exchange rate (with seasonal dummy, deflated by WPI)*

Eigenv.	L-max	Trace	$H_0 : r$	L-max90	Trace90
0.5950	48.81	112.89	0	24.63	89.37
0.4271	30.08	64.08	1	20.90	64.74
0.2644	16.58	34.01	2	17.15	43.84
0.1890	11.31	17.42	3	13.39	26.70
0.1007	5.73	6.12	4	10.60	13.31
0.0071	0.38	0.38	5	2.71	2.71
LM(1)=29.275 P-val=0.78, LM(4)=43.834 P-val=0.17					

Note: see Table 7A.1.

*Table 7A.3   Cointegration rank test for real exchange rate
(with seasonal dummy, deflated by WPI)*

Eigenv.	L-max	Trace	$H_0 : r$	L-max90	Trace90
0.5959	48.93	114.53	0	24.63	89.37
0.4409	31.40	65.60	1	20.90	64.74
0.2728	17.20	34.20	2	17.15	43.84
0.1870	11.18	17.00	3	13.39	26.70
0.1010	5.75	5.82	4	10.60	13.31
0.0012	0.07	0.07	5	2.71	2.71
LM(1)=36.120	P-val=0.46,		LM(4)=46.782	P-val=0.11	

Note: see Table 7A.1.

*Table 7A.4   Cointegration rank test for nominal exchange rate
(without seasonal dummy, deflated by WPI)*

Eigenv.	L-max	Trace	$H_0 : r$	L-max90	Trace90
0.5962	48.97	114.27	0	24.63	89.37
0.4312	30.47	65.30	1	20.90	64.74
0.2601	16.26	34.83	2	17.15	43.84
0.2093	12.68	18.56	3	13.39	26.70
0.0990	5.63	5.88	4	10.60	13.31
0.0047	0.25	0.25	5	2.71	2.71
LM(1)=29.275	P-val=0.78,		LM(4)=43.834	P-val=0.17	

Note: see Table 7A.1.

Table 7A.5 Cointegration rank test for real exchange rate (without seasonal dummy, deflated by WPI)

Eigenv.	L-max	Trace	$H_0 : r$	L-max90	Trace90
0.5976	49.16	115.39	0	24.63	89.37
0.4409	31.39	66.22	1	20.90	64.74
0.2649	16.62	34.83	2	17.15	43.84
0.2066	12.50	18.21	3	13.39	26.70
0.1000	5.69	5.71	4	10.60	13.31
0.0004	0.02	0.02	5	2.71	2.71
LM(1)=30.596	P-val=0.72,		LM(4)=44.725	P-val=0.15	

Note: see Table 7A.1.

REFERENCES

Abuaf, N. and P. Jorion (1990), 'Purchasing power parity in the long run', *Journal of Finance,* **45**: 157–74.

Agenor, Pierre-Richand and Alexander W. Hoffmaister (1996), 'Capital inflows and the real exchange rate: analytical framework and econometric evidence', *IMP Working Paper,* pp. 1–50.

Cheung, Y.W., and K.S. Lai (1993), 'Long-run purchasing power parity and the Canadian float in the 1950s', *Review of Economics and Statistics,* LXXLII, **3**: 558–62.

Dickey, D.A. and W.A. Fuller (1979), 'Distribution of the estimators for autoregressive times series with a unit root', *Journal of the American Statistical Association,* **74**: 427–31.

Dickey, D.A. and W.A. Fuller (1981), 'Likelihood ratio statistics for autoregressive times series with a unit root', *Econometrica,* **49** (4): 1057–72.

Dickey, D.A., D.W. Jansen and D.L. Thornton (1994), 'A primer on cointegration with an application to money and income', in B.B. Rao (ed.), *Cointegration for the Applied Economist,* London: Macmillan, pp. 9–45.

Dornbusch, R. (1976), 'Expectations and exchange rate dynamics', *Journal of Political Economy,* **84**: 1161–76.

Edwards, S. (1991), 'Real and nominal determinants of real exchange rate: the empirical evidence', in *Real Exchange Rates, Devaluation, and Adjustment Exchange Rate Policy in Developing Countries,* Chapter, Cambridge, Mass.: MIT Press, Chapter 5, pp. 128–156.

Engle, R.F. and C.W.J. Granger (1987), 'Cointegration and error correction: representation, estimation and testing', *Econometrica,* **55**: 251–76.

Fry, M. (1998), 'Capital inflows, the current account, monetary policy and real exchange rates', paper presented at the Central Bank of China, Taipei, Taiwan, pp. 1–27.

Glen, J. (1992), 'Real exchange rate in the short, medium and long-run', *Journal of International Economics,* **33**: 147–66.

Gonzalo, J. (1994), 'Five alternative methods of estimating long-run equilibrium relationship', *Journal of Econometrics,* **60**: 203–33.

Granger, C.W.J. and P. Newbold (1974), 'Spurious regressions in econometrics', *Journal of Econometrics,* **12**: 111–20.

Johansen, S. (1988), 'Statistical analysis of cointegration vectors', *Journal of Economic Dynamics and Control,* **12**: 231–54.

Johansen, S. (1991) 'Estimation and hypothesis testing of cointegration vectors in Gaussian vector autoregressive models', *Econometria,* **59** (6): 1551–80.

Johansen, S. (1992a), 'Determination of cointegration rank in the presence of a linear trend', *Oxford Bulletin of Economics and Statistics,* **54** (3): 383–97.

Johansen, S. (1992b), 'Cointegration in partial systems and the efficiency of single-equation analysis', *Journal of Economics,* **52**: 389–402.

Johansen, S. and K. Juselius (1990), 'Maximum likelihood estimation and inference on cointegration with application to the demand for money', *Oxford Bulletin of Economics and Statistics,* **52** (2): 169–210.

Johansen, S. and K. Juselius (1992), 'Testing structural hypotheses in a multivariate cointegration analysis of the PPP and UIP for UK', *Journal of Econometrics,* **53**: 211–44.

Lin, C.Y. (1997), 'An estimation of NT equilibrium exchange rates', un-published paper, Research Department, the Central Bank of China, pp. 1–39.

Lin, J.L., C.S. Wu and S.Y. Chen (1997), 'Financial assets and savings', paper presented in 1997 Macroeconometric Modelling, the Institute of Economics, Academia Sinica, Taipei, pp. 1–32.

MacDonald, R. (1995), 'Long-run exchange rate modeling: a survey of the recent evidence', *IMP Working Paper*, pp. 1–43.

Phillips, Peter C.B. and Perron (1988), 'Testing for a unit root in time series regression', *Biometrika,* **75**(2): 335–46.

Phillips, P.C.B. (1986) 'Understanding Spurious Regressions in Econometrics,' *Journal of Econometrics*, **33**(3), December 1986, pp. 311–40.

Phillips, P.C.B. (1995) 'Fully Modified Least Squares and Vector Auto regression,' *Econometrica*, **63**(5), September 1995, pp. 1023–78.

Sims, C.A. (1988), 'Bayesian skepticism on unit root econometrics', *Journal of Economics Dynamics and Control,* **12**: 463–74.

Whitt, J.A. (1992), 'The long-run behaviour of the real exchange rate: a reconsideration', *Journal of Money Credit and Banking,* **24** (1): 72–82.

Wickens, M.R. (1996), 'Interpreting cointegrating vectors and common stochastic trends', *Journal of Econometrics,* **74**: 255–71.

8. The choice of intermediate targets – money or interest rate: the case of Taiwan

Chung-Hua Shen

1. INTRODUCTION

The choice of intermediate targets (hereafter, IT) has been widely discussed in monetary policy literature. An IT is an intermediate between (1) the instruments and operating targets that are capable of rather tight control and (2) the ultimate target measures that can only be influenced indirectly. Three criteria (measurability, control-lability and predictability) are suggested in the literature for choosing intermediate targets (Mishkin 1995). Conventional IT focuses on the use of narrow and broad monetary aggregates. However, monetary aggregates in many countries have recently been found to lose the link with their final goals due to financial deregulations and innovations and Taiwan is not an exception. Accordingly, in addition to the monetary aggregates, the interest rate, interest spread, nominal GDP, bank loan, inflation and more are all considered as new candidates for the IT.

The current IT in Taiwan is M2 and the final goals are inflation rate, output, and exchange rate (see Shen and Hakes 1995, for a brief description of Taiwan's Central Bank Law). The top panel of Figure 8.1 plots the M2 growth rate and real GDP growth rate, while the bottom plots the M2 growth rate and inflation rate. As can be seen in the top panel, M2 appears to lose its link with output gradually. For example, while money growth follows a big downward trend after 1992, real GDP growth remains constant at around 6.2% during the same period. In particular, when real GDP recovers from the last recession (the last shaded area), money growth continues to decrease. Hence, the link between money and output becomes weak.

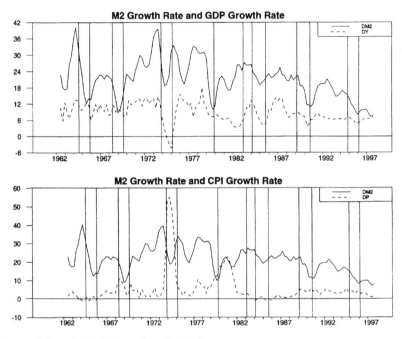

Figure 8.1   M2, CPI and real GDP

We are interested in finding an IT which can rescue this vanishing relationship.

The bottom panel of Figure 8.1, which plots the M2 growth rate and inflation rate, exhibits a more discouraging pattern than that of the top panel. The theoretical positive relation between money and inflation is either mitigated or even reversed. The decreasing money supply is not accompanied with a falling inflation rate and vice versa. One reason for this unconventional phenomenon is possibly due to the dominating supply shocks in affecting Taiwan's inflation rate. For example, two oil shocks and typhoons caused inflation to rise even when money growth fell.

The flow of foreign portfolio investment during 1988–89 also contributed to this opposite relation.[1] Shen and Hakes (1995) claim that the Central Bank of China is not concerned with inflation until it is in crisis. Hence, inflation and money growth are related, but their relationship is elusive. Under this circumstance, searching for an IT, which should have a stable link with inflation, is difficult because inflation may be affected by supply shocks and weather. Therefore, we skip inflation as our final target during the following econometric work.

This chapter plans first to study whether the broad monetary aggregate (M2 here) can still be employed as Taiwan's appropriate IT. We then investigate whether or not the interest rate measures contain predictive contents of future output. While three criteria are relevant in choosing the IT, only predictability is considered here. I plan to discuss controllability in a separate paper by comparing the monetary and financial systems internationally. Furthermore, discussing all possible ITs is not necessary for Taiwan since some of them are either fixed or in conflict with the present goal of authority. For example, targeting nominal GDP, in a loose sense, is equivalent to the 'multi-intermediate targets', which is interpreted by the press as the favor of discretionary policy. Hence, targeting nominal GDP is avoided by the central bank, though in reality it might have been doing so for years.

Granger causality is used to test whether the M2 and interest rate measures are still useful predictors of the real activity. The rolling regression with the fixed-window length is calculated to examine the sub-sample stability. The F-tests are found to reject the stable relationship between M2 and real GDP. One possible reason for this rejection is the shifting of money from banks to various mutual funds. Hence, a new monetary aggregate, M2+, is created by adding various mutual funds to M2 in order to recover the link between money and real GDP. Finally, we investigate whether or not the interest rates contain information about future economic activity. Three interest rate measures, the holding period return of term premiums, and the default premiums of the money market rates are employed.

Our results are not very encouraging. Although money aggregates and interest rate measures are related to output, they do not offer a stable relationship with output. Future research is needed to search for a stable IT.

2. DATA CONSTRUCTION

Quarterly data is used as real GDP is only available on a quarterly basis. Except for the money market rates, which were not available until the first quarter of 1981, other series start from 1961:Q3. All data is taken from ARIMOS data tape, which is available from Taiwan's Ministry of Education. The growth of each variable is computed by the so-called 'seasonal difference', which is typically employed in Taiwan.[2] The sample periods started from 1961:3 to 1997:4 for M2 and 1980:4–1997:4 for the interest rate measures.

3. THE LINK BETWEEN M2 AND REAL GNP

3.1 Whole Sample

Though it is recognized that the presence of Granger causality (here-after GC) does not necessarily imply that a variable will be useful as an IT, and conversely that the absence of Granger causality does not imply a variable cannot be used as an IT, the use of the GC to determine the appropriateness of ITs is widely evidenced (Wenninger 1990; Steindel 1990; Friedman and Kuttner 1993). Therefore, the GC of the bivariate vector autoregressive (BVAR) is used as the first step to identify the predictive contents of our candidates.

$$y_t = \sum_{i=1}^{n1} a_i y_{t-i} + \sum_{i=1}^{n2} b_i IT_{t-i} + \varepsilon_t, \tag{8.1}$$

where y_t is the real GDP growth rate, and IT_t is attempted alter-natively by using the M2 growth rate, the M2+ growth rate (see definition below), and various interest rate measures. The values of $n1$ and $n2$ are chosen by eliminating the serially-correlated error in the residuals. For simplicity, $n1$ and $n2$ are assumed to be the same.

Following Sims (1980), Litterman and Weiss (1985), Stock and Watson (1989) and Friedman and Kuttner (1993), money-income causality is assessed using a multivariate VAR model. The trivariate vector autoregressive model (TVAR) model is

$$y_t = \sum_{i=1}^{n1} a_i y_{t-i} + \sum_{i=1}^{n2} b_i IT_{t-i} + \sum_{i=1}^{n3} c_i \dot{p}_{t-i} + \varepsilon_t, \tag{8.2}$$

where $\dot{p}$ is the inflation rate calculated by the consumer price index. The stability tests are conducted via the BVAR (equation 8.1) and TVAR (equation 8.2) of money and income.

For practical consideration, the variables all transform into the annual growth rate by the seasonal difference. In Taiwan the annual growth rate of macro variables is typically non-seasonally adjusted. Hence, the annual growth rate is calculated by using the current log variable minus the variable of the same period of the last quarter. For example, the target ranges of money growth during 1998 are set to be from 6% to 12%, which is calculated based on seasonal difference. As the money market interest rate is the difference between the purchasing price and the selling price of commercial paper, they are not differenced once again.

Although the seasonal difference is employed, the seasonal cointegration approach of Lee (1992) is not attempted here for two reasons. First, the seasonal error correction term at the zero frequency is asymptotically equivalent to the conventional error correction of Johansen's (1992), as demonstrated by Lee (1992). Second, detecting the seasonal unit root at other seasonal frequencies is sensitive to lag lengths and presence of deterministic components in Taiwan (see Shen and Huang (1999) and Huang and Shen (2002) for a review).

Table 8.1 reports estimation results with lag length being equal to 2, 3, and 4, respectively. Both the individual t test and joint F test are carried out to examine the predicative contents of M2. Coefficients of M2's lagged growth rate are positive and are found to be significantly different from zero at least at the 10% level regardless of the lag lengths. Although the F tests are all significant at the 5% level, they are not significant at the 1% level. Furthermore, the individual t-tests are seldom significant. Hence, the M2 growth rate Granger causes real GDP growth in a weak sense when using the whole sample.

Table 8.1   Granger causality tests: whole sample A TVAR

$$y_t = \sum_{i=1}^{n1} a_i y_{t-i} + \sum_{i=1}^{n2} b_i IT_{t-i} + \sum_{i=1}^{n3} c_i \dot{p}_{t-i} + \varepsilon_t$$

	BVAR			TVAR		
b_1	0.137	0.132	0.135	00.108	0.136	0.154
	(0.28)	(1.80)	(1.95)	(1.71)	(1.81)	(2.14)
b_2	−0.071	−0.033	−0.102	−0.028	−0.070	−0.134
	(0.13)	(0.27)	(0.81)	(0.44)	(0.58)	(1.07)
b_3		−0.041	0.106		0.010	0.101
		(0.55)	(0.84)		(0.13)	(0.82)
b_4			−0.098			−0.050
			(1.36)			(0.69)
F-test of $\sum_{i=1}^{n2} b_i = 0$(p-value)						
	0.0140	0.0147	0.0132	0.0117	0.0297	0.0329

Note: absolute t value in parentheses.

3.2   Sub-sample

The goal of this section is to examine the stability of money-income causality statistics across subsample periods.

Taiwan's process of financial deregulations, which is first briefly accounted for, began in 1987. The movement towards deregulation was first a response to U.S. requests, but soon became a self-fueled process. During the 1980s, Taiwanese exports grew increasingly faster than its imports, which coupled with the government's exchange rate policy resulted in a vast accumulation of foreign reserves. Taiwan's balance-of-payments surplus amounted to $80 billion U.S. dollars in 1990, i.e., the third largest globally (See Shen 2000a, b).

During the mid-1980s, the burgeoning trade surplus with the U.S., together with an increasing difficulty in sterilizing the reserve accumulation, placed enormous political and economic pressure on Taiwan's monetary authority to lift its control of the exchange rate. At this same time, limits on capital remitted to and from Taiwan were also gradually raised. Because the exchange policy aimed at steadily adjusting the exchange rate (mainly against the U.S. dollar), the adjustment process was slow. The exchange rate started appreciating from 38.99:1 in June 1986, reached the highest value of 24.764:1 in April 1992 and has remained around 27:1 since then.

During this long adjustment process (three years), the policy was fully expected by investors. Short-term capital inflows, both legal and illegal, flooded Taiwan, placing even greater pressure on the NTD to rise. The inflow of hot money pushed asset prices, such as stock and real estate, away from their fundamentals. Concomitantly, M1B's annual growth rate increased substantially and reached a peak of 51% in 1989:3. The asset price bubble burst in 1990:3, forcing the growth of M1B to decrease sharply to −6% in 1990:4. At the same time, M2 fluctuated within a tolerable range, making the central bank deemphasize the M1B and use M2 as an intermediate target in July 1990.

Together with this world-wide trend, the authorities gradually began to phase out the regulations on financial markets. For example, the Central Bank of China liberalized its control of the capital account in July 1987. Because of this, the impact of foreign factors on Taiwan's interest rate should have strengthened, which may have impacted the transmission of monetary policy (see shen 1996).

Accompanied with fast deregulation, financial crises occurred frequently after 1994. The scandals of the International Bills Corporation occurred in August 1994, impacting substantially the financial market, especially the commercial paper market. The CPR even rose to 12% in one day. The financial crises of credit unions burst out in 1995 and continued to threaten Taiwan's financial system up to 1996. Credit union runs may affect both the supply of loans and money by changing the movements of deposits among commercial banks, credit unions and the postal savings office. New regulations, such as the deposit insurance, were also imposed. Loans to beneficial persons are now strictly monitored. Furthermore, money outflows occurred substantially during the two periods of missile tests by mainland China in March 1996. The M2 decreased substantially and its growth rate was below the official target range (9%–14%) for 11 months. At the same time, the growth rate of real GDP decreased only within 0.2 points. The Asia financial crisis occurred in August 1997, further impacting the deposit accounts in M2. Expecting a depreciation in the NTD, depositors shifted their local deposits to a foreign account, making the financial system very unstable. These financial turmoils may have induced an unstable relation between IT and real GDP.

We examine the stability of money-income causality statistics across the subsample periods. To accomplish this goal, the above two specifications are estimated using a rolling regression technique. First, a GC test is performed using quarterly data from 1961:Q3 to 1967:Q4. The sample size is then moved forward one quarter so that the data covers 1961:Q4 to 1968:Q1 and the test is repeated. The process of moving forward and repeating the GC test is continued until the entire data set is used to perform the test. The result is 270 F-statistics for causality, each with the same number of degrees of freedom. Finally, the p-values of the F-statistics, which are comparable across sample periods and degrees of freedom, are plotted with the date that the sample ends on the horizontal axis and the p-value.

Figure 8.2 plots the p-values and the real GDP growth. While Thoma (1994) finds that the output positively relates to the p-value using U.S. data, implying that money GCs output during recessions, we find no regularities between the p-value and the real output growth, regardless of the models. However, as can been seen in Figure 8.3, the p-values seem to have positively correlated with the stock return since 1987, when Taiwan's financial deregulations started. During this latter period, the declining stock return is associated with a decreasing p-value, suggesting that money GCs output. Conversely, when stock returns rise, the p-value also increases, suggesting that money does not GC output. One possible explanation for the regularity of these stock returns and p-values is based on Shen's (1996) explanation. Namely, money is used mainly for transaction purposes when the

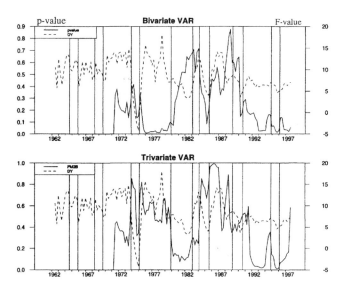

Figure 8.2 M2 p-value, RGDP growth and business cycle

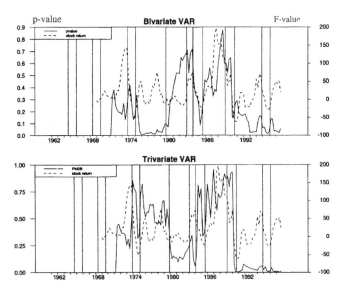

Figure 8.3 M2 p-value, stock return and business cycle

stock return is below an unknown threshold and hence is correlated with output. Alternatively, money is used for speculation purposes when the stock return exceeds the unknown threshold and hence is uncorrelated with output.

The unstable relation between money and income across the subsample possibly owes to the flow out of the time deposits to the various mutual funds. The next section pursues this issue.

4. THE LINK BETWEEN M2+ AND RGNP

The declining M2 growth rate since 1990 possibly owes to the shifting of money from the indirect financing market to the direct financing market. Returns of stock and other financial markets are higher than those of banks. During this time, various stock and bond mutual funds were permitted by the SEC to raise funds from the public. Figure 8.4 displays the growth rates of the four mutual funds-bond fund, bond/stock fund, open-end stock fund and closed-end stock fund. As we show in the figure, in contrast to the continuing decline of M2, the growth in funds have risen substantially since 1994. As a result, the shrinking money growth may be accounted for by the increase in mutual funds.

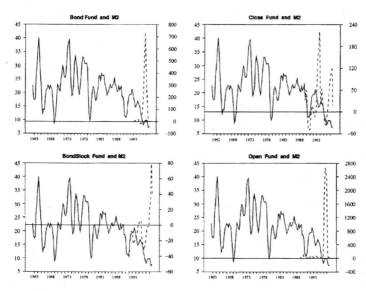

Figure 8.4 Decline of M2 and rise in mutual funds

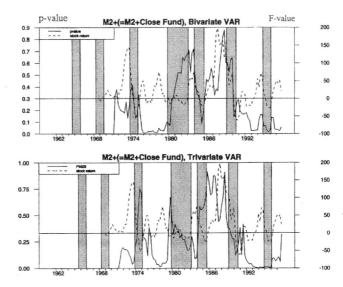

Figure 8.5 M2+ p-value, stock return and business cycle

We expand the existing M2 by including various mutual funds alternatively. However, this new monetary aggregate, M2+, only increases at most at a 0.8% growth rate of M2 and hence the differences between M2 and M2+ growth are trivial. The pattern of the *p*-value of M2+ (adding all funds), displayed in Figure 8.5, does not change significantly from that of Figure 8.3. Hence, the M2+ is also subject to the instability problem.

Since M2 and M2+ growth rates are no longer tied closely with output, the next section investigates the roles of interest rate measures in forecasting output.

5. THE LINK BETWEEN INTEREST RATES AND OUTPUT

5.1   Three Interest Rate Measures

A number of recent studies has demonstrated that interest rate spreads – i.e., the differences on given data between interest rates on alternative financial assets – have remarkable power in predicting future economic activity in the U.S. For example, Stock and Watson (1989, 1990) find that the paper-bill spread and the slope of the yield curve are two of the most potent-leading variables from the perspective of business cycle forecasting. See Bonser-Neal and Morley (1997) for a survey. However, unlike the United States, which issues regular and numerous government bonds of various maturity dates to finance expenditure, Taiwan's constant budget surplus during the data period relieved the government of the need to issue bills and bonds to finance its expenditures and hence the issuing of treasury bonds are not consecutive. The bill and bond rates are thus unable to be used in the present study.

In contrast to the thin and the nonconsecutive-issuing bond market, the money market which was established in May 1976 has increased substantially. There are four financial instruments (treasury bill (TB), commercial paper (CP), bankers' acceptance (BA), and negotiable checkable deposits (NCD)) issued in Taiwan's money market. Since a TB is issued by the government, and BA and NCD are endorsed by banks, they are equivalently default free.

The first interest rate measure is the holding period return of commercial paper. We use CP rate to represent money market rate because CP has accounted for the largest share of the money market in every year. The data available for money market rates is 1980:3.

The holding period return is calculated first by

$$\text{Holding}_m = \log(P_{t+m}/P_t) \times 30.4/\text{Maturity}, \qquad (8.3)$$

where m, which is the number of holding days, is equal to 30, 90 and 180 days, respectively. The average day of a month is 30.4, as suggested by Fama (1984). Term P_t is the purchasing price obtained by transforming the primary market rate, i.e.,

$$P_t = 1 - \text{rate} \times (\text{Days to Maturity})/365 \qquad (8.4)$$

and P_{t+m} is the selling price in the secondary market, i.e.,

$$P_{t+m} = 1/(1 + \text{rate} \times \frac{\text{Days to Maturity}}{365}). \qquad (8.5)$$

The second interest rate measure is the term premium (TP), which is calculated as the difference between the holding returns of 90 and 180 days to the 30 days. Namely,

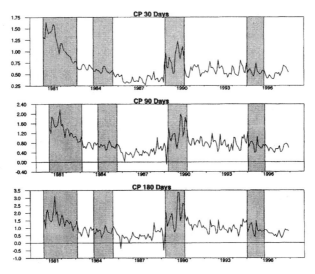

Figure 8.6 Holding period return

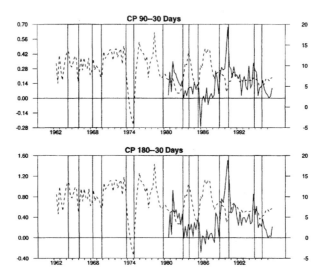

Figure 8.7 Term premium (spread of holding return) and GDP growth

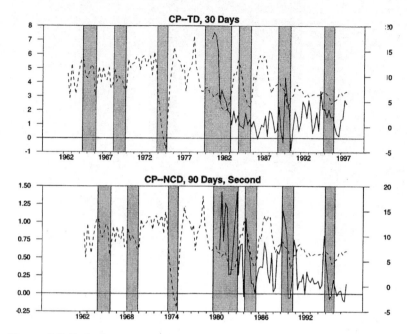

Figure 8.8 Default premium (spread of holding return) and GDP growth

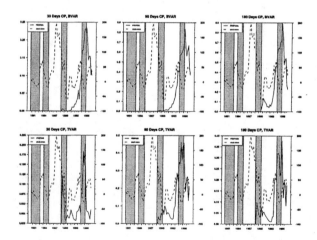

Figure 8.9 Holding return p-value, stock return and business cycle

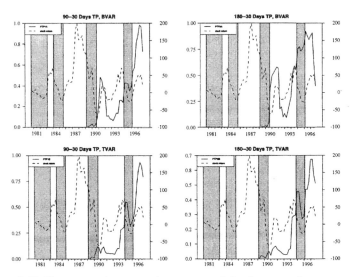

Figure 8.10 Term premium, stock return and business cycle

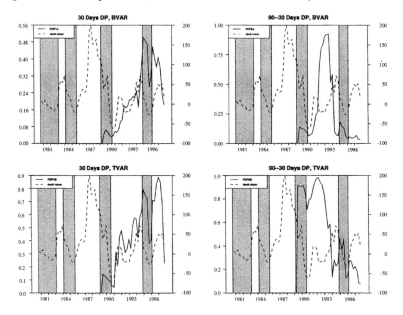

Figure 8.11 Default premium, stock return and business cycle

$$TP_{90} = Holding_{90} - Holding_{30} \qquad (8.6)$$

$$TP_{180} = Holding_{190} - Holding_{30}. \qquad (8.7)$$

The third interest rate measure is the default premium (DP), which is calculated as the difference between commercial paper and NCD (recall that the Tbill rate is non-consecutive in Taiwan)

$$DP_{30} = Holding_{CP30} - Holding_{NCD30} \qquad (8.8)$$

$$DP_{90} = Holding_{CP90} - Holding_{NCD90}. \qquad (8.9)$$

Figures 8.6, 8.7 and 8.8 plot these three different interest rate measures. Because of the data constraint, the interest rate measures start from 1980:Q4. In Figure 8.6, the holding period returns of 30, 90 and 180 days fluctuate and are much higher during the fourth and the sixth shaded areas. The returns change little in the fifth and the seventh two-shaded areas. The real GDP growth (dotted line in the figures) exhibits a different time trend from those of the holding period returns. In Figure 8.7, the patterns of term premium for 90–30 and 180–30 are similar to those of Figure 8.6 with a smaller size of change. In Figure 8.8, the patterns of default premium appear less useful in predicting future economic activity.

5.2   Interest Rate Measures and Output

Once the three different kinds of interest rate measures are obtained, the next step is to conduct the rolling regression of equations (8.1) and (8.2) using three interest rate measures to replace M2. The resulting p-values are thus plotted in Figures 8.9, 8.10, and 8.11. Judging from these three figures, the p-values are less than 5% before 1992 and greater than 1% after it. Hence, the three interest rates GC output only before 1991. The volatile interest rate measures may be reasons to deter them from predicting future output.

6. PREDICTING RECESSIONS USING INTEREST RATES

The analysis above focuses on the GC between output and the intermediate targets. The present section, however, uses the binary recession index, constructed by CEPD, to pursue the same issue. Recessions are a discrete event: we are either in a recession or we are not. Let I_t denote a 0–1 indicator of a recession, so that $I_t = 1$ if there is a recession at date t and $I_t = 0$ otherwise. Hence, two models are considered.

$$I_t = F\left(a_0 + \sum_{i=3}^{6} b_i IT_{t-i}\right) + \varepsilon_t \qquad (8.10)$$

$$I_t = F\left(a_0 + \sum_{i=3}^{6} a_i I_{t-i} + \sum_{i=3}^{6} b_i IT_{t-i}\right) + \varepsilon_t, \qquad (8.11)$$

where F is the CDF of normal distribution if the probit model is implemented, and IT_t is the intermediate targets considered above, such as growth rate of M2, holding period returns, term premiums, and default premiums. The first specification, which ignores the lagged-dependent variables, has been widely applied by researchers (Estrella and Hardouvelis 1990, 1991; Estrella and Mishkin 1995). The second specification, i.e., the lagged 3 to 6 quarter dependent variables are included in the right-hand side, has recently been applied by Dueker (1997) to consider the dynamic structure of recessions. Both specifications are estimated by the probit method.

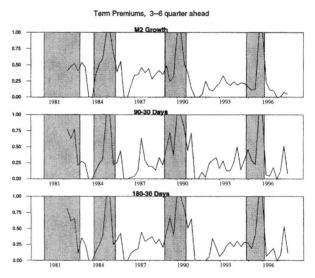

Figure 8.12 Probability of recession, probit model, term premium

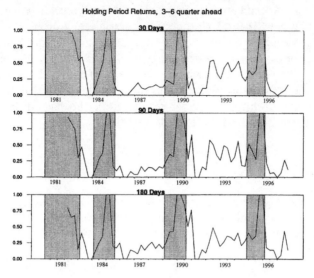

Figure 8.13 Probability of recession, probit model, holding period premium

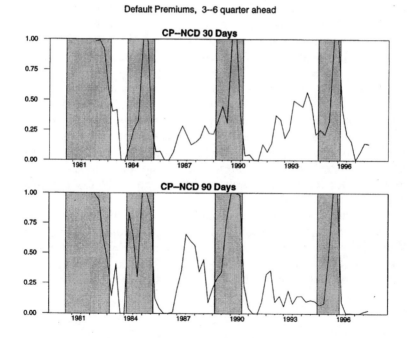

Figure 8.14 Probability of recession, probit model, default premium

The first specification predicts the 1988–90 recession with great success; however, it misses others (not graphed). Adding the lagged dependent variables on the right (the second specification) improves the fitting of recessions substantially. Figures 8.12, 8.13, and 8.14 plot the probability in forecasting recessions. Though the forecasting improves, it is far from perfect than those in the U.S. case. Furthermore, the better fitting possibly results from the lagged-dependent variable instead of the intermediate targets.

7. CONCLUSION

Conventional M2 intermediate targets lose the link with output possibly due to financial deregulations and innovations. This chapter first discusses the subsample stabilities of M2 and real GDP growth rates. The money is found to Granger cause output when the stock return is low and does not Granger cause output when stock return is high. One possible reason for this unstable relation owes to the dual characters of M2. It mainly functions as a transaction purpose when the stock return is low and functions as a speculation purpose when the stock return is high. The decline of money in recent years possibly owes to the shift of money to various mutual funds. However, when a new monetary aggregate M2+ is created to incorporate these mutual funds, the growth rate of M2+ increases trivially. Hence, monetary aggregates seem difficult to closely tie up with output.

Three interest rate measures are next attempted. The first is holding period returns, which displayed a strongly negative relationship with output during the 1988–90 recession. The relationship weakens for other recessions. The predicting power is vague possibly owing to many 'local' volatilities. The second and third interest rate measures are term and default premiums, which exhibit the similar pattern as that of holding period returns.

The two conventional intermediate targets, money and interest rates, are found to be unstable when filling the role of predictability. Whether the Central Bank of China should skip the intermediate targets and use only instrument – final targets, such as inflation target, to predict future output is a part of ongoing research.

ACKNOWLEDGEMENT

This chapter is part of the project 'The Choices of the Intermediate Target in Taiwan' prepared for the Central Bank of China. I would like to thank the researchers' comments. I, however, am responsible for any remaining errors.

NOTES

1. The foreign portfolio investment increases both the money supply and the value of New Taiwan Dollar (NTD). The latter then decreases inflation.
2. The seasonal difference is the $\log(X_t)\log(X_{t-4})$. See Shen and Huang (1999) and Huang and Shen (2002a) for studies of Taiwan money demand and Huang and Shen (1997b) for Taiwan foreign reserves.

REFERENCES

Bonser-Neal C. and T.R. Morley (1997), 'Does the yield spread predict real economic activity? a multicountry analysis', *Economic Review,* Federal Reserve Bank of Kansas City, **Third Quarter**: 37–53.

Dueker, M.J. (1997), 'Strengthening the case for the yield curve as a predictor of US recession', *Federal Reserve Bank of St. Louis Review,* **79** (March/April): 41–51.

Estrella, A. and F. Mishkin (1996), 'Predicting US recession: financial variables as leading indicators', Federal Reserve Bank of New York Working Paper No. 9606.

Estrella, A. and G.A. Hardouvelis (1990), 'Possible roles of the yield curve in monetary policy', in *Intermediate Targets and Indicators for Monetary Policy: A Critical Survey,* Federal Reserve Bank of New York, pp. 339–62,

Estrella, A. and G.A. Hardouvelis (1991), 'The term structure as a predictor of real economic activity', *Journal of Finance,* **46** (2): 555–76.

Fama, E. (1984), 'Term premiums and default premiums in money markets', *Journal of Financial Economics,* **13**: 529–46.

Friedman, B.M. and K.N. Kuttner (1993), 'Why does the paper-bill spread predict real economic activity?', in J. Stock and M. Watson (eds), *New Research on Business Cycle Indicators and Forecasting,* Chicago: Univarsity of Chicago Press.

Huang, T.S. and C.H. Shen (2002a), 'A buffer stock money demand forward looking model: seasonal cointegration cross-equation restrictions', *Journal of Econometrics (second review).*

Huang, T.S. and C.H. Shen (2002b), 'Applying the seasonal error correction model to the demand for international reserves in Taiwan', *Journal of International Money and Finance,* **18**: 107–31.

Johansen, S. (1992), 'Determination of Cointegration Rank in the Presence of a Linear Trend', *Oxford Bulletin of Economics and Statistics*, **54**(3): 383–97.

Lee, H.S. (1992), 'Maximum likelihood inference on cointegration and seasonal cointegration', *Journal of Econometrics*, **54**: 1–47.

Litterman, R.B. and L. Weiss (1985), 'Money, real interest rates, and output: an reinterpretation of postwar US data', **53**: 129–56.

Mishkin, F. (1995), *The Economics of Monetary, Banking and Financial Markets*, New York: HarperCollins.

Shen, C.H. (1996), 'The impact of financial deregulation on money demand: the case of Taiwan', *Taiwan Journal of Political Economy*, **2**: 79–108.

Shen, C.H. (2000a), 'Are the effect of monetary policy asymmetric: the case of Taiwan', *Journal of Policy Modelling*, **22** (2): 197–218.

Shen, C.H. (2000b), 'Estimation of Taiwan monetary reaction function: the nonlinear time varying parameter model', *Applied Economics*, **32**: 459–66.

Shen, C.H. and D. Hakes (1995), 'Monetary policy as a decision-making hierarchy the case of Taiwan', *Journal of Macroeconomics*, **17**: 357–68.

Shen, C.H. and T.S. Huang (1999), 'Seasonal cointegration and money demand: the case of Taiwan', *International Economic Journal*, **13** (3): 197–223.

Sims, C. (1980), 'Macroeconomics and reality', *Econometrica*, **48**: 1–49.

Steindel, C. (1990), 'Interest rates as targets and indicators for monetary policy', in *Intermediate Targets and Indicators for Monetary Policy: A Critical Survey*, Federal Reserve Bank of New York, pp. 274–304.

Stock, J.H. and M.W. Watson (1989), 'New indexes of coincident and leading economic indictors', in O.J. Blanchard and S. Fischer (eds), *NBER Macroeconomics Annual*, Cambridge, MA: MIT Press, pp. 351–94.

Stock, J.H. and M.W. Watson (1991), 'A probability model of the coincident indicator', in K. Lahiri and G. Moore (eds), *Leading Economic Indicator*, Cambridge: Cambridge University Press, pp. 63–90.

Thoma, A.M. (1994), 'Subsample instability and asymmetries in money-income causality', *Journal of Econometrics*, **64**: 279–306.

Wenninger, J. (1990), 'Monetary aggregates as intermediate targets', in *Intermediate Targets and Indicators for Monetary Policy: A Critical Survey*, Federal Reserve Bank of New York, pp. 67–108.

PART III

Banking Regulation

E52
E31
G21
G28
G34

F30

9. The microeconomic dimension of monetary policy

Delano Villanueva

1. INTRODUCTION

The banking crisis in the SEACEN region has heightened the policy makers' awareness of the need for a sound banking system.[1] The macroeconomic shocks that had buffeted several countries in the region since 1996, coupled with structural weaknesses of the banking systems, were the principal factors behind the crisis. Macroeconomic shocks (e.g., export slowdown) impacted adversely on the financial condition of domestic firms and their ability to service their debts to banks, while the latter's resilience to these shocks was impaired by certain structural weaknesses, including implicit insurance on bank liabilities, limited capital markets, and weak regulatory and supervisory systems, which encouraged banks to engage in excessive risk-taking, concentrated lending, and over-borrowing (through deposits and foreign loans).

The financial crisis, unprecedented in its severity and rapid contagion effects in the region and beyond, has taught us one important lesson, that is, it is not enough to possess good macroeconomic fundamentals – fiscal balance, high saving-investment rates, export-oriented economic structures – it is also necessary to possess a sound and robust banking system that can withstand macroeconomic shocks. If the structural weaknesses of the banking sector were unattended and unresolved, a macroeconomic shock could result in a banking crisis, which in turn could lead to a currency crisis. The critical importance of achieving and maintaining bank soundness stems from the devastating effects on the macroeconomy of bank unsoundness, as the ensuing events in the region have demonstrated so vividly (*inter alia*, defaults of domestic firms, unemployment and higher prices of imported commodities).

The traditional focus of monetary management has been the

169

macroeconomic goal of *price stability* through the pursuit of appropriate rates of growth of money and bank credit.   Perhaps the achievement and maintenance of price stability during the 1990s in the Asian region has lulled policy makers to neglect the other microeconomic goal of monetary management: *achievement and maintenance of a competitive and efficient banking and payments system*, or in other words, *a sound banking system.* Or perhaps the microeconomic goal of monetary management, viz., promotion of a sound banking system, has been viewed solely from the regulatory and supervisory perspectives, separate from the macroeconomic goal of price stability.   I shall argue that this approach to monetary management is neither tenable nor desirable. Price stability does depend on a sound banking system, and vice versa: a sound banking system depends on price stability. The macroeconomic and microeconomic dimensions of monetary management, by their nature, are inextricably intertwined. Thus, all central banks have an intrinsic interest in bank soundness, even when official oversight lies elsewhere; the multilateral financial institutions such as the International Monetary Fund and the World Bank have, albeit only recently, also intensified their policy focus on microeconomic issues such as corporate governance, market discipline, and official oversight.

In this chapter, I shall first touch on the links between the macroeconomic and microeconomic dimensions of monetary management. I shall argue that bank soundness is a *sine qua non* of price stability (or exchange rate stability), and vice versa. I shall then describe the structural weaknesses of a banking system that create conditions for a financial crisis. I conclude by describing how official oversight can buttress market discipline, given some externalities inherent in the banking industry and the *public goods* nature of banking soundness.

2. WHY IS BANK SOUNDNESS IMPORTANT FOR LOW INFLATION?

I define *low inflation* to mean a sustained modest rate of increase in some price index, say 2–3 percent per annum. Let me first say something on the importance of low inflation for bank soundness. Low inflation over the course of the business cycle can only be achieved and maintained through restrained growth rates of money and bank credit, to ensure that aggregate demands for goods and services do not exceed their supplies. Excessive money and credit expansions often are associated with a deterioration of the quality of bank assets, as standards for risk analysis and management as well as internal controls are relaxed. An increase in the share of non-performing assets is a consequence – an initial step, if uncorrected, towards bank unsoundness or insolvency. Additionally, the increase in the overall rate of inflation has adverse effects on the financial condition of banks via three channels: (1) asset price inflation reverses course when the bubble bursts; e.g., a negative macroeconomic shock leads to bank borrower defaults and asset price deflation, which in turn reduce the bank's net worth to zero or perhaps negative levels (insolvency); (2) overall inflation may send the wrong relative price signals and thus induce a distortionary effect on the allocation of bank credit, thus raising the inefficiencies of bank operations; and (3) inflation tends to decrease the attractiveness of bank deposits, thus reducing the resources available for banks to earn profits and strengthen their capital.

Now, the importance of bank soundness for low inflation: A sound banking system is necessary for monetary policy signals to be transmitted appropriately to the rest of the economy. An unsound banking sector will render uncertain the linkages between monetary policy instruments and their intended effects. Additionally, those effects will be diluted by unsound banks that could not respond through timely changes in their operations. Increased moral hazard and adverse selection will further distort the behaviour of bank owners, directors and managers and interfere with the monetary policy transmission mechanism. All these would result in inefficiencies in the allocation of bank credit, with adverse consequences for the economy at large.

A fragile banking sector places another constraint on monetary policy in view of the lender-of-last-resort function of a central bank. A banking system in distress will need central bank liquidity support, but this may run counter to a predetermined rate of increase in money and credit prescribed by the *low inflation* objective.

Conversely, a sound banking system helps ensure that changes in monetary policy instruments work themselves out and that their effects on the banking sector are as intended and most effective. Sound banks also contribute to the efficiency of credit allocation, and thus to realising the maximum rate of growth of potential output.

3. BANK SOUNDNESS IN A GLOBAL FINANCIAL MARKET

In a world of free cross-border capital movements and under a floating exchange rate system tempered by movements of reserves to reduce sharp daily fluctuations in the exchange rate while letting it drift in any direction in the longer term, capital flows influence domestic monetary conditions through the exchange rate or monetary base or both. Under these conditions, attempts to adjust monetary policy to exogenous shifts in capital flows (inflow or outflows) will be destabilising, while fiscal policy adjustments will be stabilising.[2] To illustrate, I will discuss the effects of unexpected changes in net capital inflows and outflows.

Suppose that the small open economy is in internal and external balance. Shifts in market sentiment for whatever reason drive net capital inflows into the country. The exchange rate tends to appreciate, and to avoid sharp appreciation the central bank purchases foreign exchange. Foreign reserves and money supply rise, and nominal income goes up. To dampen the rise in aggregate demand, monetary policy is tightened through lower net domestic assets (NDA) or higher required reserves or both. The result would be a further appreciation of the exchange rate and further capital inflows. By contrast, a tightened fiscal policy (reduced government spending and/or increase in taxes) tends to depreciate the exchange rate, reverse the capital inflows, lower money supply and ultimately lower nominal income. The opposite sequence is triggered by exogenous net capital outflows. The exchange rate will depreciate, and to moderate the depreciation, the central bank sells foreign exchange. Foreign reserves, money supply, and nominal income fall. To counter these deflationary tendencies, monetary policy is relaxed through higher NDA or lower required reserves or both. The result would be a further depreciation of the exchange rate and further capital outflows. Again, by contrast, an easing of fiscal policy through higher government spending and/or lower taxes would tend to appreciate the exchange rate, reverse the capital outflows, raise money supply and ultimately raise nominal income. Thus, in globalised and integrated financial markets, and under a 'dirty float', countercyclical monetary policy tends to be destabilizing, while countercyclical fiscal policy appears to be stabilising.[3]

The severity of constraints on monetary and exchange rate policies posed by capital flows will also depend on the soundness of the banking system. Like in the closed economy, bank unsoundness imposes a constraint on monetary policy in two contexts. In a flexible exchange rate regime, an exchange rate depreciation that may be required for macroeconomic adjustment may be resisted for fear of worsening the financial condition of already weak banks with significant foreign asset/liability mismatch. The possibilities of capital flight, deposit withdrawals and increased external debt servicing burdens of bank customers and thus their reduced ability to repay bank loans, would add to the reluctance to depreciate the exchange rate. Under a fixed exchange rate regime, the central bank's lender-of-last-resort would be constrained one way or another. There would be no lender-of-last-resort under a currency-board arrangement, while in a central bank arrangement with an exchange rate target, provision of lender-of-last-resort facilities to weak banks may run counter to the fixed exchange rate objective.

Although liberalised capital accounts are generally beneficial for economic growth in the long term, they can pose problems for monetary policy and the banking system in the short term. For example, capital inflows through the banking sector can lead to an excessive expansion of very risky lending, particularly in the presence of (implicit or explicit) insurance by the government on such foreign borrowings. Sterilisation operations to contain the growth of bank credit may result in high interest rates, which could put additional pressure on already weak bank balance sheets. Additionally, open capital accounts are a quick channel for the propagation of banking and financial crises across countries. The Basle Committee on Banking Supervision exemplifies a policy response to the problems posed by the international dimension of bank supervision. Harmonised national regulatory systems also serve to ensure sound and competitive activities of internationally active financial institutions. The Basle Committee's pioneering achievements notwithstanding, the convergence of national regulatory systems beyond the G-10 countries has a long way to go.

4. MICROECONOMIC DETERMINANTS OF BANK UNSOUNDNESS

An *unstable macroeconomic environment* is a major source of banking system fragility. Sharp fluctuations in real income, interest rates, exchange rates, asset prices and inflation rates make assessment of credit and market risks extremely difficult. Besides, in the developing countries there are often no significant markets that exist in the industrial countries to diversify such risks. The other sources of banking system fragility are *microeconomic* in nature, six of which are: (1) free or underpriced insurance/guarantee schemes on bank liabilities; (2) lack of transparency in banking; (3) weak regulatory and supervisory systems; (4) weak corporate governance in both financial and non-financial sectors; (5) concentrated bank ownership and connected lending; and (6) shallow long-term private bond and equity markets.

4.1 Externalities and Insurance on Bank Liabilities

The *public goods* characteristic of banking (reflecting the key importance of public confidence in banks) has led to explicit or implicit insurance on bank liabilities – deposits and/or foreign borrowings – to prevent sudden withdrawals of deposits or recall of short-term foreign credits. The enormous social costs of a systemic bank failure provide the rationale behind such official insurance and guarantees.

This said, free or underpriced government insurance on bank liabilities poses a moral hazard problem, isolating holders of bank liabilities (local depositors and foreign creditors) from the risks borne by banks and inducing them to overborrow and take on excessive risks in their loan portfolio, distorting credit allocation and raising the probability of a banking crisis and possibly a currency crisis.

The overborrowing syndrome (local deposits and foreign borrowing) may be illustrated in Figure 9.1. A private bank earns a net marginal private revenue shown by the curve DEL2. Maximising its own profit, it is motivated to increase loans to the point where the net marginal bank revenue is zero – loans L2. This lending activity, however, imposes an external cost of FL2 dollars on the government which insures the bank's liabilities, as shown by the line AEF. The private bank's failure to internalise this external cost will motivate the bank not only to overborrow but also to take on excessive risk in its loan portfolio.[4] The net social revenue is net private revenue minus external costs, shown by the curve CL1. The socially optimal bank lending is L1, where net private marginal revenue equals net marginal external cost (point E), or where net marginal social revenue is zero (at bank lending equal to L1). If the private bank is required to pay an insurance premium of EL1 dollars, it will willingly extend bank loans up to L1, because its net marginal revenue is greater than the net marginal cost of insurance/guarantee. But the bank will not extend loans from L1 to L2, because the private revenue (area EL1L2)

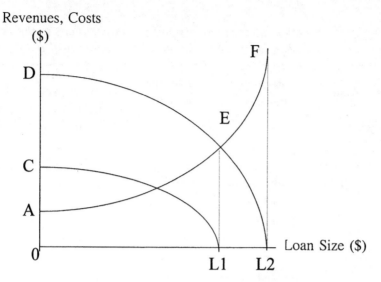

Internalising an externality can motivate optimal behaviour

Figure 9.1 Consequences and corrections of externalities

is smaller than the insurance payments (area L1EFL2). Thus, the private bank will be motivated to produce the socially optimal bank loan size L1. It should be noted that socially optimal lending requires a *risk-adjusted* insurance premium.

How then can one design an insurance scheme on bank liabilities (to ensure public confidence in banks) that minimises its moral hazard effects (reduced market discipline by bank creditors, excessive risk-taking by banks, etc.)? A concrete example of one such incentive-compatible official safety net is provided by the prompt-corrective-action provisions of the Federal Deposit Insurance Corporation Improvement Act of 1991 (FDICIA), which was motivated by the staggering taxpayer losses (at least US$150 billion) incurred in the U.S. savings and loan crisis. The intellectual impetus originated from Benston and Kaufman's[5] Structured Early Intervention and Resolution (SEIR). The objectives were twofold: (1) to keep deposit insurance for banks but to impose mandatory sanctions when certain capital-zone and leverage thresholds were violated by banks; and (2) to reduce the regulatory discretion on corrective measures and closure of banks. Table 9.1 summarises the prompt-corrective-action features of FDICIA. Some notable reforms include: (1) deposit insurance premiums paid by banks are risk-weighted and depend on bank capital and bank examination rating; (2) as a bank's capital falls

Table 9.1   Summary of prompt-corrective-action provisions of the Federal Deposit Insurance Corporation Improvement Act of 1991

Zone	Mandatory Provisions	Discretionary Provisions	Risk-Based Total	Risk-Based Tier 1	Leverage Tier 1
1. Well capitalised			> 10	> 6	> 5
2. Adequately capitalised	1. No brokered deposits, except with FDIC approval		> 8	> 4	> 4
3. Undercapitalised	1. Suspend dividends and management fees	1. Order recapitalisation	< 8	< 4	< 4
	2. Require capital restoration plan	2. Restrict interaffiliate transaction			
	3. Restrict asset growth	3. Restrict deposit interest rates			
	4. Approval required for acquisitions, branching, and new activities	4. Restrict certain other activities			
	5. No brokered deposits	5. Any other actions that would better carry out prompt corrective action			
4. Significantly undercapitalised	1. Same as for Zone 3	1. Any Zone 3 discretionary actions	< 6	< 3	< 3
	2. Order recapitalisation*	2. Conservatorship or receivership			

Table 9.1   *continued*

Zone	Mandatory Provisions	Discretionary Provisions	Risk-Based Total	Risk-Based Tier 1	Leverage Tier 1
	3. Restrict interaffiliate transactions* 4. Restrict deposit interest rates* 5. Pay of officers restricted	if it fails to submit or implement a plan or recapitalise pursuant to order 3. Any other Zone 5 provision, if such action is necessary to carry out prompt corrective action			
5. Critically undercapitalised	1. Same as for Zone 4 2. Receiver/ conservator within 90 days* 3. Receiver if still in Zone 5 four quarters after becoming critically undercapitalised				< 2

Note: * Not required if primary supervisor determines action would not serve purpose of prompt corrective action, or if certain other conditions are met.

Source: Board of Governors of the Federal Reserve, United States of America.

below multiple capital-zone tripwires, progressively harsher sanctions are imposed on it by regulators – no dividends to be declared, slower asset growth, changing management; (3) regulators' discretion with respect to adopting 'prompt corrective actions' is sharply curtailed (least-cost resolution); and (4) public approval for 'too large to fail' bailouts to banks should come from the most senior economic officials (e.g., Governor of the Central Bank and Minister of Finance).

A credible exit policy for problem banks, which is critical to an effective deposit insurance scheme and lender-of-last-resort facility, is implied in Table 9.1 (see capital-zone trip wire number 5, in particular). To counter moral hazard and regulatory forbearance, the significant precommittment features of the FDICIA have been adopted in Chile and are being considered for implementation by Japan this year.

4.2 Lack of Transparency in Banking

Key to effective corporate governance, market discipline, and official oversight is transparency in banks' financial data, particularly loan loss provisions. A realistic valuation of bank assets requires the introduction of internationally accepted accounting standards, including the application of principles for consolidation of financial groups' or conglomerates' operations, loan classification, provisioning, and income recognition rules.[6]

Public disclosure of reliable, comprehensive, and timely information on the financial condition of banks enhances market discipline. This is an area where little progress has been achieved in developing countries. The integrity of financial data gets worse when the information is most needed, i.e., in times of banking difficulties. Thus, quantitative and qualitative information that goes beyond standard financial statements should be disclosed, such as structure of bank ownership, risk concentration, policies and practices of risk-management systems. The establishment and development of rating agencies should also contribute to the process.

4.3 Weak Regulatory and Supervisory Structures

A major objective of regulation and supervision of banks is to minimise the adverse moral hazard effects of official safety nets (insurance on bank liabilities and lender-of-last-resort facility) on risk-taking and to encourage banks to internalise the externalities of failures.[7] Strong regulation and supervision of the financial system complements efforts to strengthen corporate governance and market discipline. In many developing countries, regulatory rules have been codified, in some instances reflecting the core principles for effective supervision as enunciated by BIS. The problem lies in enforcement, first in respect of the rules themselves and second with regard to the implementation of corrective measures when needed.

4.4 Weak Corporate Governance

Most bank problems can be traced to unsound management that allows banks to absorb low quality assets and take on excessive risks, and that lacks adequate internal information and control systems to monitor, detect, and resolve problem loans and inappropriate risk positions. Quantitative regulation is never enough to ensure sound banking. Management requires a high degree of integrity, competence, and experience in banking. Sound management should be able to *identify, measure, monitor,* and *control* risks, including credit, market, operational and reputational risks.[8] In addition to adequate systems and control procedures, banks should have a high-quality and independent internal audit function to ensure that processing systems are reliable and protected from fraud and that sufficient separation is made between business-generating and accounting functions, especially in trading.

4.5 Connected Lending

In many cases, particularly in the developing countries, banking problems can be attributed to connected lending – large loans to parties connected to the bank (directors, managers, shareholders, and their families), which can easily become non-performing. Connected lending is an indication of a breakdown of market discipline and should be disclosed and subject to official oversight (in terms of limits and/or the supervisory authority's right to deduct such connected lending, if not undertaken on an arm's-length basis, from bank capital).

4.6 Inadequate Financial Infrastructure

Non-existent or shallow private long-term bond, equity, foreign exchange and money markets, combined with poor payments and settlement systems, are other structural weaknesses of financial systems in developing countries. The preponderance of bank loans in financing economic activity in the developing world increases the vulnerability of corporate borrowers to a liquidity crunch and/or interest rate hike. The relatively immature financial structure places a disproportionate burden of risk-sharing on banking institutions. Particularly for banks whose portfolio is dominated by fixed-interest rate loans, increases in short-term interest rates both on deposits and foreign credits make banks more vulnerable to cash-flow problems. Increases in non-performing loans at a time of higher funding costs will deteriorate the financial condition of banks and thus will weaken their ability to withstand shifts in macroeconomic policies or exogenous shocks.

Payments systems should be able to contain systemic risks to the payment and clearing system brought about by a failure of a bank, as in real time gross settlement systems. Efficient foreign exchange, money and capital markets allow banks to manage their liquidity, raise capital and issue debt in proportions that will minimise their vulnerability to macroeconomic shocks. Sound banking also requires an efficiently designed and enforced set of financial contracts, loan recovery, realisation of collateral, and bankruptcy. In many developing countries, deficiencies in the judicial systems tend to offset the benefits of improved corporate governance and bank supervision.

5. HOW OFFICIAL OVERSIGHT CAN REINFORCE CORPORATE GOVERNANCE AND MARKET DISCIPLINE

Official oversight encompasses prudential regulation and supervision. Regulation includes laws, decrees, and administrative orders intended to control bank entry, behaviour, and exit (licensing, capital adequacy, asset limits, liquidity ratios, accounting rules and internal and external audits, liquidation). Supervision includes monitoring the banking system soundness, adequacy of internal control and risk management procedures and financial data, and banks' compliance with prudential regulations.

Sound banking requires sound bankers. Prudential regulations can reinforce good corporate governance by strict licensing requirements – 'fit-and-proper' owners, directors, and managers; strong risk-weighted capital standards; appropriate loan-valuation and classification practices and accounting standards; limits on insider lending, foreign exchange exposure, and maturity mismatch; internal and external audit standards; and separation of dealing and back-office functions.

Market discipline requires market participants to possess as much information as possible to assess the soundness of bank and market sanctions on erring banks. Prudential regulations can reinforce market discipline by requiring enhanced public disclosure of bank financial information and a transparent legal framework that defines the rights of bank owners, creditors, and depositors as well as facilitates exit of unsound banks.

Prudential supervision can reinforce corporate governance through on-site and off-site inspections. While off-site examinations provide indicative assessments that banks are in compliance with all prudential regulations, only on-site visits can verify them. The accuracy of reported capital adequacy can only be verified on-site, as can exposures to credit, liquidity, interest rate, foreign exchange, and off-balance sheet risks, and insider lending limits. Also, assessments of the quality of bank management and the adequacy of internal controls and internal audit can only be done on-site. As important, there must be clear legal authority for supervisors to encourage voluntary compliance of prudential regulations, punish noncompliance and compel corrective actions, including closure, mergers, and liquidation.

Finally, prudential supervision can reinforce market discipline by verifying that accurate and timely information on banks' financial condition is disclosed to market participants and that unsound banks are forced to exit the market. A good example of such prudential supervision is the FDICIA of 1991 (see Table 9.1) that requires banks to take prompt corrective actions when certain levels of undercapitalisation are reached, including speedy closures and liquidation. After all, the closure of individual banks without a systemic fallout indicates a well-functioning supervisory framework.

ACKNOWLEDGEMENT

This chapter, which is in the approved list of SEACEN research topics for 1998, was presented at the International Conference on the

Conduct of Monetary Policy held in the Academia Sinica, Taipei on 12–13 June 1998, and jointly sponsored by the Central Bank of China, Taipei and the Institute of Economics, Academia Sinica. The author is grateful to his SEACEN colleagues, Tan Wai Kuen, Peter Lee, Nid Quah, Vincent Lim, and participants in the Taipei conference for useful comments.

NOTES

1. I consider near-banks, like finance companies in Thailand and merchant banks in Korea that do banking business, to be *de facto* banks even if *de jure* they are not.
2. See Galbis, Vicente (1975), 'Monetary and exchange rate policies in a small open economy', International Monetary Fund Staff Papers, July, pp. 313–43.
3. These are standard results in the literature on a small, open economy.
4. In good times, the private bank keeps all profits, and in bad times walks away from losses, the bulk of which is covered by the government.
5. Benston, George and George Kaufman (1988), 'Risk and solvency regulation of depository institutions: past policies and current options', Monograph Series in Finance and Economics, New York: New York University Press.
6. The International Accounting Standards Committee is developing such standards; the Basle Committee has also established a task force to contribute to their development.
7. 'The presence of the safety net, which inevitably imparts a subsidy to banks, has created a disconnect between risk-taking by banks and banks' cost of capital. It is this disconnect that has made necessary a degree of supervision and regulation that would not be necessary without the existence of the safety net' (Alan Greenspan, speech at a meeting of the Institute of International Finance, Washington, DC, April 29, 1997).
8. One of the Basle Committee's core principles for effective banking supervision is that 'Supervisors should encourage and pursue market discipline by encouraging good corporate governance (through an appropriate structure and set of responsibilities for a bank's board of directors and senior management), and enhancing market transparency and surveillance'.

G-21
G-28
P31,
P34
L33

10. Enterprise restructuring and banking reform: lessons from Eastern Europe since 1990

Ronald W. Anderson

1. GROWTH AND FINANCIAL TRANSITION

An admittedly simple, but useful, way of looking on the economics of transition is that the ex-socialist countries of Central and Eastern Europe (CEE) are complex, industrialized societies which nevertheless have a per capita income level which is significantly below the levels of the OECD countries. The task of transition is to change the organization of these economies so as to drastically reduce this gap. Thus the broad objective of transition is to promote growth. An indication of the magnitude of the problem is given in Table 10.1 which lists the EBRD estimates of GDP per capita for selected transition countries as well as the average for the G-7 countries. In the second column we have calculated the real growth rate that would be required in order to attain the G-7 1992 level by the year 2010. The required growth rate varies from 6 to 11 per cent per year. These are very high rates. The highest annual growth rate so far attained by a transition country is 6–7 per cent. If we assume the listed countries were able to maintain a sustained 5 per cent growth rate we see the Czech Republic would require 20 years to get to the G-7 1992 level whereas Romania would require 39 years. GDP growth has important shortcomings as a measure of economic progress. Furthermore, the current estimates of GDP in Central and Eastern Europe must be taken as only approximate. Therefore, not too much should be read into such calculations as these. Nevertheless, they are useful in reminding us that the transition economies of CEE face a very serious growth challenge.

Table 10.1   Income comparisons for selected transition countries

	GDP per capita 1992 (in US dollars at purchasing power parity exchange rates)	Growth rate to match G-7 1992 by 2010	Years to match G-7 1992 at 5 per cent growth rate
Romania	2,750	11	39
Poland	4,880	8	28
Slovak Republic	5,620	7	25
Hungary	5,740	7	25
Czech Republic	7,160	6	20
G-7	19,600		

Source: EBRD, Transition Report 1994 and own calculations.

Achieving sustained growth requires the development of a broad range of supporting institutions. The financial sector is at the core of such institutional development. In a broad cross-country comparison King and Levine (1993) find financial depth to be the single most important factor explaining differences in growth rates across countries. They show that countries with a greater proportion of credits intermediated by commercial banks grow faster, as do those with a greater share of credits extended to the private sector. The study also identifies significant links between these two measures and efficiency in the economy as a whole.

Economic growth requires both development of new institutions and transformation of existing ones. The bias of socialism was reinforced by strong and complex institutional arrangements. Redirecting transition economies to grow the private sector and shrink (in relative terms) the public sector requires deep and large-scale institutional change. In what follows we review the efforts since 1989 to develop financial sectors within the formerly socialist economies of Central and Eastern Europe. Most of our analysis has been restricted to Hungary, Poland and the Czech Republic, three countries with somewhat similar experiences since World War II and which started their transitions to the market with fairly similar income levels and institutions. Despite these similarities, the three countries have taken different strategies to adapting their economies to the market. In this sense, they have carried out a natural experiment in the development of market institutions in an economy directed by socialist planning.

Reviewing their experiences is interesting in identifying what policies have worked and what have not. This may provide some useful lessons that may be helpful in guiding policy decision in a country such as China which is today confronted by some of the problems which Eastern European economies faced in 1990.

2. FINANCIAL ASPECTS OF STABILIZATION IN TRANSITION

The suddenness of the political changes which swept the socialist countries of Central and Eastern Europe from 1989 to 1991 exposed their economies to a number of very important, system-wide shocks. There was a risk that the economies would veer off toward high inflation, severe recession or both before the natural stabilizers that exist in a market economy could be put into place. Thus one of the first priorities of policy making in transition was to stabilize the economy. The fact that these economies were exposed to more than one shock made the task of stabilization complex.

Liberalization was the source of many shocks. *Price liberalization* was aimed at allowing consumer and producer prices to adjust to market-clearing levels.[1] Given very large discrepancies in relative prices between the socialist economies and capitalist economies these adjustments were often very severe.[2] An economy in transition is in many instances subjected to *major* changes in the *state budget*. Prior to 1989 many socialist economies had made efforts to remove direct subsidies to loss-making enterprises. However, few such enterprises had been shut down and many of the structural losses were covered from the state budget or the banking system. Many of the reforming governments which came to power in 1989 or after placed high priority on *removing direct subsidies*. When implemented, this exposed their economies to a contractionary shock which threatened major job loss and loss of sales to suppliers. In order to allow competitive forces needed for a market to function, many of the reforms sought to promote the growth of the private sector by *removing barriers to entry*. The hope of course was that the growth of the private sector would help to offset contractionary forces. In particular, labor shed from inefficient manufacturing industries could be absorbed by the service sector which had been neglected under socialism and where large untapped demand would be found. However, increased competition would force existing firms to speed their adjustments and thereby could serve to reinforce contractionary tendencies.

Transition countries were also exposed to major changes in their foreign economic relations. The economic by-product of the fall of the Yalta order was the *break-up of the system of foreign trade* that had applied to these countries. Under the Council for Mutual Economic Assistance (CMEA) foreign trade flows among socialist countries were determined through an administrative bargaining process at terms which were divorced from those prevailing in the world's hard currency trade. This broke up starting in 1991 so that from that time on, foreign trade of the former socialist countries both among themselves and with the West was conducted on a hard currency basis. This was profoundly disruptive to trade. All of the transition economies were open prior to 1991. Consequently, there was no way that the governments of these economies could have avoided this shock. And there were only limited policy tools, mainly border measures (such as tariffs or quotas) and exchange rate policy, available to help moderate or modulate the shock.

3. FINANCIAL LIBERALIZATION

In the traditional socialist economy the state is present in almost all segments of the economy. Given this origin, the naive liberal prescription for transition is very simple: take the state out of the contracting between private parties. However, the reality of post-socialist economies makes this prescription difficult to follow in an immediate way. In the first place, socialist habits in contracting are not those known in a mature capitalist economy. In part, this may be because of difficulties in the prevailing contract law. At least as important is that there may be a lack of an enforcement mechanism. When enforcement is difficult, it is natural that contract terms are routinely the subject of renegotiation.

A further difficulty in liberalizing exchange is that in a post-socialist economy there may be a lack of clarity of ownership. When ownership rights are not clear, contracting between agents cannot be expected to produce efficient results.[3] To see how this can affect financial contracting in a transition economy consider the case of a new firm which seeks a bank loan to acquire and operate equipment. If it is difficult to establish that the seller of the equipment is its owner under the law, the sale may not be valid. If so, the equipment would not be a security for the loan. Uncertainty of this sort may be sufficient for lenders to decide not to grant the loan.

Given the structure of the socialist system, liberalizing existing financial institutions essentially means bank reform. The object of liberalization in this area is to remove the state from setting interest rates on deposits and on bank loans. This is accomplished by *introducing two-tiered banking*. One part of the ex-monobank becomes the central bank. Commercial banking activities are diverted to independent institutions either carved out of the ex-monobank or newly created. Individuals are given the freedom to hold deposits in the bank of their choosing, and banks are free to set rates on deposits as they wish. At the same time, borrowers are allowed select their bank and to negotiate the rate and other terms of their loan agreement.

Liberalizing the banking sector is unlike liberalizing other economic activities because banks are the conduits of monetary control. At times central banks of the capitalist economies have exercised monetary control through restrictions on the quantity of credits that banks are authorized to make. Another quantitative credit tool is the provision of refinance credit. Such tools tend to give the central authorities control not only of overall monetary conditions but also of the allocation of funds among potential borrowers. Clearly, this works against the principle that credit decisions should reflect the free negotiation between private borrowers and lenders, and for this reason in most mature capitalist countries, central banks have increasing relied on less indirect policy tools such as reserve requirements and open market operations. Refinance credit is restricted to short-term liquidity provision such as Lombard credit or discount credit.

Given that the central bank in a transition economy may be struggling to establish its mastery in monetary control, it may oppose rapid liberalization throughout the banking sector. In particular, the market for government securities may be very underdeveloped so that open market operations are infeasible. Furthermore, policies aimed at influencing market interest rates may be ineffective if financial discipline is not in force. A distinct but similar concern is that rapid liberalization may disrupt operations of state-owned enterprises with long-standing debts and continuing needs for credit. This may provoke liquidity crises for such firms even if they are solvent. Thus in banking reform as elsewhere the objectives of liberalization and stabilization tend to come into opposition.

Perhaps the most pervasive socialist banking practice and the most difficult to change is the passive behavior of creditors. This is one of the main factors contributing to what has come to be known as the *'soft budget constraints'* faced by socialist enterprises.[4] An enterprise with revenues insufficient to allow it to service its outstanding debt was not likely to receive any severe sanction for this shortcoming. Certainly the bank could not force the liquidation of the firm in order to recover the amounts owed. Instead, it was more likely that additional credits would be accorded to allow it to meet its production and other objectives. As a result, the banking sector at the start of transition had no experience in disciplining its borrowers; rather banks experience was that tolerating non-performing loans was sanctioned by the state. Furthermore, giving the banks the means of enforcing contracts requires the implementation of effective bankruptcy laws. Even if these laws exist, they may be administered, either intentionally or not, in a way that makes bankruptcy very costly. In such a circumstance, the rational course may be to allow the enterprise to continue operations in the hopes that something will be recovered in the future. Enterprises tend to recognize this, thereby reducing their incentives to service their debts.[5]

In addition to these possible difficulties in pursuing liberal banking reforms, we should mention the widely-held view that it may be inappropriate to leave real interest rate determination to market forces alone. Often this line of argument comes in the form of recommending subsidized long-term credit. The idea is that markets may apply an inappropriately high discount rate to projects because of risk aversion.[6] The Japan Development Bank is sometimes suggested as an example of the successful public intervention in the provision of long-term finance.[7] Others may argue that interest rates should be determined by the market but that the state should provide loan guarantees to borrowers who would otherwise be cut off from credit. Again, rationale for this policy may be that the market is applying an inappropriate risk premium to some borrowers.

Whatever the merits of these arguments in favor of credit subsidies, other considerations may suggest that, if anything, they can be even more distortionary and difficult to eliminate than direct subsidies from the state budget. Since they operate by distorting prices, credit subsidies do not appear on any government budget. Therefore, it is difficult to identify who receives the subsidies and who is paying the bill. Since they are difficult to account for and their incidence is unclear, there may be little effective resistance to granting such subsidies. Other forms of intervention in banking relations may produce subsidies that are similarly difficult to detect and to quantify. For example, in granting loan guarantees, the state gives borrowers access to credit at lower rates than they would have otherwise. The costs of this emerge only in the future and only in those cases where the borrowers experience difficulty. In the same vein, if the state indirectly pursues a policy that encourages extending credits to state owned enterprises which do not service their debts, there is an implicit guarantee.

Since 1990 decisive steps have been taken toward liberalizing the economies of Hungary, Poland and the Czech Republic. Most price controls were removed early on in the transition process. At the same time, in the financial sector competitive rate setting became more prevalent. Much of the public debt was securitized with prices being determined by trading on a secondary OTC market. Banks were given the freedom to set rates on deposits and on bank loans. This liberalization of finance was not complete. Rates on certain types of credits, in particular, refinance credits were linked to reference rates which were set administratively. Generally, these rates were below market and were accorded to specific sectors or firms selected by the state. In effect, with the removal of direct budgetary subsidies, the state turned to credit subsidies as a less transparent means of supporting sensitive sectors. While the trend has been toward reducing such credit subsidies, there were still significant amounts of refinance credits outstanding in the mid-1990s.

4. ESTABLISHING PROPERTY RIGHTS: PRIVATIZATION

In virtually every former communist country of Eastern and Central Europe there was widespread recognition that the transition to the market economy must involve the privatization of state-owned enterprises. Economic efficiency is clearly the principal benefit sought through privatization. Socialism was inefficient because resources were controlled by agents and organizations who did not have a clear interest in using them well. In essence under socialism there is no 'advocate' for capital.[8] In principle, privatization changes this because then the firm's capital and land belong to agents who can legally use them in a self-interested way. Thus it is in their interests to see that the return on capital is maximized.

With this idea in mind at the outset of transition many argued that it was important to privatize state-owned enterprises rapidly; whereas the precise form of privatization was of secondary importance. However, this view ignores the distributional implications of privatization. In part, because of these, the choice of privatization method became a hotly debated and highly politicized question. As a result in some transition countries privatization has been anything but rapid.

There have been a very large number of proposed methods to privatize state-owned assets of the former socialist economies.[9] These can be grouped into three broad categories:

1. **The sale of state assets to the public for money.** This may or may not be open to foreigners. It may be carried out by auction, negotiated sale or other means. It may involve leverage or not.

2. **Turn over firms to employees.** This may involve all employees or only subgroups (e.g., managers). It may require employees to pay for their stakes. They may be permitted to borrow to finance their purchase (i.e., leveraged buy-out). Plant and equipment may be transferred to the employees or they may be retained by the state and leased to the employees. It may involve mixed public/employee sales with employees paying lower prices.

3. **Free-of-charge transfers to the public.** This is intended to give the citizens specific claims on the assets which they previously owned collectively. They may be given specific assets (e.g. restitution of properties expropriated by the state). They may receive vouchers which are claims on assets. They may use vouchers to bid for specific assets. Vouchers may be tradable or not. Assets may be bunched together to spread risks. This may involve intermediaries (mutual funds). The population may be required to pay a small amount of money for the claims.

All three of these general approaches can be applied to one firm at a time on a *case-by-case* basis. However, there has been an emphasis on carrying out the privatization process rapidly on a massive scale, and to this end a number of former socialist countries have simplified procedures as part of a process of *large-scale privatization*. The Czech Republic and Russia stand out in this regard.

Depending upon the precise details of the privatization method employed these approaches can have very different consequences for the distribution of ownership and control both within the citizenry and between foreigners and the domestic population. Similarly, they can lead to different relations between owners and managers. In particular, an important issue is whether post-privatization there are significant ownership groups with a clear incentive to monitor management who might otherwise pursue their own private objectives. If privatization results in the shares of the firm being held by a very large number of individual owners, it may be that no one owner will have the incentive to undertake the effort to follow the affairs of the firm very closely. On the other hand, a privatization process which bestowed a controlling interest in an enterprise on a single individual or a very small group of investors would probably be extremely inegalitarian. The alternative which attempts to reconcile a wide distribution of financial wealth with the concentration of control rights involves financial intermediaries.[10] However, this leaves open the issues of what form such intermediaries should take and whether the intermediaries themselves will be subjected to effective monitoring.[11] Perhaps equally important is the question of whether the privatization is merely a matter of form with little substantial change in the control of the real assets. For example, before privatization many socialist enterprises' productive assets were owned by the state but control rights were vested in workers' councils. If privatization takes the form of an employee buy-out with plant and equipment owned by the state to be leased backed to the employees, then there is very little effective change in the way the firm is operated.

This discussion makes it clear that a country's approach to privatization has direct implications for the development of the country's financial sector. Privatization that endows the population with shares or bonds necessarily tends to create a securities market. Privatization through mutual funds may also do this if both the funds and the population trade on a secondary market. On the other hand, privatization that has the banking sector as the main creditor of industry reinforces the intermediation process but does little to develop securities markets. Finally, selling state assets to large foreign enterprises does little to develop the domestic financial sector. We now briefly review the experience in privatization in the Czech Republic, Poland and Hungary.

4.1 Czech Privatization

The Czech strategy toward transition reflects the strength of vision represented by Vaclav Klaus a former National Bank researcher who served initially as Minister of Finance and then until 1997 as Prime Minister. The distinctive characteristic of this strategy is its single-minded focus on privatization of state-owned enterprises. Privatization was started in the federation in 1990 and was virtually completed in the Czech Republic by the end of 1995. A variety of methods have been used and can be grouped into three broad categories: restitution, small-scale privatization, and large-scale privatization.

Restitution was intended to return to their former owners properties taken over by the state since 1948. This included the return of apartments, offices, industrial buildings, and agricultural or forest land. These were to be returned to private owners. In addition some properties destined for public use were transferred to municipal governments which since 1990 have been reconstituted as independent authorities. The thorny issue of restitution properties which were incorporated into larger enterprises was handled by requiring that a fraction of the large enterprise shares be placed at the time of the privatization in a restitution fund to be held against future claims.

Small-scale privatization was aimed at transforming small business units into proprietorships. This program commenced in January 1991 and was completed by the end of 1993. Some 20,000 retail stores, restaurants, and service facilities were sold in this manner (see Mladek 1994).

Large-scale privatization was the method used to privatize most large enterprises which made up the major part of state property. At the beginning of 1991, the Czechoslovak government earmarked approximately 6000 large enterprises for privatization: 4400 in the Czech Republic and 1600 in Slovakia (see Svejnar and Singer 1994). There have been two waves of large-scale privatization. The first was initiated in 1991. The second wave was completed in 1995.

As a result of these programs, the Czech economy was transformed from one which in 1989 conformed closely to the classical model of Soviet style planning to one which in 1995 was dominated by privately-owned enterprise. This remarkable transformation involved a number of important innovations and, for better or worse, has determined how the economy in general and the financial system in particular will operate for years to come.

From the earliest stages of the Czechoslovak transition there was a widespread support for using vouchers as the most equitable means of transferring resources from the state to its citizens. While other methods have been used as well, the use of vouchers has been a distinctive feature of the Czech mass privatization experience. This has meant that share ownership has been within the reach of the entire adult population, thus giving a strong boost to the development of direct channels of finance. However, the privatization program has involved the creation of some new intermediaries as well.

There are broadly three steps involved in the Czech large-scale privatization process:

1. *Selection of privatization plans*: Any group or individual was free to propose a privatization plan to the ministry of finance. This involved a business plan and a proposed means of distributed shares (e.g., sells 10 percent of shares to outsiders for money through an auction, sell 30 percent of shares to employees for money, place 60 percent of shares to be sold for vouchers). Existing management obviously submitted many plans, but in many cases the plan that was selected originated from a potential investor group.
2. *The transfer of properties to the National Property Fund*: The NPF was the legal entity that held the shares of SOE's after they were 'commercialized', i.e., converted to joint stock companies or limited liability companies. This is a public entity which has significant autonomy from the Czech State. In particular, income from privatization is used by NPF according to certain guidelines and does not directly enter the state budget.
3. *The sale of the properties to the private sector:* The NPF was charged to a company according to privatization scheme that had been selected by the Ministry of Finance for that company.

As a consequence of the privatization process, the NPF has been funded essentially by transfers of assets from the state. Many people incorrectly assume that privatization in the Czech Republic took place exclusively through the use of vouchers. This is far from correct, and the NPF generated huge amounts of income from assets sales. For example, NTF had generated a total cash income of CZK 90.3 billion through the end of 1993 which was equivalent to 9.8 percent of Czech GDP in that year. This bestowed the fund with enormous power to influence the Czech economy in one way or another. To varying degrees these funds have been used as follows:

1. Covering liabilities of enterprises earmarked for privatization;
2. Compensation of banks for losses realized through bankruptcy proceedings;
3. Covering the operating expenses of enterprises that have been privatized if the NPF has retained a stake and if there are authorized claims outstanding;
4. For providing security on credits to the enterprises in which the Fund is holding at least 50 percent share;
5. Compensation of environmental damage from a former state-owned enterprise;
6. Proceeds from the privatization of the Czech Railroad Company could be used in the development of railroad transport.

The first four of these uses are various forms of subsidies directed toward what remained essentially the state enterprise sector. Potentially this could have allowed budget constraints of these enterprises to remain very soft for some considerable time after official budgetary subsidies were stopped and these enterprises formally entered the privatization. In anticipation of its revenues from privatization the NPF funded its activities through the issue of bonds. Many of these bonds were used to recapitalize the banking system, as will be described below. The NPF is powerful also as the largest single shareholder in Czech industry. Thus the NPF has been able to serve as a buffer during the early transition period, preventing the instability of the banking system or excessive disruption of enterprises.

When Czech state-owned enterprises were transformed into joint stock companies their shares were initially held by the National Property Fund. These shares became publicly held securities when they were auctioned for vouchers. After the auction, share certificates were issued to the purchasers and shares could then be bought and sold on the secondary market for money. The vouchers themselves could not be legally traded. The shares purchased in this way are common stock, meaning that, in addition to receiving a share of the company profits when dividends are paid, the holder has a voting right at shareholders' meetings. Thus the new Czech stock market has the potential for determining who controls Czech corporations. The development of this market has involved the creation of some new Czech institutions. The main steps in the development of the Czech stock market are shown in Table 10.2.

In the Czech mass privatization program, vouchers were given to individuals. For slightly over CZK 1000 crowns an adult received 1000 voucher points. The represented about one week's wages for the average working person. As a result the cost was more than a symbolic amount but still it was accessible to most Czechs. Ultimately, 75 percent of those eligible participated in the first-wave program and an even higher percentage participated in the second-wave program (see Filer and Hanousek 1994). An individual could either participate directly in the auction or could place some or all of his or her points in an investment fund. Thus the Czech program did not impose a system of mutual funds, but it allowed them to come into existence. In the first round of privatizations more than 70 percent of all voucher points were invested through mutual funds.

Table 10.2   The chronology of the creation of the Czech stock market

October 1991	Start of the first wave of voucher privatizations. All adult Czechoslovak citizen-residents were entitled to one book of 1000 voucher points which could be purchased for CZK 35 ($1.20) plus a mandatory registration fee of CZK 1000 ($33.30) the equivalent of about one week's average wage.
January 1992	First-wave privatization project submissions closed.
February 1992	Registration of newly created Investment Privatization Funds completed.
May 1992	First-wave privatization projects selected. New joint stock companies registered. First round of voucher bidding begins.
October 1992	Deadline for submitting second-wave privatization projects.
December 1992	Fifth and final round of first-wave voucher bidding ends.
April 1993	Opening of the Prague Stock Exchange.
June 1993	Shares transferred to purchasers. Secondary trading starts.
October 1993	Start of sale of second-wave vouchers to Czech citizen-residents. CZK 50 per book plus CZK 1000 to register.
November 1993	Registration of Investment and Mutual Funds completed.
March 1994	Announcement of companies included in second-wave voucher privatization. First round of bidding started and completed with transfer of shares sold.
December 1994	End of sixth and final round bidding of the second wave.

Source: Mladek (1994) and Ministry of the Privatization.

The intermediaries that grew out of voucher privatization were *investment companies* (ICs) and *investment privatization funds* (IPFs). ICs were companies authorized to found and manage IPFs. IPFs themselves were authorized to receive voucher points and were organized as joint stock companies similar to closed-end mutual funds in the US and elsewhere. The ICs themselves could be owned by another institution. Indeed, many of them are owned by banks.

The operations of the voucher privatization program were managed by the state. All shares were dematerialized and were registered on a central computer system. Bidding proceeded in rounds. In each round the program manager announced a price and the number of unsold shares for each firm. While the details of price setting by the voucher program manager were not public, it seems that it was basically something close to a partial adjustment model with adjustment based on the excess supply or demand. At the start of the auction the total number of rounds was not announced. The first-wave auction lasted five rounds over a seven-month period. About 92 percent of all shares placed in the auction were sold. Virtually all voucher points were spent (see Filer and Hanousek 1994). In June 1993, some time after the first-wave voucher auction was completed, share certificates were signed over to their new owners and trading began on the secondary market. The marketplace is made up of two different stock exchanges and an over-the-counter market.

From this description we see that financial market development in the Czech Republic was given a giant push forward through the mass privatization program. Starting from an economy with no publicly traded firms and no investors, the system has been transformed into one where close to two thousand larger-sized firms are publicly traded joint-stock companies.

4.2 Polish Privatization

Table 10.3 presents some measures of the relative importance of the public and private sectors in Poland. The private share of GDP is estimated to have grown steadily from 28 percent in 1989 to over 50 percent by 1993. Similarly, by 1993 over 50 percent of employment was in the private sector. While some of this high fraction is the result of the large number of private farms in Poland, the trend toward strong growth of the private sector is clear. We now examine in more detail the institutional changes that are behind these trends in order to see in what ways the Polish financial sector has facilitated or impeded the reallocation of economic resources.

Much of the early literature on the transition of Eastern and Central Europe assumed that privatization would be the fast route to shrinking state control of productive resources. In Poland, despite the early and nearly universal recognition of the importance of privatization, its implementation has been slow. There have been several shifts in policy direction. Furthermore, the process of privatization in Poland emphasizes collective decisions by affected parties, a practice which has undoubtedly slowed the speed of privatization.

Polish privatization law envisages two alternative routes: 1.'corporatization' or the transformation from a state-owned enterprise to a state-owned corporation (either joint-stock or limited liabilities company) whereby the Minister of Privatization executes the function of the owner and appoints a supervisory board of which 2/3 are representatives of the state and 1/3 of the company and 2. the 'liquidation' route with the dissolution of an enterprise and the privatization of its assets.

The law states that following corporatization, companies should be privatized within two years. There are two broad alternatives for accomplishing this: individual privatization and mass privatization. The basic procedure for privatization that was employed through 1994 was based on initiative taken by the founding organ of the enterprise with the consultation of labor unions and workers' councils. Since the latter are effectively disenfranchised through the process, there was naturally a reluctance to accept privatization. Poland has experimented with a number of methods.[12] The first to be tried was capital privatization. This consists of transforming the firm into either a joint-stock company or a limited liability company which is then sold. Under Polish privatization law employees may purchase 20

Table 10.3   Private sector development (share in percentage)

	1989	1990	1991	1992	1993
GDP	28.4	35.0	45.3	49.7	50+
Employment	43.9	45.1	50.2	53.7	57.5
Employment excluding private agriculture	29.6	30.9	36.6	40.4	45.2

Source: OECD Economic Survey, Poland (1994).

percent of the shares of the company at a discounted price. The amount of the discount is 50 percent of the price for the general public or an amount equal to the total wages paid to employees in the previous year, whichever is less. Alternative privatization methods include employee buy-outs and liquidations.

In the early stages of the privatization program, among those firms which were not liquidated, the most common form of privatization was an employee buy-out. This suggests that employee power to block privatizations effectively allowed them to concentrate property rights in their own hands. The process was further facilitated by a feature under Polish privatization law which allows the state to maintain ownership of productive assets and to lease them to employee-owned privatized companies.

It is perhaps not surprising that piece-meal privatization has been relatively slow and that the process has not removed all fuzziness in firm objectives. Indeed, it was the anticipation of just such an outcome which led many analysts to call for a mass privatization process where traditional power blocs would be neutralized.

In Poland, mass privatization has been the subject of constant debate since 1989, but it was only in 1995 that mass privatization got underway. Fifteen closed-end mutual funds called National Investment Funds (NIF) were created. Some 500 state-owned enterprises were commercialized, and the shares in these companies were distributed to the NIFs. Each NIF was awarded some 33 percent of the shares of about 35 companies and about 2 percent of the shares in each of the remaining companies in the mass privatization program. The idea was that each NIF would serve as a strategic investor in a limited number of companies. In this way, it was hoped that they would exert effective control over management and would be instrumental in retructuring the films they hold.

The state was the initial owner of the NIFs, but ownership was transferred to Polish citizens for a nominal charge. Specifically, each adult was able to acquire a privatization fund certificate for about $8. Each privatization certificate could be redeemed for one share in each of the 15 NIFs. These shares can be bought and sold for money. Since July 1996 they have been traded on the Warsaw Stock Exchange. Thus an individual investor can choose to concentrate his holdings in one or a few of the NIFs. It should be noted that one possible strategy for a company included in the mass privatization program is to go public either to raise new capital or to allow the NIFs to cash out. In fact, relatively few of the 500 companies in the program are currently listed on the Warsaw Stock Exchange.

In awaiting the implementation of Polish mass privatization, a large number of Polish state enterprises were allowed to operate for six years into transition without any major restructuring. In most cases this probably has meant little effective control by outsiders. Many of the largest of Polish enterprises, including most of the banks, are still not privatized. For the 500 firms that have now been processed by mass privatization i is not clear that they have been brought under effective control by outside investors. Each of the NIFs itself has very dispersed ownership. Furthermore, management teams of the NIFs were selected by the Ministry of Finance and do not have equity participation in the fund. In principle, the NIFs compete to keep their shareholders. However, if all the funds continue to keep broadly diversified portfolios, they will all have about the same performance, and private investors will have little reason to shift from one fund to another. In this way, managers can continue to collect their fees without making the effort to exert control in firms where they hold shares.

4.3 Hungarian Privatization

The privatization process in Hungary began in the middle of the 1980s and by the mid-1990s it was still far from being finished. It exemplifies the Hungarian 'gradualist approach' to transition policy. It has proceeded in fits and starts which resulted not so much from the measured application of a single vision but rather from the conflicting efforts to pull the program in one direction or another. In part, this was a by-product of the 1980s attempts to reform the economy through the decentralization of initiative to enterprises. This gave rise to a wave of 'spontaneous' privatizations initiated by the firms' managers themselves. Subsequently, the state has attempted to take back the control of the process and to some extent has been successful. In 1990 its goals were ambitious. From a state sector comprising 2200 enterprises valued at 1900 billion forint, about 900 companies were expected to be rapidly privatized representing a value of 700 billion forint. The priority was firstly given to the maximization of privatization income, particularly in foreign currency given the lack of international reserves of the country and the burden of the external debt. However, the principles of the process were never terribly clear. Furthermore, the state responded to criticisms claiming that it was selling too cheaply by going slowly. Thus, in practice much privatization continued to be initiated by the firms or by investors. Also after a period of selling essentially for cash, often to foreigners, the government attempted to give access to small domestic investors. In 1991 it initiated a 'Compensation Program' which awarded vouchers to individuals with claims on properties that were nationalized after 1939. In addition, it attempted to encourage small-investor participation by giving loans at preferential terms to employees purchasing shares in their company.

What has been the net result of all these efforts? The State Property Agency (SPA) was given the responsibility for more than 2000 public enterprises with an estimated book value of 2000 billion forint. After about five years they had disposed of 1248 of them. Half had been privatized. Most of the others had been liquidated. These figures show that despite the slow beginning and the numerous changes of direction in the state's active privatization efforts, a large fraction of the state enterprises have at least been commercialized or closed down. Much of this activity has occurred since 1993. For example, of the 1200 state-owned enterprises that had been transformed by the SPA into joint-stock or limited liabilities companies as of November 1994, 506 were transformed in 1993 alone.

Another view of privatization activity is given by Table 10.4 which reports the revenues of privatization. The acceleration in the privatization process since 1992 is clearly demonstrated by the evolution of their total income. While through 1992 most of the income derived from foreign sales, these foreign sales dropped off sharply in 1993 and fell away almost entirely in 1994. During that year, the foreign exchange sales amounted to 10.9 billion forint which was one-tenth of the corresponding figure for 1993. The drop of foreign exchange sales partly reflects the fact that some of the state's most valuable enterprises had been sold previously. Also, it testifies to the existence of a significant political reaction to the initial government policy of selling to foreigners. The opening of the privatization process to domestic investors was accomplished largely through the use of credit and compensation vouchers. Thus the cash proceeds have fallen from 133.2 billion forint in 1993 to 36.1 billion forint in 1994. Furthermore, whether or not the institutions will ever actually receive cash for much of the 85.9 billion forint sales on credit remains somewhat in doubt. Should the value of the shares bought on instalment credit fall below their purchase price, investors may choose to not make their payments. Overall, privatizations produced a total value of 415 billion forint. This is far short of the 700 billion forint in book value that the state set out to privatize in 1990. The reasons for the shortfall are that some assets proved to

Table 10.4   Composition of revenues from sales of the Hungarian State properties (in billion forint)

	1990	1991	1992	1993	1994	1990–94
Cash	0.67	30.37	66.74	133.19	36.06	267.03
E-loan	–	1.01	9.07	21.70	30.23	62.01
Compensation Vouchers	–	–	2.64	19.54	63.68	85.86
TOTAL	0.67	31.38	78.45	174.43	129.97	414.9

Source: NBH Annual Report (1994).

be worth less than their book value and that some of the properties still on the state's books are large with considerable value at least in accounting terms.

More than the half of the annual income from privatization (55 percent in 1992 and 67 percent in 1993) was used to support the government budget via state debt amortization or funds outside the budget such as the Employment Fund and the Agricultural Development Fund. This budget support means that part of the privatization receipts is used to cover current expenditures of the state.

5. IMPOSING DISCIPLINE IN FINANCIAL CONTRACTING: HARD BUDGET CONSTRAINTS

Privatized enterprise is viewed as an important step toward achieving economic efficiency and growth. However, enterprises, either pubic or private, will waste resources if offered subsidies to do so. Thus the removal of direct state subsidies is the first and most obvious step toward increasing the economic discipline of enterprises. By and large, in Poland, Hungary, and the Czech Republic, direct budgetary subsidies to state-owned enterprises were drastically reduced from 1989 to 1992. However, there were some exceptions. As we have already noted, in the Czech Republic some proceeds from privatization were used to subsidize loss-making enterprises while they were being prepared to go through mass privatization. Still these exceptions have been relatively few in number and limited in their duration.

While direct subsidies were dramatically reduced in the early phase of transition, other institutional forms of the 'soft budget constraint' emerged which effectively cushioned some of the shock brought on by liberalization. One of these was the use of credit subsidies. These came either in the form of providing access to refinance credits at below market rates or by the public entities providing loan guarantees to certain classes of borrowers. The second form of indirect support in the form of *de facto* tax relief. Many enterprises in distress allowed tax arrears to grow but were not vigorously pursued by the taxing authorities. This was particularly the case in Poland where a loss-making enterprise would still be liable for tax on its wage bill if their wage rate increase exceed the statutorily allowed amount.

Finally an enterprise, either private or state-owned, may find that they can avoid or delay paying for some inputs. For example, its supplier may be a loosely-run state enterprise. Alternatively, even a privatized enterprise may feel that it has little alternative but to ship to a customer that is unable to pay immediately. Thus, using trade credit by letting payments arrears mount is one way for a firm to keep its budget constraints soft. During the period from 1990 until 1992 many commentators were alarmed by the growth of trade credit. The fear was that this was emerging as a new form of generalized budgetary indiscipline which would undermine efforts to force enterprises into making tough restructuring decisions. In fact, subsequent analysis with better data has shown that the level of commercial credit is not particularly high by international standards (see Schaffer 1997).

Rising tax arrears or trade credit may be manifestations of a more general tendency of creditors to be tolerant with a distressed enterprise when contract and bankruptcy laws are badly written or poorly administered. In the early stages of transition it was evident that inefficient bankruptcy laws were typical throughout Eastern Europe. In the face of this, there have been dramatically different responses in different countries.

In the Czech Republic a corollary of the emphasis placed on mass privatization has been that financial distress has been de-emphasized. In part, this implies that bankruptcy law reform and other related institutional changes were given low priority. Beyond this there may have been an active policy of avoiding bankruptcies for fear they might erode political support and thereby threaten privatization efforts. The consequence of this is that as of 1997, bankruptcy remained a relatively cumbersome procedure which affords creditors relatively few rights.

Hungary has taken an approach that was diametrically opposed to this. Already in the 1980s there had been some serious efforts made to harden Hungarian budget constraints. In September 1986, a bankruptcy law was adopted. This was directed at facilitating negotiations between creditors and debtors leading to an out-of-court settlement of claims. As a last resort, courts intervened to initiate liquidation proceedings. The provisions of the bankruptcy law were largely used to liquidate small enterprises on a modest scale. Between 1986 and 1991 there were about 1000 bankruptcy filings, only 50 of which involved state-owned firms. A new bankruptcy law was enacted on 1 January 1992 which altered radically the regime in force in Hungary for resolving financial distress. While still favoring negotiation between creditors and the firms over liquidation, the new law was modified to take a form similar to Chapter 11 of the US bankruptcy code. Specifically, the firm can obtain temporary shielding from its creditors thus allowing an opportunity for restructuring and reorganization. Managers of bankrupt firms retain their jobs after filing and have the first opportunity to present a reorganization plan. Creditors then vote on the plan and have the opportunity to present alternative plans. If an agreement cannot be reached the procedure reverts to liquidation. Priority under liquidation was changed to give tax penalties a lower status than taxes themselves. Given that tax penalties can be very large relative to other claims, this change improved the probable payoff to unsecured creditors including other firms and thereby increased their incentive to initiate bankruptcy. A very controversial feature of the law was to make it a criminal offence for firm officials not to declare bankruptcy when they had an outstanding debt with scheduled principal or interest payment more than 90 days overdue, independently of the amount of the deficiency. By forcing the debtor himself to declare bankruptcy even in the absence of strong pressure from the creditors, the legislative intent was clearly to harden the budget constraints of the state-owned enterprises. Another controversial provision of the bankruptcy law was the requirement of unanimous consent of creditors to implement the restructuring plan. This provision implied very long and complex negotiations to obtain the creditor agreement and gave too much power to marginal creditors to stop the process. The strict new bankruptcy code was not the only factor increasing the chances that a distressed firm would end up in bankruptcy court. Starting in 1992, the Hungarian social security administration, one of the main creditors of the bad debtors, started bankruptcy proceedings against these enterprises.

Table 10.5   Bankruptcies and liquidations in Hungary

Year	1989	1990	1991	1992	1993	1994*
Bankruptcy filed	n.a.	n.a.	n.a.	4169	987	151
—— closed	n.a.	n.a.	n.a.	2703	1924	340
Liquidations filed	n.a.	n.a.	n.a.	9891	7242	3940
—— closed	141	233	526	4936	5115	2984

Note: * First through third quarters.
Source: Bonin and Schaffer (1995).

The effects of these changes were rapid and dramatic. Table 10.5 shows that in 1992 after the new law went into effect there were some 4000 filings for bankruptcy (the temporary protection from creditors) and almost 10,000 filings for liquidation. While most of the firms involved were small, many were large so that the potential impact on Hungarian national output was significant.[13] The National Bank of Hungary presents different figures of bankruptcies and liquidation given that they concern only the incorporated economic organizations and not the individual entrepreneurs. Between 1992 and the end of 1994, the central bank has recorded 3147 bankruptcies and 6671 liquidations. Liquidations primarily affected limited liability companies and cooperatives which accounted for 90 percent of liquidated businesses.

In fact, most bankruptcies and liquidations ended up being settled administratively and did not generally involve shutting down the firm. Nevertheless, the feared consequences of this wave of bankruptcies on the employment and on the portfolio quality of the banks led the government to water down the law and to limit its scope of application. In July 1992, the government launched the debtor consolidation scheme offering a protection against bankruptcy for enterprises classified as being of 'national interest,' and in July 1993, the bankruptcy law was amended to remove the institution of mandatory self-declared bankruptcy and change several other significant features of the law. The self-bankruptcy procedure can be initiated only where it is supported by the majority of the creditors. In order to accelerate the procedure, the amendment reduced the required majority for approval of a reorganization agreement from 100 percent to a two-thirds (in value) and to one-half (in number) of mature claims plus one-fourth (in number) of not-yet-mature claims.

Despite these steps to moderate the force of the law, the Hungarian approach represented a very aggressive and bold attempt to force restructuring on Hungarian enterprises. It was motivated to a significant degree because it was feared that uneconomic firms were surviving without restructuring because there were able to force creditors to extend further credits. The measures were effective in the sense that a very large fraction of the liquidations cases were initiated by creditors other than the banks or the tax authorities. It is difficult to say if Hungary went too far, that is, that many of the bankruptcies and liquidations were economically inefficient. However, the perception that the measures were excessive did tend to contribute to a feeling that the aggressive disruption of the economy was ill-advised.

Poland developed its own distinct strategy toward bankruptcy reform. Essentially it aimed at streamlining bankruptcy procedures on the one hand and linking it to bank recapitalization on the other. Since the late 1980s in Poland, the legal means for dealing with financial distress include liquidation, bankruptcy, and judicial reconciliation. Liquidation has proved relatively more widely practiced than the other two procedures. The term 'liquidation' is usually taken to mean that the firm's productive assets are broken up and sold off to the highest bidder in order to pay creditors according to absolute priority of claims. In fact, in Poland legal liquidation has been used as a part of a more informal process of negotiation among interested parties in distressed firms, the outcome of which may maintain the assets in place. Once it is clear what form the restructured firm is to take the firm is formally liquidated with its assets acquired by the new firm or by the creditors who then lease to the new firm. In contrast, formal bankruptcy has been less widely used for resolving financial distress in Poland. One possible reason for this is that under bankruptcy law tax liabilities are given higher priority than financial liabilities. Furthermore, the government has an automatic lien over all property of any party in arrears. Since 1990, a great many enterprises accumulated very substantial tax arrears.[14] If tax liabilities are large relative to the value of the firm, banks may believe that as junior claimants they have no incentive to provoke a bankruptcy proceeding.

One further means of resolving financial distress that has been available from the outset of Polish transition is court reconciliation. Under this procedure a firm may restructure its financial claims, but not its tax liabilities, upon reaching agreement with creditors. Some features of the conciliation procedure were borrowed in the Financial Restructuring Act of 1993. We shall see below that the modified procedure, called bank conciliation, emerged as an important means of financial restructuring in Poland.

We have stressed privatization and bankruptcy as the two major ways that state-owned enterprises are restructured to achieve efficiency. This idea is challenged by some on the basis of macro-economic evidence. In particular, they point to the fact that despite being slower to privatize than was the Czech Republic and being slower to use bankruptcy procedures than was Hungary, Poland was the first transition country to emerge from the regional recession of the 1990s. This seems to suggest that it had been possible for state-owned enterprises to adapt to the new, liberalized economic environment.

In Poland several studies have looked at firm level data to shed light on this issue. Pinto et al. (1993) surveyed 75 large SOEs covering the period from June 1989 through June 1992. They find that, even though their formal ownership and organizational structure had not been changed, these SOEs as a group had been surprisingly aggressive in adapting to the new conditions of the transition economy. It was estimated that between mid-1989 and mid-1992, employment in these firms fell by 27.2 percent. Labor was shed both by profitable firms and loss-making firms. The survey suggests that during the course of the three years covered, the firms' decision making was placed increasingly on a commercial basis. For example, initially in the transition period, the use of inter-enterprise credit rose very strongly but was later reduced substantially. One possible reason for this was that firms gained a clearer idea of the risks associated with this type of credit. The authors of the study thus argue that it is not private ownership per se which is the key to making enterprises efficient. They emphasize the importance of hard budget constraints and the expectations of future privatization of the enterprise can be effective means of inducing change. It should be noted however that while the firms may have been cut off from direct subsidies, tax arrears rose substantially for the firms covered so that budget constraints were indirectly allowed to remain soft.

Pinto and Van Wijnbergen (1994) reconsider the same data to carry out some simple tests of whether there had been significant shift in firm behavior. They note that the main changes in behavior came after they had faced more severe credit constraints. They interpret this as evidence that Polish banks became more aggressive monitors of state enterprises and that tightening of the financial budget constraints could do much to promote efficient state enterprises in advance of privatization. In fact, the credit constraints in Poland became binding when in 1992 the Finance Ministry forbade banks to advance loans to state enterprises which were not servicing their outstanding loans

*Table 10.6   Polish domestic, non-governmental credits outstanding, 31
December 1994 (percent)*

	Regional Commercial Banks	Specialized banks	Cooperative banks	New Commercial Banks	Total
1. State owned enterprises	64	41	2	9	40
2. Privately owned enterprises	30	52	82	72	51
3. Bills of exchange	1	1	0	3	1
4. Households	4	6	16	16	8
5. Total 1–4	100	100	100	100	100
Total credits (billion zlotys)	133,972	178,366	28,206	74,843	415,387
As percent of grand total	32	43	7	18	100

Source: NBP.

Table 10.7   Distribution of credit creation

	1991	1992	1993	1994
1. State owned enterprises	60.55	−48.55	29.89	29.86
2. Private enterprises	34.30	137.96	55.96	58.17
3. Bills of exchange	0.0	6.69	1.50	−1.00
4. Households	5.15	3.91	12.66	12.97
Total household and enterprise credit creation (billion zlotys)	73,387	57,097	83,047	83,697

satisfactorily. Thus the initiative came from the authority of the state
and was not the result of the decentralized decisions of profit minded
bankers.

These results are important in that they cast doubt on the overly
simplified view that state-owned enterprises are inevitably the source
of great waste. However, the limitations of the data mean that the
results should not be pushed too far. In particular, the sample covers a
small fraction of the more than 5000 SOEs in Poland, and it specifically
excludes some of the largest and most politically sensitive of these on

the grounds that they would not be representative. However, this is precisely where the inefficiencies are likely to be greatest. Second, the period covers the earliest stage of transition when the widely-shared expectation was that early privatization was very likely for most state enterprises. Given the slowness of the privatization process in Poland and the political backlash to rapid liberalization, the prospect of privatization for the remaining state en   rises subsequently became less clear. This change of expectations could have had an important impact on the behavior of firm managers who no longer need to be as concerned about pleasing their future private owners nor proving management ability so that they can do well on the job market. Third, the only action of the firms which unambiguously indicated restructuring was their willingness to shed labor. This is very crude and reflect only one aspect of improving efficiency. The ability to perceive and undertake good investment projects is another which is total absent from the analysis.

How can one account for this set of apparently contradictory evidence? It seems likely that dynamic private firms are simply bidding away resources from the public sector. Where have they obtained the financial means to do this? Inevitably, some of the growth has been self-financed as small start-up firms in most countries grow from retained earnings. However, the credit flows data (Tables 10.6 and 10.7) indicate that the banking sector, with the exception of the large regional commercial banks, has strongly expanded lending to the private sector.

6. CLEANING UP BAD LOANS: BANK RECAPITALIZATION

In the socialist system enterprises were directed according to the priorities of the state. In decision making, profitability was only one consideration and often not the most important one. Furthermore, the profitability of an enterprise reflected the prevailing price structure which was set administratively. Economic liberalization and the removal of direct subsidies meant that many state enterprises had become unprofitable immediately after the start of transition implying that much of the plant and equipment of these enterprises was worth less than it cost to produce them. This shrinkage of the asset base implied the loss of financial capital in the enterprise. However, enterprises were also financed by credits from the banks and from other enterprises. For many firms the declines in asset values were likely to be large enough to make it impossible to pay back all these loans. This is the origin of the 'bad loan problem' which was widely recognized at the start of transition as one of the major policy problems to be addressed.

Even though this bad debt problem was recognized early on, most economists probably underestimated its magnitude; otherwise the depth of the transition-induced recession that was experienced by the CEE countries would not have been as surprising as it has been. The collapse of credit was very likely one of the important causes of this sharp decline in economic activity (Calvo and Coricelli 1993), and even if it was not one of the causes, it was surely a result. Within a few months of the introduction of liberalization measures, a great many firms became financially distressed in the sense that they were unable to service their debts without a major restructuring. With a lag, as new accounting methods were applied, this showed up in the form of a ballooning mass of non-performing credits on the books of the banks. By 1992 it should have been apparent to all that dealing with the bad debt problem was urgently needed to clear the way for growth.

In addition there were clear microeconomic reasons for dealing with bad debts quickly. At the start of transition, firms were burdened with a stock of old bad debts. If left untreated, this would distort incentives in granting new credits. In particular, finance theory teaches us that debt overhang can create serious problems of moral hazard for firms and can give rise to either underinvestment (Myers 1977) or excessive risk-taking (Jensen and Meckling 1976). In the CEE countries even if firms are privatized or managers of SOEs can be induced to maximize profits, the debt-burdened enterprises may fail to undertake the investments that would help them grow, or they may undertake risky projects which frequently leave creditors with new bad loans ex post. If left untreated, the bad debt problem is a major obstacle to privatization, since private owners will be deterred from buying into financially-distressed firms and banks.

In theory it seems that the state has considerable power to address the problem.[15] In particular, both the enterprises who are unable to service their loans and the banks and other enterprises which hold them are owned by the state. If the state consolidated the balance sheets of all of these state-owned institutions it would find that the debts would cancel. In the end it would be left with real assets, i.e., the plant and equipment of the enterprises, which constitute the net worth of the state. As owner of both the banks and the enterprises involved, the state should be able to bring about a clean-up of the accounts of these enterprises. In effect this would involve a general moratorium on old debts. This would allow the state enterprises to undertake the adjustment to the new economic environment unhindered by its old obligations. Furthermore, these enterprises could then be privatized more readily since purchasers would be acquiring in essence the assets of the old enterprises but not the liabilities.

Despite this apparent simplicity of dealing with bad debts, the countries of Eastern Europe did not move quickly to do so. It is important to ask why this has been the case. In part the reasons that there was no simple centralized solution to the bad debt problem are the same that previously had made central planning so difficult to implement in these countries. *Information was imperfect*; there was no complete and accurate account of which outstanding credits were good and which were bad. Serious efforts to get this information in Poland, Hungary and the Czech Republic, took several years to produce results. Furthermore, there were *bureaucratic distortions of incentives*. Even though property rights were fuzzy in the SOEs, managers clearly had an incentive to have their financial liabilities forgiven but were loath to give up on their financial assets. Beyond this, authorities in Eastern Europe were reluctant to pursue a policy of debt forgiveness for fear that it *would create very bad precedents* for the future. From the perspective of improving contract enforcement, nothing could have been worse than for the state to start the transition process with a policy of general debt forgiveness. The outcome that the policy makers would like is to clean up the old debts while still encouraging financial discipline in the future.[16] Therefore, it may declare that any debt forgiveness is a one time only affair. However such declarations may not be entirely convincing. Somehow the state would like to tie its hands so that such declarations would be credible. Unfortunately, there are no obvious institutional means of making such commitments credible.

Bank recapitalization is central to dealing with the bad debt problem in a transition economy. Under-capitalized banks are unreliable in evaluating risks and granting credits, are incapable of playing a role in merchant banking and securities markets development, and pose a threat to macroeconomic stability. After the creation of two-tier banking, bank capitalization has been a top priority for bank reform in CEE.

Basically two sorts of policy interventions could improve the health of the banks. Either efforts could be made to improve the quality of the assets. For example, government securities could be swapped for loans which threaten default. Alternatively, the state could intervene in order to assure the performance of the existing loan portfolio. The second class of measure would work on the liability side of the ledger. The state might give the banks capital infusions. Or it can give the banks access to cheap funds either by subsidizing deposit rates or through low-rate credits from the central bank. None of these policy interventions is entirely innocuous. In bond-loan swaps, who ends up holding the old, bad loan? Guaranteeing service of enterprise loans involves a subsidy which could distort firm behavior. Similarly, subsidized deposit rates drives a wedge between lending and borrowing rates. And if banks benefit from capital infusions now, will they not come to expect the same in the future?

Hungary was the first Eastern European country to move toward bank recapitalization. On the basis of an audit of loans initiated before the introduction of two-tiered banking in 1987, the government in 1991 agreed to guarantee one quarter (10.5 billion forints) of the bad loans picked up in the audit. In retrospect, this proved too little, too early. After the introduction of the draconian bankruptcy law in 1992, the Hungarian government initiated a bank consolidation program in which the banks were able to swap bad loans for Treasury consolidation bonds. Subsequent to the transfer of these bonds, haggling between the government and the banks resulted in the government agreeing to improve the terms and conditions of the bonds. Thus by 1993, the Hungarian government had done much to establish its reputation as a soft bargainer by first by moving the date for loans open to bail-outs from 1987 to 1992 and by renegotiating the terms of securities it had issued. After this the government started a bailout of 14 major state-owned industrial enterprises. Subsequently, after much lobbying, the list was expanded to include 78 firms. In 1993, the government initiated a second bank consolidation scheme. These measures have hardly satisfied the calls for further bailouts.

The efforts to recapitalize banks were initiated in the Czech Republic in 1991 (at that time still Czechoslovakia), one year after the introduction of two-tiered banking. The most distinctive feature of their approach was the use of a specialized consolidation or 'hospital' bank. This consolidation bank took non-performing loans off the books of qualified, state-owned banks, giving high grade bonds in return. Thus the commercial banks were restored to health and the resolution of the bad loans was placed into the hands of a specialized bank. At its inception the Czech consolidation bank was capitalized through an infusion of funds from the National Property Fund (NPF). Subsequently, the NPF repeated this several more times.

The distinctive feature of this process has been that privatization revenues have been used as the main source of funds for bank recapitalization. The main state budget has not been drawn upon. The commercial banks that have been able to write off bad debts through the process have now gone through mass privatization. In principle, by 1994 the recapitalization of the Czech banking system was complete. The commercial banks' capital and reserves were supposed to be sufficient to support their loan portfolio which undoubtedly contained some very risky assets. Thus, officially they are to find their own way in the marketplace. However, the consolidation bank still is owned by the state and the NPF still commands a huge amount of resources in the form of securities, enterprises yet to be privatized, and strategic stakes in privatized companies. In particular, the state has retained blocking minority stakes in the major banks that have been privatized. The risk was that in the future bad business conditions might threaten these banks. In this case the resources of the NPF could be called upon to bail out these banks using the consolidation bank as an intermediary as in the past.

In fact, a banking crisis did emerged in the Czech Republic after the privatization of the major banks. In 1994–95 the failure of three medium-sized banks plus some smaller banks effectively depleted the deposit insurance funds and left the banking sector vulnerable. In 1996 additional small banks failed, but the big shock to the system came in August 1996 when Kreditni Banka (the sixth largest commercial bank) failed. The public sector moved rapidly to stabilize the banking sector by assuring that Kreditni's depositors would make only limited losses. However, confidence was clearly shaken so that in September Agrobanka (the fifth largest) began to experience massive withdrawals. Even though it was argued that this bank's loan portfolio was sound, the state intervened directly by placing the bank under central bank administration and by announcing that all deposits were guaranteed. The details of the Kreditni Banka bailout demonstrate how difficult it is to establish arm's length banking regulation in transition economies and are an interesting lesson of how things get done in the new Czech Republic. Official deposit insurance funds covered only 80 percent of individual deposits up to 100,000 crowns. However, Ceska Pojistovna, the largest Czech insurance company and Kreditni's largest single shareholder, announced that it would cover losses on other deposits up to 4 million crowns. Why a shareholder should do this is perhaps explained by the fact that Pojistovna was going to finance this operation through an exceptional share issue to its own largest shareholders. These are Investicni a Postovni Banka and Komereni Banka (both large privatized commercial banks in which the state has retained a large share), Ceskoslovenska Obchodni Banka (which has not been privatized), and the National Property Fund. This is not the first time that the new institutions of the Czech Republic have worked together to find *ad hoc* solutions to the unforeseen problems that emerge in a transition economy, and in some ways this is one of the strengths of the Czech system. However, it shows that a stable, competitive, private banking sector that deals with credit risk on a routine basis is yet to be achieved.

The Polish program of bank recapitalization went into operation in 1994, five years after the introduction of two-tiered banking. Besides being slow in coming, the Polish program is notable in that it was decentralized, not involving a specialized bad-loans bank or agency, and that it integrated structural changes aimed at making the resolution of firms' financial distress more efficient. The centerpiece of the program was the Financial Restructuring Act of 1993 which (a) allowed for the recapitalization of seven of the regional commercial banks that had emerged from the mono-bank and (b) introduced bank conciliation, a fast-track procedure for resolving financial distress. Seven of the original regional banks participated in the program, the other two having previously been recapitalized as part of their privatization. The starting point of the program was a 1991 audit of loans to SOEs. In return for a commitment to restructure a portfolio of 15 trillion old zloty of qualified loans within one year using bank conciliation or some other method, the seven banks received a capital infusion of 11 trillion zloty in the form of Treasury bonds. Much to the surprise of many observers familiar with Poland's failure to get privatization off the ground and with the slowness of conventional bankruptcy procedures in Poland, almost all the loans selected were restructured in approximately the period called for. The incentive structure of the program probably contributed to this; the amount of recapitalization was linked to the assessed value of the portfolio thus giving the banks the incentive to maximize the ex post realized value. Overall, the program has been widely recognized as one of the best conceived and best executed aspects of Poland's microeconomic policies in transition.

Unfortunately, as the recapitalization program was being put into place, it became apparent that the bad loan problem of the specialized banks, specifically PK-BP and BGZ, were larger than that of the regional commercial banks. Furthermore, the underlying distress reflected complicated structural problems which would not be amenable to resolution in the way that bank enterprise loans were.

In the case of PK-BP, the bad loans were large credits granted to housing cooperatives. The terms of the loan linked repayments to the incomes of cooperative members. Furthermore, if cooperatives were delinquent, Polish law gave the bank few practical means of forcing performance. In the case of BGZ, large credits had been extended to private agriculture and to large state farms during 1991 and 1992. By 1993 a large fraction of these loans were non-performing. Part of the difficulty was BGZ's legal structure gave the state a minority voice on the board with the majority interest being held by cooperative banks to which BGZ granted credits. Until today, BGZ management views its primary mission as aiding agricultural development, with profit maximization being an alien concept subsidiary to, if not incompatible with, its main mission. The scale of the problems of PK-BP and BGZ are huge. During 1990–93 the operating tosses of PK-BP were covered by the state budget though the purchase of 29 trillion zloty of accrued interest. In 1994 as an afterthought to the 1993 Financial Restructuring Act, the government injected 6 trillion zlotys of Treasury bonds. In the case of BGZ in 1994, the government injected 12 trillion zlotys of Treasury bonds; however, it is estimated that this fell at least 13 trillion short of the minimum amount needed to bring BGZ up to international capital standards. Furthermore, the ownership structure of BGZ and the organization of the banking cooperatives are highly politicized issues that remain largely unresolved. As a consequence, many observers fear that before the bailout is over, it may cost much more than the total of 25 trillion zlotys of bad loans that have been identified already.

These descriptions make it clear that in transition it is a basic error to think that the bad debt problem is only a problem of cleaning up the loans used to finance the negative net present value projects taken on by SOEs in the past. Also important, perhaps *most important*, are the new investments undertaken in transition which are not profitable. The fact is that transition exposes enterprises and banks to large, systematic risks. This certainly was the case for 1990–95. For example, in Table 10.8 we see that the bad loans on the books of commercial banks in Poland and the Czech Republic continued to rise through 1994 even though a number of measures had been undertaken to relieve them of the old, pre-transition loans. Following bad loan statistics over time is made difficult by frequent changes of definition and reclassification of loans, and this is simply because of improvements in reporting. Nevertheless it is clear that the bad loans problem was not eliminated by the policy measures aimed at addressing them. Transition risks will probably remain large

Table 10.8   Bad loans in selected CEE countries

	1991	1992	1993	1994
As percent of bank loans to enterprises and individuals				
Hungary	9.4	20.7	42.6	30.2
Poland	16.5	26.8	27.4	29.0
Czech Republic	2.7	19.3	22.1	38.8
As percent of total assets				
Hungary	4.1	7.5	15.7	11.0
Poland	6.9	10.2	9.7	9.8
Czech Republic	1.2	10.4	10.5	20.1
As percent of GDP				
Hungary	3.5	5.4	11.9	7.9
Poland	2.2	3.3	2.7	3.2
Czech Republic	1.9	14.3	16.9	30.4

Source: National banks of Hungary, Poland, and the Czech Republic.

during 1996–2000 as well. These risks cannot realistically be hedged by agents either through contracts or through diversification. If these agents were really convinced that there was no hope of government bailouts either of creditors or of borrowers in the future, the free-market solution to the problem would simply be to ask for high levels of collateral or to add a very heavy risk premium onto to the rate of interest required by a loan contract. This would tend to discourage investment and serve as a drag on growth. Indeed, this probably has happened: by most measures real rates have been quite high in Poland, Hungary and the Czech Republic since 1990. However, the hope for future bailouts may well have kept rates lower than might have been the case otherwise.

This poses an important dilemma for policy makers. Efforts have already been extended to treat the bad debt problem. However, transition risks are still large. A too-cautious approach to granting credits as reflected in excessive risk premia will stifle growth. The consequences of excessive risk avoidance are made even more severe because they would tend to fall most heavily on small and medium sized enterprises which potentially are the driving force behind private sector development. The prospect of bailouts can help to alleviate this problem and stimulate growth. However, if bailouts are made too easy, this will be a clear invitation to relaxing financial discipline and to excessive risk-taking. In the face of this, one extreme policy response is to say that no bailouts will be granted in the future. This extreme view stance is probably not believable. The only way to build credibility would be to let large politically important institutions fail when they become distressed. Even if the government in power is courageous or foolhardy enough to be tough in this way, the question is whether it is worth the economic cost given the chilling effect it would have on growth. The alternative extreme is to be very soft. This would essentially be backsliding toward the pre-transition situation where financial contracts had little, if any, bite at all. Between these two extremes, the middle ground would appear to be to make no provision for future bailouts but simply say that the future bailouts can be granted if the distressed sectors can demonstrate sufficient cause so that the political sphere will be moved to intervene. This puts in place a hurdle to be cleared which means that bailouts will not too easy. However, this also politicizes finance and probably favours the continued financial development of the state-owned and the ex-state-owned banks. In turn, this would be an invitation to a certain amount of costly, rent-seeking activity. In fact, at this stage, most of the CEE countries occupy this middle ground.

There are important policy implications of these observations. First, the governments of the CEE countries should not try to pretend that bad debts are a problem of the past. Instead, they should recognize that the risks of transition will continue to give rise to bad debts in the future. In anticipation of this, they must concentrate their efforts on preparing the private sector to deal with these problems without general assistance of the state. Thus places where bankruptcy law development has lagged (e.g., the Czech Republic), it should now be given much greater emphasis. In any event, the overriding message should be that if the economy's new market institutions cannot solve future credit problems, a future bailout by the state will come only with great difficulty and in a way that will only partially compensate creditors.

This review of the steps taken toward bank recapitalization in transition countries contains several lessons that are important for policy. First, despite being in principle a mere problem in budgetary accounting, the bad loan clean-up has turned out to be relatively complicated. In particular, it has proved difficult to establish firm dividing lines between old and new loans. Second, in a period when a major policy objective was to harden budget constraints by removing subsidies and improving incentives for contract enforcement by private parties, the recapitalization essentially went in the opposite direction by rewarding the weak, the myopic and the politically favoured. This sets an important challenge for governments in the next phase of transition, namely, how to prevent recapitalization from turning into a new form of chronic budgetary softness. Third, if the incentive structure of a recapitalization program is designed properly, a decentralized approach can result in massive portfolio restructuring in a relatively short period of time. Thus efficiency may not necessarily require creating specialized state-owned receivers which pose monitoring and control problems of their own.

7. CONCLUSION

We have surveyed the development of the finance in Eastern Europe since the fall of the Berlin Wall. We have specifically dealt with the Czech Republic, Hungary and Poland. Our focus has been on three problems which we view at being at the heart of the financial transition namely: privatization, increasing discipline in financial contracting, and on the resolution of the bad loan problem. For reasons of space we have been only indirectly touched upon other important topics including, central banking, prudential regulation, deposit insurance, and securities market development.

Rather than summarize what has already been a brief summary of these complicated issues, we conclude by putting forward a number of important policy lessons of this experience. We believe that our discussion here is suggestive of these lessons. For further support for these views we direct the reader to the fuller account in Anderson and Kegels.

- *Good and bad reasons to privatize.* Privatization is above all a means of giving explicit title to productive capital that had been held collectively under socialism. In this way it is an important step toward creating effective monitors for management. It is not essentially a way to reduce the government's fiscal deficit.
- *The role of vouchers.* Mass privatization using vouchers can be an important step toward creating a equitable distribution of wealth at the outset of transition. It can also have the benefit of maintaining political support for privatization even if the process will result in job losses.
- *Treatment of distressed enterprises.* Bankruptcy is a cumbersome

means of bringing about massive enterprise restructuring. A sharp tightening of bankruptcy laws early in the transition process can severely undermine economic growth. However, good bankruptcy laws are needed to allow restructuring of privatized firms.

- *Incentive effects of bad loan clean-up.* A bad loan clean-up program should be carefully designed and of a sufficient scale. A series of partial clean-ups can become a new form of indirect subsidies which would weaken financial discipline.
- *On hospital banks.* Banks can be recapitalized and bad loans cleaned-up without the use of a specialized hospital bank. A state-owned hospital bank prolongs the state allocation of credit and undermines the development of the market.
- *On getting credit flowing toward new private enterprises.* In the pre-privatization phase of transition, administrative constraints on lending to state enterprises with non-performing loans can be an effective way of redirecting credits toward the emerging private sector.

To what extent might these lessons apply to countries outside Eastern Europe? For example, might they be relevant to China, a country which is just now at the stage to approaching enterprise reform, banking reform, and bad loan clean-up on a country-wide basis? Undoubtedly good policy making must be based on each country's particular circumstances. However, the experience of Eastern European countries suggests that despite the many differences in the conditions, they were all required to confront these issues in one way or another. Thus we believe that policy makers elsewhere in the world may well benefit from seriously considering the relevance of these lessons to their own circumstances.

ACKNOWLEDGEMENT

This chapter draws very heavily upon Anderson, Berglöf, and Mizsei (1996) and, especially, Anderson and Kegels (1998). I thank my coauthors for their cooperation and their many useful insights. The opinions expressed in this chapter and responsibility for all errors are my own.

NOTES

1. Nuti (1992), describes the liberalization measures taken by the post-socialist countries of Central and Eastern Europe.
2. For example, in 1989 the price of bread (expressed in terms of units of wheat) was about 3.5 times higher in West Germany than in East. At the same time the price of washing machines in West Germany was one half of that in East Germany. See, Kornai (1992), Table 8.4.
3. In such a case, the basic conditions of the Coase theorem are not fulfilled. See Coase (1960).
4. See Kornai (1992), Chapter 8.
5. In the parlance of game theory, the banks have no 'credible commitment' to enforce the terms of the loan agreement. For a theoretical analysis of this see, Dewatripont and Maskin (1990) and Maskin (1994).
6. For a theoretical statement of this position, see Arrow and Lind (1970).
7. For a description of the Japan Development Bank, see Harada (1994).
8. In an influential article in the early days after the fall of communism in eastern Europe, E. Hinds argued, 'In effect, having socialized enterprises owning themselves means that nobody owns them. Thus there is no direct advocate for capital in these enterprises. Workers are supposed to be the surrogate advocates, but they have little interest in preserving and increasing their enterprises' capital (Hinds, 1991).
9. General references concerning privatization in eastern and central Europe are Frydman et al. (1991a, b) and Bolton and Roland (1992).
10. See Diamond (1984) for an analysis of the advantage that a financial intermediary has in monitoring firms.
11. For example, the Polish approach to mass privatization has featured having state assets allocated to mutual funds and in turn citizens receiving vouchers which they can invest in the competing mutual funds (see Frydman and Rapaczynski 1991a). This approach has been criticized on the grounds that it does not create strong incentives for the mutual funds to compete with one another and therefore results in passive ownership.
12. A detailed discussion of Polish privatization can be found in Frydman et al. (1993).
13. Bonin and Schaffer estimated that the employment in firms declared bankrupt in 1992–93 amounted to 12 to 13 percent of enterprise employment.
14. In Poland the tax liability of a firm is not eliminated as its operating net revenues fall to zero. The reason is the *'popywek'* whereby taxes are assessed on salary increases in excess of an official index. Thus firms can be profitable before tax but loss-making after tax.
15. See Begg and Portes (1993), for a statement of the problem and a proposed centralized solution involving debt forgiveness.
16. This is expressed by Begg and Portes by saying that the *stock* of old loans should be written down so that the *flow* of new credits will be managed in a disciplined way.

REFERENCES

Anderson, R.W. and C. Kegels (1998), *Transition Banking: Financial Development in Central and Eastern Europe*, New York: Oxford University Press.

Anderson, R.W., E. Berglöf and K. Mizsei (1996), *Banking Sector Development in Central and Eastern Europe*, London: CEPR and Institute of East-West Studies.

Arrow, K.J. and R.C. Lind (1970), 'Uncertainty and the evaluation of public investment decisions', *American Economic Review*, **60** (3): 364–78.

Begg, D. and R. Portes (1993), 'Enterprise debt and financial restructuring in Central and Eastern Europe', *European Economic Review*, **37** (2–3): 396–407.

Bolton, P. and G. Roland (1992), 'The economics of mass privatization: Czechoslovakia, Germany, Hungary, Poland', *Economic Policy*, **0** (15): 275–303.

Bonin, J.P. and M.E. Schaffer (1995), 'Banks, firms, bad debts and bankruptcy in Hungary 1991–94', paper presented at the meetings of the American Economics Association, Washington, DC, January.

Calvo, G., and Coricelli (1993), F., 'Output Collapse in Eastern Europe: The Role of Credit', IMF Staff Papers, **40**(1), 1993.

Coase, R. (1960), 'The problem of social costs', *Journal of Law and Economics*, **3**: 1–44.

Dewatripont, M. and E. Maskin (1990), 'Credit and efficiency in centralized and decentralized economies', mimeo.

Diamond, D.W. (1984), 'Financial intermediation and delegated monitoring', *Review of Economic Studies*, **51** (3): 393–414.

Filer, R.K. and J. Hanousek (1994), 'Efficiency in newly emerging capital markets: the case of Czech Voucher privatization', working paper, CERGE, Prague.

Frydman, R. and A. Rapaczynski (1991a), 'Markets and institutions in large-scale privatization: an approach to economic and social transformation in Eastern Europe', in V. Corbo, F. Coricelli and J. Bossak (eds), *Reforming Central and Eastern European Economies: Initial Results and Challenges*, World Bank Symposium, Washington, DC: World Bank, pp. 253–74.

Frydman, R. and A. Rapaczynski (1991b), 'Privatization and corporate governance in Eastern Europe: can a market economy be designed?', working paper, New York University Economic Research Reports, **91-52**: 48.

Frydman, R., A. Rapaczynski and J.S. Earle (1993), *The Privatization Process in Central Europe: Central Economic Environment, Legal and Ownership Structure, Institutions for State Regulation, Overview of Privatization Programs and Initial Transformation of Enterprises*, CEU Privatization Reports, Vol. 1, Budapest, London and New York: Central European University ress, 262.

Harada, Y. (1994), 'Lessons from Japanese policy-based finance', in *Transition: Private Sector Development and the Role of Financial Institutions*, EBRD working paper, 13.

Hinds, M. (1991), 'Issues in the introduction of market forces in Eastern European Socialist Economies', *Managing Inflation in Socialist Economics in Transition*, Economic Development Institute Seminar Series, Washington DC: World Bank, pp. 121–53.

Jensen, M.C. and W.H. Meckling (1976), 'Theory of the firm, managerial behavior, agency costs, and ownership structure', *Journal of Financial Economics*, **3** (4): 305–60.

King, R. and K. Levine (1993), 'Finance, entrepreneurship, and growth: theory and evidence', *Journal of Monetary Economics*, **32** (3): 513–42.

Kornai, J. (1992), *The Socialist System: The Political Economy of Communism*, Princeton, NJ: Princeton University Press.

Maskin, E. (1994), 'Theories of the soft-budget constraint', paper presented at Institutional Dimensions of Transition, conference held at ECARE, Brussels, 7 May 1994.

Mladek, J. (1994), 'Mass privatization in the Czech Republic', The Czech Institute of Applied Economics, Prague.

Myers, S.C. (1977), 'The determinants of corporate borrowing', *Journal of Financial Economics*, **5** (2): 147–75.

NBH Annual Report (1994), Prepared by the Economic Department of the National Bank of Hungary.

Nuti, D.M. (1992), 'The role of the banking sector in the process of privatization', Commission of the European Communities, Economic Papers, 98.

Pinto, B., M. Belka and S. Krajewski (1993), 'Transforming state enterprises in Poland: evidence on adjustment by manufacturing firms', *Brookings Papers on Economic Activity*, **0** (1): 213–61.

Pinto, B. and S. Van Wijnbergen (1994), 'Ownership and corporate control in Poland: why state firms defied the odds', working paper, University of Amsterdam.

Schaffer, M.E. (1997), 'Do firms in transition economies have Soft budget constraints?: a reconsideration of concepts and evidence', CERT working paper, Heriot-Watt University.

Svejnar, Jan and Singer, M. (1994) 'Using Vouchers to Privatize an Economy: The Czech and Slovak Case', *Economics of Transition*, **2**(1), 1994, PP. 43–69.

Index

Abuaf, N. 133, 145
Agenor, Pierre-Richard 139, 145
Agricultural Developments Fund,
  Hungary 201
agricultural land, Czech Republic 192
  development of, Poland 214
Agrobanka, Czech Republic 212
Amano, R. 92, 97
Arrow, K.J. 219, 220
Asia, currencies and economies 103, 104
  financial crisis 3, 7, 8, 9, 41, 93,
    98–127, 153
  monetary authorities 111
assets, 111, 119, 121, 137, 152, 171, 173,
  178, 179, 180, 208
  state-owned, sale of to public 190, 193

bad debt, in Eastern Europe 215, 216
balance of payment equilibrium 131
Bank of Canada 26, 28, 29, 42, 44, 45
Bank of England 6, 9, 26, 45, 87, 88, 89,
  91, 93, 96, 97
  Monetary Policy Committee 3
Bank for International Settlements, Basle
  3, 44, 45, 104, 126
Bank of Japan 39
banking, in Eastern Europe 183–221
  regulation 8–9
  sound 170, 172, 181
  two-tiered 211
bankruptcy 180, 193, 206
  and enterprise restructuring 217–18
  law reform and development 188,
    202–05, 211, 216, 218
banks, borrowing 171
  capital 175, 179, 205, 208, 217
  consolidation scheme, Hungary 211
  credit 98, 109, 170, 171
  liabilities 174–8
Barro, Robert 65

Basle Committee on Banking
  Supervision 173, 182
Bean, C. 96, 97
Begg, D. 219, 220
Belka, M. 221
Benston, George 175, 182
Berglöf, E. 218, 220
Bernanke, Ben S. 13, 15–17, 29, 44, 45
Blanchard, O.J. 166
Bolton, P. 219, 220
bonds, inflation forecast 62
  issue of 194
  markets 60, 62, 125, 157, 174, 180
  rates 61, 63
Bonin, P. 219, 220
Bonser-Neal, C. 157, 165
Brazilian central bank 118, 119
bread, price of, in Eastern Europe 219
Bruno, Michael 65
budget, accounting 216
  constraints, Eastern Europe, 203, 210
  deficits, low 114
  projections, US 64
  subsidies 201
  surplus 157
Bundesbank 15, 16, 17, 22, 24, 25, 39,
  42, 43, 87, 96
bureaucracy in Eastern Europe 210
business, cycle 22, 34, 157

Calvo, G. 209, 220
Canada 13, 23, 42
  inflation-control target 43, 63
capitalist economies 185, 186
capitalization of Czech banking system
  212
Cechhetti, Stephen G. 43, 46
Central Bank of China 152, 164, 165
central banks 24, 29, 41, 87, 88, 103,
  123, 131–4, 139, 149, 172, 187